A MATHEMATICS ACTIVITY CURRICULUM
for Early Childhood and Special Education

A MATHEMATICS ACTIVITY CURRICULUM
for Early Childhood and Special Education

Lloyd I. Richardson, Jr.
University of Missouri, St. Louis

Kathy L. Goodman
Early Learning Center, San Diego

Nancy Noftsinger Hartman
Special School District of St. Louis County, Missouri

Henri C. LePique
Special School District of St. Louis County, Missouri

Macmillan Publishing Co., Inc.
New York
Collier Macmillan Publishers
London

Macmillan Publishing Co., Inc.
866 Third Avenue, New York, New York 10022

Collier Macmillan Canada, Ltd.

Library of Congress Cataloging in Publication Data

A Mathematics activity curriculum for early childhood and special
    education.

    Includes index.
    1.   Mathematics – Study and teaching – Elementary.
I.   Richardson, Lloyd I.
QA135.5.M3677 1980   372.7   79–15677

ISBN 0-02-399710-9

Printing: 2 3 4 5 6 7 8   Year: 2 3 4 5 6

Contents

CHAPTER 1

Rationale and Organization

1.1   Introduction

The purpose of this book is to provide the teacher with a set of activity lessons with which to build a prenumber mathematics program and to supplement the early childhood math curriculum through grade 3. The titles for the chapters identified as prenumber concepts are Topology, Shape, Color, Size, Classification, and Seriation. Also a chapter entitled Numerals and one chapter on Numberness are included. The latter chapter is for those children who begin to conserve number early. This chapter offers an appropriate sequence for beginning one-to-one relationships and addition concepts for the teacher who does not regularly deal with a child who conserves. Chapters on Addition, Place Value, Subtraction, and Multiplication complete an early childhood mathematics program on the elementary school level.   These chapters do not provide a comprehensive curriculum; rather, they are included to supplement an existing school text. Within each chapter, topics are sequenced to coincide with the child's development.

**Early work with shapes and boundaries is a natural part
of the young child's life.**

The preschool teacher is provided a framework linking mathematical readiness to elementary school mathematics programs. When a child attends elementary school, mathematics and reading will be the primary content concerns. Although a great deal of information is available regarding preparation of a child for reading experiences, much less is available for mathematical readiness.

There seems to be a basic void in activity-oriented developmental lessons for children before starting the study of numerals and number. A comprehensive early childhood mathematics curriculum does not exist in a form usable by teachers. Certainly scattered activity suggestions are available as are books of a theoretical nature. Many early childhood books are aimed at language development, perceptual and motor skills, and cognitive development. The activities in this book draw from each of these areas, but their primary aim is longitudinal development of the child's mathematical abilities.

The term "mathematics" usually conjures up images of counting objects or adding and subtracting with numerals. Although crucial when the child studies arithmetical operations, these activities have a limited role in a prenumber math curriculum. Until a child can conserve number, these activities are learned only rotely and/or superficially. To clarify why conservation is a turning point in a child's development and why lack of it prevents successful math experiences with numeration, let's look at an example defining conservation of number. A child who does not conserve is influenced by appearances. A set in which objects are placed close together "appears" to have fewer objects than a set in which the objects are spread out.

"less"   "more"

A child would have difficulty working with numbers of objects when the groups of objects were forever changing their quantity just by being re-arranged in space. One can only stress the importance of delaying arithmetic work with numbers until a child conserves.

Verbal challenges extend and expand the potential of each activity, if indeed the activity is appropriate for the child's level of maturation. Questions and comments that provide the teacher and child a mutual form of communication about experiences and that seek to encourage problem-solving abilities are especially important. Thinking up questions on the spur of the moment as the lesson progresses is difficult for most teachers; thus important questions are provided where the authors feel they are crucial to the activity. When appropriate, the authors provide direction to the teacher through questions posed.

Chapters dealing with prenumber math activities are appropriate for children ages $2\frac{1}{2}$ to around age 6 or 7. These activities will also be useful to the child enrolled in special education classes functioning on the prenumber level. Chapters dealing with arithmetical operations are most appropriate for children who have conserved number.

HOW TO USE THE BOOK

1.2   Chapter selection

The chapters have been sequenced to correspond to a child's development in acquiring math concept understanding. This sequence reflects current mathematics education research and the work of Piaget.

Basically, the book focuses on activities for the preoperational and concrete operational child (those readers not familiar with the terms are referred to Reys and Post, 1973). A child in the preoperational stage is characterized as very egocentric and is generally incapable of viewing a situation from more than one perspective. During this stage the child begins to move from viewing the world topologically (open-closed curves) to viewing the world Euclideanly (points, corners, lines) as in dealing with shapes. Once the child discriminates shapes, work with learning shapes should be provided.

According to research, the child discriminates color soon after shape—coming so close that either color or shape could be presented first. The child then becomes increasingly adept in working with progressively more difficult concepts of size, classification, seriation, and patterning. A child can work with numerals (chanting them, recognizing them, writing them) long before numeration activities can be comprehended appropriately. A separate chapter on numerals is therefore included before the chapter on numeration. One must keep in mind though that the abilities to use numerals in chanting or recognizing situations does not imply that a child can understand numberness. When the child can conserve, he/she moves from the preoperational to the concrete operational stage on the number concept.

The numeration chapter is intended for the conserver of number and concentrates on mathematical operations. It was decided that, even though sufficient numbers of elementary school mathematics programs concentrate on mathematical operations, exemplar activities should be included here that enhance acquisition and mastery of the mathematical operations. A final chapter deals with patterns and other math games.

Not all activities in a particular chapter are to be used before teaching activities from subsequent chapters. Primarily the chapter ordering follows

Reys, Robert E. and Thomas R. Post. *The Mathematics Laboratory.* Boston: Prindle, Weber & Schmidt, Inc., 1973.

the developmental sequences of children. As an example, shapes should be taught before size. Once the introductory activities from the shape chapter have been taught, the teacher may do introductory activities from the size chapter. Then activities from both the shape and size chapters may be taught at different times during the same day. Thus *all* the shape activities are *not* finished before doing *any* size activities.

An exception to mixing activities from two chapters is discussed in detail in the shape chapter. Basically naming shapes and colors can be confusing unless one or the other concept has been well learned prior to the introduction of the other.

1.3   Activity selection

The mathematical content is sequenced so that prerequisite topics are presented before topics utilizing the prerequisites. For example, in the topology chapter, the topic "open-closed" is presented before "inside-outside," as the latter topic assumes the concept of closure as a prerequisite skill. The mathematical content sequence appears as section headings within the chapter.

Vocabulary activities are included throughout and are necessary to student success. Learning the shape and color names is a mathematical discrimination, as abstract names are applied to properties of objects. This is analogous to applying the number name, numeral, to the property of the set of objects.

Activities were chosen and sequenced using certain guidelines selected from the work of Jerome Bruner and Robert Gagne. Bruner suggests that a pupil progresses through three modes in developing an understanding of a mathematical concept. The three modes are

enactive   a concrete model of the concept, usually involving manipulative or physical materials.

iconic   a semiabstract model, usually involving pictures of the situation.

symbolic   an abstract model of the concept.

These three modes have been incorporated throughout the development of each concept in this book. In every section, the authors have attempted to involve the pupil first in activities in the enactive mode with a progression to activity involvement in the symbolic mode when feasible. To facilitate selecting activities in one of these modes, the appendix catalogues every activity as to whether it is concrete, semiabstract, or abstract. Refer to the appendix for assistance in choosing an appropriate mode.

Incorporating the ideas of Gagne, the activities have been ordered so as to begin with the easiest task and progress sequentially to the problem-solving capability desired.

Bruner, Jerome S. *Toward a Theory of Instruction.* Cambridge: Harvard University Press, Belknap Press, 1963, 28.
Gagne, Robert. *The Condition of Learning,* 2nd ed. New York: Holt, Rinehart & Winston, 1970.

The authors have attempted to sequence the lessons so that work with a mathematical concept progresses from familiar objects to mathematically symbolic objects. Incorporated, when appropriate, is the assumption that when a pupil encounters a mathematical concept, the concept should first be embodied in an activity utilizing materials and objects familiar to the child (taken from his environment). Second, presentation of the concept should utilize mathematically symbolic objects (shapes and numerals) but allow manipulation and touching. Third, the presentation should utilize these symbolic objects in a mathematically symbolic setting. Perhaps an example is in order. In the chapter on numeration a presentation on one-to-one correspondence (all in the enactive mode of Bruner) would progress as follows:

1. set of hats (cowboy hat, fireman hat, nurse cap, baseball hat) with set of people (cowboy, fireman, nurse, baseball player) (both sets familiar, from environment)

2. set of fruit (orange, apples, bananas) matched with shapes including circle, square, triangle (set familiar to the child with mathematically symbolic objects)

3. set of circular shapes matched with sets of triangles

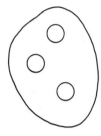 

1.4   Activity format

The format chosen for activity description includes concept, materials, group size, procedure, questions, notes, and diagram (where appropriate).

Concept: Briefly describes the objective of the activity.

Materials: Describes the supplies necessary to conduct the activity.

Group size: Indicates the authors' thinking when conceptualizing the activity. This does not preclude using the activity with larger or smaller groups.

Procedure: Explains the presentation of the activity and coordination of materials presentation with teacher questions.

Questions: Lists significant questions to ask during the activity.

Diagram: Drawing of the activity to facilitate construction from materials or special feature for organizing the materials if verbal description could be confusing.

Note space: An area for the user to make notes regarding modifications or special items to be remembered. Once the activity is completed, variations or pertinent modifications observed by the user should be marked in the space below the activity for future reference. When the activity is again used (with another class, another pupil, or another sibling), the user will have a record of past experience and desired modifications.

Activities included in this book have been field tested in a preschool or special education setting. The questions posed and procedures described are, in many cases, those that resulted from the field testing. Each activity has been given a name for facilitating communication both within the book and with the children.

1.5   Using the appendix

All the activities included in the book are listed in the appendix. The purposes of the appendix are to aid the teacher in choosing appropriate activities to fit the needs of a special child, to facilitate making lesson plans, and to provide an index of activities by name and number. The appendix may assist teachers in special education who need to identify skills when writing Individual Educational Plans (IEPs).

The appendix is divided into three types of information—the mode of the activity presentation (concrete, semiabstract, abstract), the learning mode (visual, auditory, and tactile/kinesthetic), and the mode of the child's response (verbal, gross motor, fine motor, or with writing and drawing). Any one or all of these types of information may be included to develop lesson plans.

A complete description of this appendix is included in the appendix itself, and the reader should refer to this section.

Topology

2.1   Introduction

There are many possible geometries in mathematics, one of which is topology. Traditionally people are familiar with Euclidean plane geometry because it is the usual geometry taught in schools. However, the young child first views the world from a topological point of view, then matures to viewing the world Euclideanly.

Topology is the study of intrinsic qualitative geometric properties without regard for number or measurement. These properties are independent of location, shape, or size. The properties do not change when the object under consideration is bent or stretched, as long as no tearing occurs. Consider the rubber band in Figure 2–1 as it is stretched.

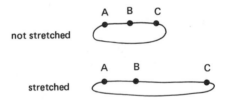

Figure 2.1

Note that the property of B between A and C is preserved when the rubber band is stretched.

As another example consider the closed circuit formed by a rubber band regardless of how it is stretched or bent. All of the forms the rubber band takes on in Figure 2.2 are called *equivalent*.

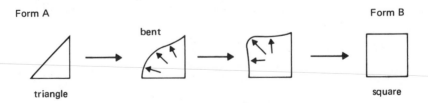

Figure 2.2

In topology a triangle is equivalent to a square because one can be transformed into the other without tearing the boundary. The only change occurs as the hypotenuse is stretched sufficiently and realigned to form the square.

Many theorists have shown that children's first geometric work is from a topological standpoint. Later, around age $3\frac{1}{2}$ to 4 years, the child begins to discriminate shapes or to view the geometric world from a Euclidean frame of reference. These topological concepts do not diminish in stature as Euclidean geometry develops but, rather, are refined and form the foundation for later geometric work.

In developing topological properties, the important properties are proximity, separation, enclosure, surrounding on a boundary, and betweenness. The activities in this chapter attempt to develop the child's topological perspectives. These properties form the basis for work with sets, number, mathematical vocabulary, and spatial relations.

2.2 Proximity (near, far)

The spatial perception of proximity is the earliest topological relationship developed by the child. The child distinguishes between those objects near and those farther away; for instance, the child could differentiate between the ball next to his chair and the one by the door.

Proximity is a relative relationship. The judgment of whether something is near or far is relative to what is used as a measure or guideline. Children discriminate proximity on two levels. On the first level the child compares the proximity of two objects both of which are in the same line of sight. On the second level the child compares the proximity of two objects that are not lying in the same direction. The second level is more difficult as

"Place the horse in the grassy area."

the child must retain a visual, mental image of the location of one object and then compare that image with the position of the other object. Remember that mathematical discriminations rely on a correlation of the child's maturation with his or her ability to utilize mental images when representing a comparison.

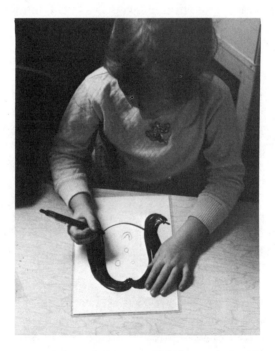

Proximity and order are apparent in drawing — looks like my teacher to me!

THE HOT SEAT

Concept: Identify nearest item given a choice between two.

Materials: Chair ("hot seat").

Classroom objects.

Group size: Any size group.

Procedure: Designate a chair the "hot seat" and place it at any point in the room. Have children take turns sitting in the "hot seat." Name two objects in the room; the child must tell which is nearer to him or her and which is farther from him or her.

The "hot seat" can be moved from time to time.

Variation: Name one object and have the child tell you whether it is near or far.

Questions: Can you name an object near you? Far from you?

BEANBAG BUDDIES

Concept: Manipulate objects in near and far situations.

Materials: Beanbags or pairs of similar objects.

Group size: Two, small group, or class.

Procedure: Call the names of two children and state "near" or "far." They both put their beanbags as near to each other or as far away from each other as they can.

Have group or whole class put their beanbags (buttons, pencils) "near" and then "far apart."

You may wish to have the children remain seated and move their objects from where they are.

Questions: What is the farthest we can move them? Nearest?
Is one of these beanbags nearer to Jeanne's than Bill's?

"near"

"far"

MAGIC SHOES

Concept: Discriminate near and far, using children's shoes.

Materials: Children's own shoes.

Magic wand (optional).

Group size: Any size group.

Procedure: Have children take off their shoes. Tell the children that their shoes have become "magic shoes." The shoes can listen to directions and "walk" wherever they are told.

The teacher or a child may be the magician and wave the magic wand, saying, "Jerry's shoes, go near the pencil sharpener." "Paul's shoes, go far from the pencil sharpener."

Children use their hands to walk the shoes to the correct place.

Variation: Shoes can be hidden; direct child to find them by indicating if the child is "near" or "far" from the shoes.

Questions: Jerry's shoes are near the sharpener. Name an object that they are far from; name one that they are near.

PLAYGROUND DIRECTIONS

Concept: Place self near to or far from playground objects upon direction.

Materials: Playground equipment.

Group size: Small group.

Procedure: Give each child a direction to stand near to or far from different objects or places on the playground. Children who respond correctly may stay where told; subsequent children may be told to move relative to these first children. (This last part might be successful with children who are 5 years old or older, as younger ones do not like to be left out of any activity.)

MONSTER, MAY I?

Concept: Given directions from the teacher, the child steps toward or away from the teacher. Identify nearest and farthest child from teacher upon completion of the steps.

Materials: None.

Group size: Class.

Procedure: Line the children up in a row facing you. Tell the class to take great steps away from or toward you until you say "stop." Ask who is the nearest and who is the farthest after each direction. Give directions to individual children to move forward or backward.

Questions: How do we find the nearest? Farthest? Why?

MARBLE GAME

Concept: Tell whose marble is nearest the target and whose marble is the farthest from the target.

Materials: Marbles or balls (or jar lids with children's names written on the lids).

Ramp made from a piece of plywood or cardboard.

Bull's-eye on paper (tape to floor to keep in place).

Group size: Small group.

Procedure: Have each child pick his or her own ball (or use the lid with his or her name). Make sure that each knows which one is his or hers. Each child rolls the ball down a ramp toward the bull's-eye. The child who is nearest could get a point; the farthest could also get a point. Have the children take turns seeing who can get nearest.

Questions: Is it better to roll the ball fast or slow? What is the best way to get near to the target?

CARD SHARP

Concept: Given a picture of an object, the child places himself or herself near to or far from the object as directed by the teacher.

Materials: Deck of cards with pictures of school equipment (as from a catalog of school supplies): chairs, windows, chalkboard, desk, etc.

Group size: Class.

Procedure: Put the deck of cards in a stack turned upside down. Let each child take a turn drawing a card, then placing himself or herself near the object drawn. Play also with the word "far." Then play with both at the same time—each draws a card and then someone tells him/her to move near to or far from the object. The child moves to the proper position.

Variations: This can be played like "Simon Says" with your giving verbal directions and the children placing themselves near to or far from something according to their instructions.

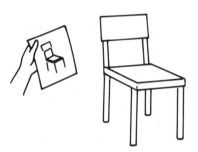

POINT TO A PICTURE

Concept: Point to the picture that is near or far as directed by the teacher.

Materials: Assorted pictures (animals, toys, vehicles, etc.).

Group size: Three to four children.

Procedure   Have each child point to different pictures in the room (either held by children or placed about the room) and say "near" or "far." Let the child decide which picture is near and which is far.

JUG PICTURES

Concept: Name which picture is near and which picture is far when looking through a tube or a milk carton.

Materials: Plastic gallon milk cartons with pictures of anything mounted inside.

Group size: One or more children depending on the number of jugs.

Procedure: Place pictures in the slots in the jug. Have the child look in the milk carton through the spout. Ask the child to tell you about the picture farthest away, and then the nearest one.

pictures in slots

pictures to be
inserted in slots

DETECTIVE

Concept: Identify near and far objects in a picture.

Materials: Large picture or poster of a city scene, a park, farmyard, or other suitable panorama.

Group size: Any size group.

Procedure: Give near or far clues to guide children in guessing the object of which you are thinking.

    The child who guesses the correct object is a good detective and may be allowed to pick and whisper to you the next object to be guessed. Repeat the procedure with the remaining children.

Questions: Can you guess the object that is near the tree, but far from the car? Can you guess the object that is nearer to the car than the squirrel is?

EARTH AND SKY

Concept: Place objects in correct proximity to the earth or the sky.

Materials: Flannelboard.

Cutout objects for the flannelboard, i.e., stars, flying birds, rabbits, ducks, sun, flower, tree, plane.

Grass and cloud cutouts.

Group size: Four to six children.

Procedure: Place clouds near the top of the flannelboard and grass near the bottom. Each child takes a cutout object and places it in correct relation to grass and sky.

Note: Some objects may be placed correctly either way, for example, an airplane. Ask the child why he or she placed the object in a certain position.

Variation: This activity can also be drawn on the chalkboard, or pictures with tape on the back can be placed on the chalkboard in correct relationship to sky and earth.

WORKSHEET: NEAR AND FAR

Concept: Draw figures in correct proximity given names of objects to be drawn.

Materials: Duplicated worksheets showing familiar objects.

Crayons.

Group size: Class.

Procedure: Give directions for the child to draw objects near to or far from objects on the worksheet.

Say, "Draw a boy." "Make a red balloon near the boy." "Draw a blue cloud far from the tree." "Draw a yellow flower near the rock." "Make green grass near the car."

DRAW A DUPLICATE

Concept: Copy pictures with objects in correct proximity.

Materials: Chalk, crayons, or pencils (blocks are an alternative).

Paper.

Group size: Any size group.

Procedure: Draw objects on the chalkboard or lay out objects on a table. Some should be near to each other, others far apart. Have the children draw a picture of the objects with correct relative position to each other. Say, "Where is this bird? Draw it." "Where is this other bird? Now, draw it." "Where is the sun? Is it near something else?"

Variation: Instead of drawing, the children can arrange felt cutouts on their desk tops to copy the teacher's flannelboard arrangement.

DOT PICTURES

Concept: Connect dots by drawing a line from a starting point to the nearest dot, then the dot nearest it, etc.

Materials: Paper.

Pencil.

Crayons to color in finished picture.

Group size: Class.

Procedure: Make dittos or permanent dot-to-dot pictures that can be erased and used over. Beginning pictures should have large differences in distances between dots so the child can discriminate nearest more easily. Differences can be made more minute as the child develops skill.

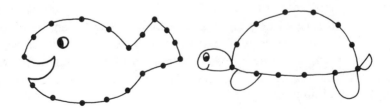

2.3   Separation

Separation skills are the perception of whether objects are touching or not touching; "attached" or "unattached" also describes the relationship. Development of these skills begins with simple observations such as "the door is separated from the wall" and "the block is separated from the floor." These skills become more refined until the child can deal with imposing the relation on the objects (e.g., placing buttons so they touch) or making separation judgments about objects when the relation is imposed on the objects and does not naturally occur in the child's environment (e.g., two children walking with an orange between their shoulders).

Physical objects that are touching can frequently be moved as a single unit. This causal relationship provides a foundation for numerous activities in the separation section. Other activities rely only on the perception of touching or separated in their degree of "nearness." These activities include discriminations of whether a train engine is attached to the cars or separated from them.

BUTTONS

Concept: Manipulate objects in separation situations.

Materials: Two pieces of paper or two spaces outlined on the two inside sides of a file folder.

Buttons, bottle caps, or anything similar.

Group size: One or two children.

Procedure: Ask the child to place all the objects on one sheet so that they are touching; all the objects on the other sheet are placed so that they are separated.

Questions: How can you tell if something is touching? Can you think of things in the room that are touching now? Not touching? Can you think of other ways to put the objects together so that they are touching? Not touching?

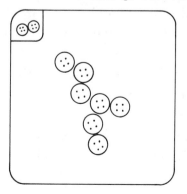 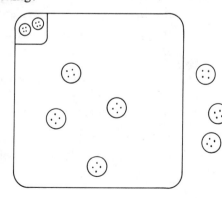

THE LITTLE ENGINE THAT *COULD*

Concept: Discriminate attached from unattached objects.

Materials: Toy train pieces or teacher-made train pieces (cars should be different colors or be easily distinguished some other way).

Group size: Four to six children.

Procedure: Display a train and have children decide if the cars are attached to the engine. Then change the display and allow children to determine if the engine (or cars) are attached. At times have the cars attached and at other times have one of the cars unattached.

Questions: Can the little engine pull the train as you see it? Why? Why not?

THE OATMEAL TUNNEL

Concept: Discriminate between attached (touching) and unattached objects.

Materials: Cars, toy trucks, or animals.

String or yarn.

A tunnel made from a box or halved oatmeal container.

Group size: One to three children.

Procedure: Tie strings to all the cars. Lay the cars and their strings out so that the strings pass through the tunnel. Add a few extra strings that go through the tunnel from the cars to the child but are not attached to the cars.

Have a child choose a string coming out of the tunnel. Next, have the child pull the string to find out if it is attached to (touching) a car or if the string is unattached.

Let the child try a few strings. Next, when a child begins to pull a string, ask if the string has a car or not. Ask the child how he or she can tell.

Questions: Which car will the string pull? How can we find out? Have child close eyes and pull a string: Can you tell if you have a car or not? How?

THE ORANGE THAT SEPARATES

Concept: Maintain separation through a physical experience and identify the object held between two people.

Materials: Balls or oranges.

Group size: Class.

Procedure: Seat the children in pairs facing each other with a ball between each pair.

Ask, "Can you hold the ball up in the air with both of you touching the ball? Try it." "What will happen when you separate from the ball or stop touching the ball? Do it." "Try holding the ball between you with elbows, hands, shoulders." "What will happen each time one of you moves or separates from the ball?"

Variation: Let the pairs of children try walking around with the ball between them in some way. Try walking around with each of three or four people separated by a ball.

Questions: What was the hardest thing we tried? Who was able to hold it the longest? Can we think of other things to hold (big, or little)?

GLUED PEOPLE

Concept: Maintain separation through a physical experience and identify the middle person in a group of three as the one who separates the other two.

Materials: Mats, hoops, or something to identify areas in a room.

Group size: Class.

Procedure: Have the children work in threes and let each group stand in a defined area. One child is the middle child and the one who separates the other two children. (Allowing the middle child to wear something to distinguish him or her as the middle child is optional.) At the naming of a body part, have the three children touch with that body part. The three children are then touching, such as hands to hands, toes to toes, knees to knees, head to head, etc. Direct the three children to move to another designated spot while trying to maintain touch continually. Repeat the activity.

Questions: Was it hard to move around the room touching? What was the hardest thing to maintain touch with and move? What was the most fun?

YARN RUNNERS

Concept: Maintain separation through physical experience and identify the object held between two people.

Materials: Yarn cut into 3-foot (or 1-meter) lengths or scarves.

Group size: Any size group.

Procedure: Allow children to pair off with one string for each pair. With each child holding an end of the yarn, have them try to run, skip, or walk fast without one of the children dropping an end. Let them try to walk backward.

Variation: Run relays with the pairs of children. Or blindfold the pairs of children and have them move on instructions.

Questions: Why does the yarn get dropped? How can we make sure that we don't do this? What would happen if we had longer strings? Shorter? Try it.

JOIN 'EM UP

Concept: Join or separate figures as directed.

Materials: Flannelboard or table top.

Assorted felt shapes.

Group size: Four to six children.

Procedure: Give each child two pieces. Tell the child to join the pieces of felt. Point out to the child that joining means making them touch. The next piece can be separated from the first two. Say, "Put your piece on the board, but place it so that it does not touch any of the other pieces." Then ask, "How close can you get them before they touch? Show me." "Can you place this piece (handing the child a piece) on the board so that it touches the others?"

KISSING COUSINS

Concept: Discriminate pictured forms as separated or touching.

Materials: Cards with designs that have touching boundaries or separate boundaries.

Group size: One to two children.

Procedure: Have the child sort pictures of shapes into those that are touching and those that are separated.

Questions: How can we tell if something is separate or touching? As you look at the picture, are the shapes touching or not touching?

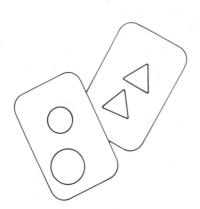 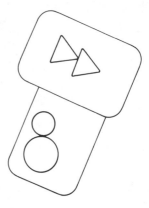

TWINS

Concept: Discriminate joined and separated objects on a worksheet.

Materials: Duplicated worksheets showing pairs of objects, some pairs joined and the others separted.

Crayons.

Group size: Class.

Procedure: Direct the children to color only the pairs ("twins") that are joined together. Say, "See the two birds? They are twins. Are they joined together? Are they touching?" "If they are joined, color them. If they are separated, do not color them."

2.4   Separation and order

Spatial relations of separation and order fall into two categories in this section of topology activities. The two sections are

1. Objects are separated (not touching or touching) by a given order. The order is positional (above, below, next to) and proximal (nearest to or farthest from).
2. Parts of a whole are separated by a given order. The parts may all be attached and yet separated in space. The parts of a body or the features of a house are cases in point. In the activities the child's task is to put parts of a whole together in their correct order.

CHECKERS

Concept: Order objects to duplicate a pattern.

Materials: Any small objects that are readily available.

A 15-centimeter-square piece of paper.

Group size: One or two children or small group.

Procedure: On your square present a simple pattern to the child with some objects touching and others not touching. Have the child duplicate the pattern. Ask, "Can you place the checkers on your board so that it looks like mine?" Do this enough so that every child has an opportunity. Then make the pattern slightly harder as in Figure 2. If the child seems to have difficulty, do some readiness work with arrangements such as that in Figure 3.

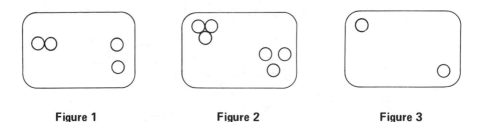

Figure 1   Figure 2   Figure 3

JUGGLER

Concept: Duplicate patterns from one size to another with the order of objects proportionally similar.

Materials: Any objects that can be represented on a small scale in two sizes with manipulative objects (kites, balls, balloons, animals, etc.).

Two sizes of paper for background.

Group size: One or two children.

Procedure: Make a pattern with the smaller objects on the small sheet of paper. Let the child try to duplicate it with the larger objects on the large sheet. Look for the nearness of objects. Reverse the size making the model with large objects, letting the child copy with the smaller objects. At first use only three objects.

Easier variations: Draw trees, clouds, people, etc. in proportion on the sheets so that the child can group the objects in proximity to some outstanding feature.

Teacher card   Child card

CHOO CHOO TRAIN

Concept: Join or separate objects as directed.

Materials: Toy train or a teacher-made milk carton train (a half-gallon carton can be the engine, and half-pints can be cars). Cars should be different colors or be distinguishable some other way.

Group size: Four to six children.

Procedure: Starting with the engine, have a child join cars as directed by you. Ask, "Can you join the red car to the blue car?" "Join the green car to the red one." "Separate the blue car and put it on the sidetrack." Also direct the child to leave some cars separate as in the last direction. When mentioning the color name, either hand the car to the child or point to the car if the child does not yet know colors.

Variations: (1) Assemble felt cutouts on a flannelboard in place of the toy train. (2) Make a "real" train by painting cardboard boxes that children could sit in. One child, the yard master, can direct joining the cars.

IT'S A GRAPE DAY!

Concept: Recognize separate parts of a whole object.

Materials: Grapes on the stem.

Group size: Class.

Procedure: Show the grapes to the class. Talk about the parts of the bunch of grapes that they can see. Ask the questions below. Let children pull off the grapes to eat.

Questions: How is one grape separated from another? What does each grape touch? What does the stem touch?

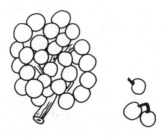

HIP CONNECTED TO THE THIGH

Concept: Name attached parts of the body.

Materials: None.

Group size: Class.

Procedure: Call out body parts to students and have them respond verbally. If you say "toe," the child could say "foot" or touch his or her foot. There may be more than one correct answer and all should be accepted.

Questions: Did we all think of the same parts? Can anyone think of another body part that is connected to the leg? Can you touch both parts at the same time?

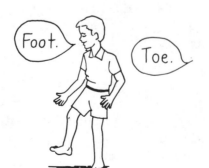

toe/foot/ankle
head/neck/hair/ear
fingers/hand
shoulder/neck/arm/chest

MAKE A FACE

Concept: Place features on a face in correct topological position relative to each other.

Materials: Felt cutouts of a face and facial features.

Mirror.

Group size: Four to six children.

Procedure: Give the child the felt face and have the child put the eyes, nose, and mouth in correct places. Say, "See the face. Here is the nose. Where does the mouth go? Over here? Down here?"

At first, you may place the nose for the child, and the child places the mouth and the eyes.

If there is disagreement or for self-checking, the child should look in the mirror or at another child.

Questions: Are your eyes closer to your nose or to your mouth?

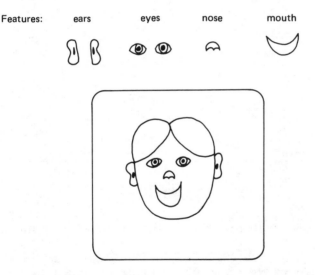

BODY BEAUTIFUL

Concept: Put all body parts in the correct topological positions.

Materials: Felt human figure cut into these parts: head, two ears, neck, trunk, two arms, two hands, two legs, two feet, two eyes, nose, mouth, and hair.

Outline of the body correctly assembled (optional).

Group size: One to four children.

Procedure: Have the child assemble the person with all parts in correct order. Should the child need help, have him or her place a single body part on a body already partially assembled. Have other children, who are ready, arrange correctly a total body from scrambled parts.

Variation: Parts may be assembled on a flannelboard, for a group activity, or on a table, for an individual activity.

An outline of the assembled body may be provided for self-checking or for an initial teaching experience.

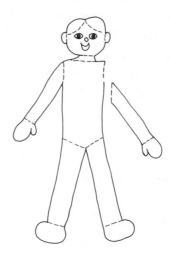

CLOWN

Concept: Put body parts together in correct topological position.

Materials: Puzzles on cardboard (see diagram). Or magazine pictures of people pasted on cardboard and cut similar to the drawing (dotted lines indicate additional places where puzzle could be cut to make puzzle more difficult).

Group size: One or two children.

Procedure: Lay the puzzle pieces out so that the child can see each piece rightside up. Allow the child to take the mixed-up body parts and put them together.

The puzzles are good to use with a child who does not yet have the motor skills to express topological understanding in drawings.

Give children more experiences with the concepts by using different puzzle characters.

Questions: Where is your shoulder? Where is your hand? What is this called (point to the whole arm)? Does your hand join your shoulder or your arm?

BUILD THE HOUSE

Concept: Assemble a house with the parts in correct proximity to each other.

Materials: Flannelboard.

Felt cutouts of house pieces: frame or wall, roof, chimney, windows, doors, doorbell, mailbox, sidewalk, bushes.

Group size: Four to six children.

Procedure: Begin by placing the frame of the house on the flannelboard. Then place the other pieces in correct position.

Some variations will occur.

Questions: Where does a window go? Does it touch the bottom of the wall? The top? Why not?

2.5   Enclosure (open, closed)

Judgements about a boundary's being open or closed constitute discriminations concerning enclosures. A child's ability to discriminate closed boundaries serves as a prerequisite to later work with sets. Difficulties with topological perceptions of open and closed figures are often revealed in a child's confusion with letters such as C and O. The child must be provided activities that develop a strategy for assessing whether a boundary is open or closed.

There are two strategies for discriminating open from closed figures. One strategy involves choosing a starting point on the boundary and trying to follow the boundary in one direction around to the starting point. If traversing the boundary allows one to return to the starting point, then the figure is called *closed*. Notice that, in moving along the boundary, no line may be used more than once. The second strategy involves determining if one can move from the inside of the figure to the outside (or vice versa) without crossing the boundary. If one can find a break (or opening), then the figure is called *open*. In Figure 2.3, curve A is closed and curve B is open.

Curve A   Curve B

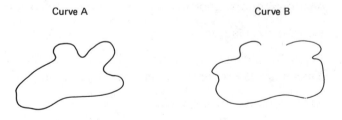

Figure 2.3

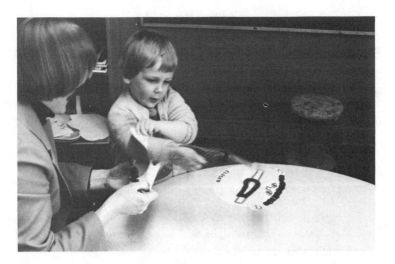

Putting the open shapes in "Big Mouth" is always popular.

Initial activities include boundaries that provide a tactile as well as a visual boundary. Note that a child might be able to use one of the strategies and correctly identify an open or closed figure and yet not perceptually perceive it as such. Hence, the activities with very simple open and closed figures should be used first. As the child gains experience using the strategy through tactile activities, ability to evaluate open or closed figures perceptually should develop.

Sometimes a decision is difficult to make.

WALK THE SHAPE

Concept: Use reference point to determine whether shape is open or closed.

Materials: Ropes or chalk or masking tape.

                 Beanbags.

Group size: Any size group.

Procedure: Lay shapes out on the floor. Some are open, some are closed. Drop a beanbag on the boundary of each.

                 Have a child begin at the beanbag and try to walk on the shape all the way around back to the beanbag. Discuss whether the walk was successful.

                 Try to elicit from the children that it is possible to return on a closed shape but not on an open shape.

Questions: Where did you start from? Can you get back to the beanbag? Why? Can you get back if the shape is open? How could you fix it to get back? Can you get back if the shape is closed? Is your shape open or closed?

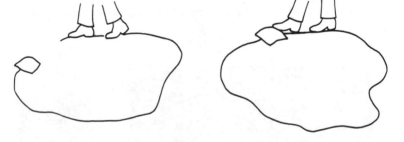

BEAN BAG MAZE

Concept: Discriminate open from closed figures.

Materials: Beanbags.

                 Masking tape.

Group size: Class.

Procedure: Lay out masking tape shapes on the floor. Have the children take turns throwing beanbags at the shapes. The object is to throw a beanbag into open shapes so that the bag can get out again. The beanbags that land in closed shapes can't get out until all the beanbags are "captured." When a child has thrown a beanbag, the child may throw another if one can be found in an open figure.

Questions: Are you going to try to throw the beanbags in the closed or open shapes? Why? What happens when the beanbag lands in the closed shapes? Can you find a beanbag in an open figure?

 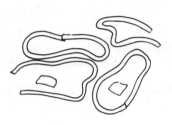

ROPE MAZE

Concept: Discriminate open from closed shapes. Find way out of a maze of open shapes.

Materials: Rope or tape, chalk, or yarn taped to the floor.

Objects for "treasures" (optional).

Group size: Class.

Procedure: Make one or more mazes starting with simple ones and working toward more complex ones. Have a child start in the center of the maze and find a way out or start outside and find a way in to a "treasure." Be sure that the child understands that he or she cannot step over ropes; the child must find openings. Children can look down and see openings more easily with floor mazes than they can with mazes on paper.

You can make some mazes closed ones.

Variation: Blindfold the child and have him or her try to crawl out of the maze laid out on the floor with ropes.

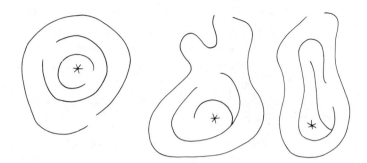

OUT OR IN—WHO WILL WIN?

Concept: Identify closed shapes from open shapes regardless of the configuration of the boundary.

Materials: Long rope with ends tied together and short rope with ends untied.

Group size: Class.

Procedure: Place the long rope with ends tied on the floor in the center of the room. Say, "I want Helga and Demetrius to get inside the roped area and shut their eyes. When I tell them, they must try to escape, but they cannot cross over the rope. They must state if they can or cannot escape. If they are right, they get to choose the next players."

Change the configuration of the rope boundary. Then, children open their eyes and try to escape. Occasionally interchange the open for closed ropes.

change to

change to

BEANBAG RALLY

Concept: Discriminate open and closed pathways.

Materials: Cans or boxes.

Beanbags or any substitute, i.e., clothes pins, balls.

Rope.

Group size: Small group or class.

Procedure: Set up an obstacle course with cans along the route and use rope to mark the path. The route can be open or closed. Have each child move along the obstacle course dropping a beanbag into each can along the way. After all children have finished the course, ask if the course was open or closed.

Run the obstacle course in reverse, having the children take one beanbag from each can along the way.

Change the course from open to closed or vice versa.

Questions: Tell me why the course is open? Closed?

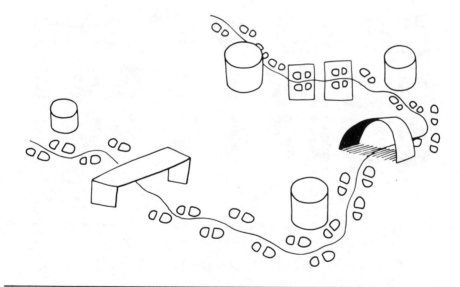

BIG MOUTH

Concept: Sort open and closed figures.

Materials: Two large plastic or felt faces with oversized mouths, one "open" and the other "closed."

Assorted open and closed felt shapes.

Group size: One to four children.

Procedure: Sort open shapes onto the open mouth and closed shapes onto the closed mouth. For self-checking, correct shapes can be pictured on the reverse side of each face.

A mesh bag (like those that onions come in) can be taped behind the open mouth. The shapes can then be inserted through a hole or slit in the open mouth.

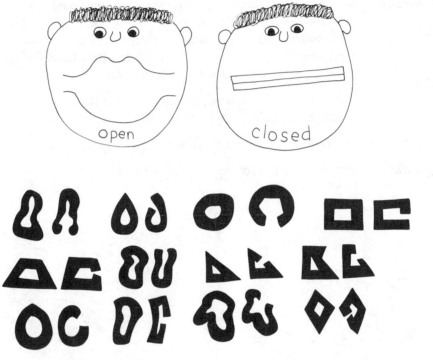

BLIND MAN'S SHAPES

Concept: Discriminate open and closed figures by touch.

Materials: Blindfold.

Assorted open and closed felt figures (same as used for "Big Mouth"). Put a tactile reference point on each shape using little balls of masking tape or even staples.

Group size: Four to six children.

Procedure: Blindfold a child. Give the child a figure and have him or her use a finger to trace around the figure using reference tape as a starting point. Have the child tell you whether the figure is open or closed.

Variation: Children in pairs, with one blindfold per pair, may present the figures to each other.

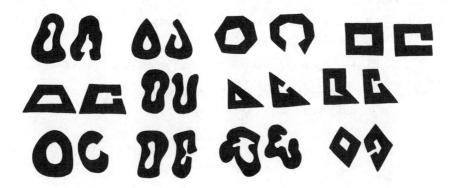

OPEN OR CLOSED

Concept: Discriminate objects that have open boundaries from those that are closed.

Materials: Bracelet, ring, Lifesaver candy, horseshoe magnet, hula hoop, rope, string of beads.

Group size: Four to six children or class.

Procedure: Put the objects on a flat surface one by one. Ask each child to decide if an object is open or closed by determining if he or she can reach the inside without crossing a boundary. Ring— no, you have to cross a boundary. Horseshoe—yes, you can put something inside through the opening. Then, make sets of closed and open objects.

GEOBOARDS

Concepts: Construct closed curves given a geoboard and rubberbands.

Materials: Geoboard.

Rubberbands.

Group size: Four to six children.

Procedure: Ask the children to make as many closed shapes as they can think of on their geoboards.

Later, ask if anyone can make an open shape on a geoboard.

Questions: Can you make a shape bigger and keep it a closed shape? How could you make a closed shape open?

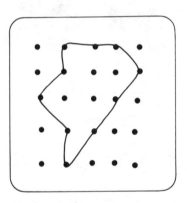

THE OK CORRAL

Concept: Construct and discriminate open and closed shapes.

Materials: Six toy horses.

Six squares of fabric, tagboard, or plastic, each with a fence outline drawn on it: Three fences open, three fences closed. Inside each fence is an X. Outside each fence is drawn an apple.

Toy fence sections (inch cubes will work), enough to cover exactly the fence outlines.

Three small felt apples (optional).

Group size: One to four children.

Procedure: Have the child match sections of fence onto the outlines. (You may need to assist in the fence building.) Next, let the child place a horse on each X. Have the child determine whether each horse can get the treat of an apple. If the corral is open, the child walks the horse over to the apple in the corner of the square. If the corral is closed, the horse must stay inside. No fence jumping is allowed.

If the child succeeds, permit him or her to feed the felt apples to the horses inside the corrals.

As a variation, if the child insists that the horses can jump over any fence, snails can be substituted for horses.

Questions: Can you fix the fence of the closed corral so that the horse could get out to the apple? Can you fix the fence of the open corral so that the horse can/can not get out?

KEEP YOUR PET IN THE YARD

Concept: Discriminate open and closed shapes.

Materials: Gameboard as in the diagram.

Deck of 12 to 20 cards, each showing a pet animal either surrounded (by a closed shape) or partly surrounded (by an open shape). The reverse side of each card can be marked with a happy or sad face to make the game self-correcting.

Group size: One to four children.

Procedure: Show the gameboard and explain that the happy face shows a child who has kept the yard gate closed so the pet could not run away; the sad face shows a child whose pet got away because the yard gate was left open.

Have the child sort the cards into two piles on the gameboard, placing closed yards on the happy face side and open yards on the sad face side.

It is not necessary for the child to read open and closed (written on the gameboard) as the smiling and sad faces serve as cues.

Questions: Why would you be sad if your pet got out of the yard? Can you sort the pictures onto the happy face if the pet cannot escape? Onto the sad face if the pet can escape?

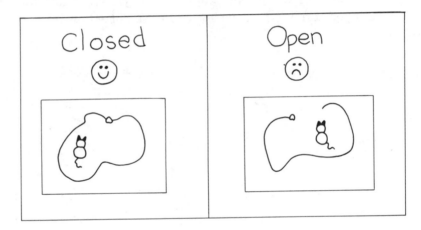

LION MAZE

Concept: Distinguish objects surrounded by a boundary from those that are not. Recognize that the boundary of a closed shape cannot be crossed.

Materials: Drawings of lion cages in mazes, some open and others closed.

Lion markers.

Group size: One or two children.

Procedure: Tell a story about a zookeeper who went to call Mommy or Daddy and left some of the lions out of their cages. Have the child put the lions back into the cages that are open.

Questions: Can you find the open cages? How can you tell which ones are open? Can you close the cages so the lions cannot get out?

OPEN-CLOSED CONCENTRATION

Concept: Match pairs of open shapes and pairs of closed shapes.

Materials: Deck of 40 cards—half showing open shapes, half showing closed shapes.

Group size: Two to five children.

Procedure: Shuffle the cards and place them facedown in five rows of eight cards each. Have the children take turns picking up two cards. If one shape is open and the other is closed, the child must return both to original facedown position and the turn ends. If both shapes are equivalent, the child must name them correctly "open" or "closed"; if correct, he or she keeps them.

Play proceeds to the next child. The child with the most cards is the winner.

For young children, use three rows of three cards to eliminate confusion and increase the number of cards as the child gains experience.

Variation: (1) Use this as an independent activity by having one child sort the cards into those that are open and those that are closed. (2) Also, for young children the teacher can show a picture and let the child state "open" or "closed."

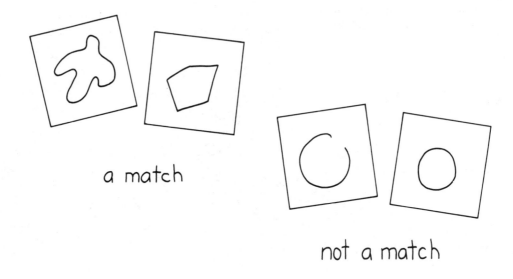

a match

not a match

THE MAIL CARRIER IN YOUR NEIGHBORHOOD

Concept:　Discriminate open and closed shapes.

Materials:　Neighborhood drawings (see diagram).

A toy mail carrier's car or an envelope with a drawing of a mail carrier's car (mail is kept inside).

Paper to represent mail.

Group size:　One to two children.

Procedure:　Ask the child to park the mailcar somewhere in the neighborhood and begin to deliver mail "on foot." Tell the child that each house gets mail so that the child can see where mail has been delivered. Note that the child is not to deliver mail to a house twice or walk past a house to which mail has already been delivered.

If the mail carrier delivers mail to all the houses and finishes at the parked car, then he or she has walked around a closed shape. If the child does not end up at the starting point, then he or she must walk back to the car and the shape was open.

Questions:　"Will this mail route still be closed if you park somewhere else and deliver the mail? Try it. Will this mail route still be open if you park somewhere else and deliver the mail? Try it."

BAREFOOT BABY

Concept: Construct pathways of open and closed shapes.

Materials: Playing cards with designs as follows: one card with a picture of a baby on each side (use pictures that represent the racial make-up of your class) and approximately ten cards with foot-prints to match (see drawing).

Group size: One to three children.

Procedure: Have children share cards evenly. Lay the card with the bare-foot baby on the table first. Allow each child to take a turn, laying down a card matching heels to toes so that a pathway of footprints is laid out on the table.

Open shapes will be made more often than closed. Ask the children to try to make a closed shape. Have them work together to bring the footprints back to the baby. This is not a competitive game.

As a variation, have the children try to make the baby walk in a straight line toward some object (open shape).

Also, the children can try to make open and closed shapes using only three or four cards.

Questions: If the baby walks around to the starting place will the shape of the pathway be closed or open?

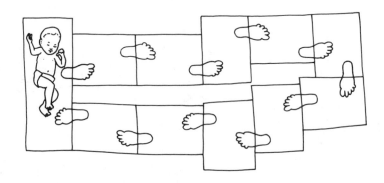

HOP HOME

Concept: Find a closed pathway to get back to the starting point.

Materials: Gameboards with diagrams such as those shown below.

Markers.

Group size: One or two children.

Procedure: Give each child a marker representing "his or her house." Then have the child "hop" along the path (dark spots are rest points) to see if it is possible to get back to "his or her house" without going back over the path.

The child does not actually hop on the gameboard (unless you have constructed it large enough) but, rather, moves a marker along the path simulating hopping.

Variation: Use frogs hopping from one lily pad to another on curved lines.

Questions: Can you hop backward and get home? Did you hop on a closed pathway or an open pathway? Can you find another way to get home (another pathway)?

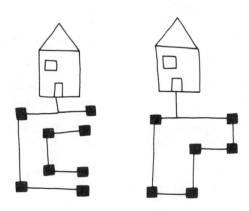

OPEN-CLOSED WORKSHEET

Concept: Identify open figures and closed figures.

Materials: Duplicated worksheets with assorted open and closed shapes.

Crayons.

Group size: Class.

Procedure: Give each child a worksheet and demonstrate the correct procedure on the chalkboard or chart paper. Ask the children to
find the closed shapes, point to them, and color them.

Open shapes are to be marked with an X.

Variation: Have the children turn their worksheets over and
draw their own closed and open shapes.

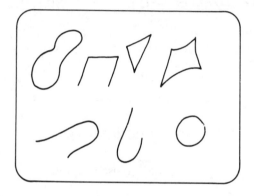

HOLES

Concept: Identify and mark shapes that include a closed boundary.

Materials: Paper with the printed alphabet on it.

Pencil or magnetic, wooden, or cardboard letters.

Group size: Any size group.

Procedure: Have the children find the letters of the alphabet that have a
"hole," or closed boundary, on them.

Notice that the word hole means an area completely enclosed
by a boundary. It does not mean a hole in the boundary.

Do this with either upper- or lower-case letters or both.

Let a child sort the letters into two piles or put a circle around those letters.

Another option is to have the child color inside the closed boundary of the letters.

Ⓐ⒝CⒹEFGHIJKLM
NⓄⓅⓆRSTUVWXYZ

ⓐⓑcⓓⓔfⓖhijklm
nⓄⓅⓆrstuvwxyz

HOLES IN YOUR NAME

Concept: Identify shapes that have closed boundaries.

Materials: Paper and pencil.

Crayons or magnetic, wooden, or cardboard letters.

Group size: Any size group.

Procedure: Have the children write or spell their names or give them sheets with their names written on them. Let them find the letters in their names that have holes and color them. Find out who has the most holes, who has the least.

Give the child a choice of coloring the holes in his/her name or drawing a face in each closed letter.

Make a bar graph using the colored letters from each person's name. This provides a comparison method.

Questions: Does anyone not have holes in their name? (Use last names or the name of someone in their families for those who do not have holes in their first names.) Can you think of words that might have "holes"? Might not have "holes"?

DRAW IT AGAIN, SAM

Concept: Use repeated open or closed shapes to make a design.

Materials: Pencil, chalk, or crayon.

Paper or chalkboard.

Group size: Small or large group.

Procedure: Ask the child to draw an open or a closed shape and then repeat the shape over and over to make a design. Demonstrate with open and closed shapes.

You could give the children choices of shapes to choose from. Keep in mind the children's drawing abilities.

The designs may be colored by those children showing an interest in doing so.

Questions: What happens to the shape? Does it become larger or smaller?

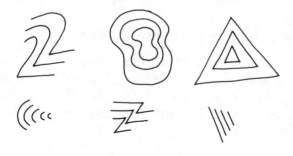

HIDDEN PICTURES

Concept: Find and differentiate open figures and closed figures.

Materials: Paper with drawings (see diagram).

Crayons or magic markers.

Group size: Any size group.

Procedure: Ask each child to find and point to a closed figure. Then, have the child color the closed figures to find the hidden pictures.

Children might be able to make designs. Have them draw and color their own patterns.

Questions: Will your pictures look alike if you all color the closed shapes? Why? Why not?

2.6 Surrounding by a boundary (inside, outside)

The prerequisite to recognizing the inside and outside of a figure or object is the ability to recognize a closed boundary. A closed figure has two regions (an inside and an outside) separated by a boundary. Initial activities allow the boundary to be distinguished by tactile experiences as in the previous section.

When the fence isn't closed, the horse gets an apple.

ROPE SHAPES

Concept: Discriminate inside, outside, and boundary of a closed shape.

Materials: Jump ropes, string, or masking tape.

Group size: Four to six children.

Procedure: Lay out a simple closed curve on the floor. Give directions to the children to stand inside, outside, or on the shape.

Questions: Can you make part of you inside and part of you outside the shape?

ANIMALS PLAYING

Concept: Place objects inside or outside specified areas.

Materials: Gameboard with colored areas representing a pond (blue), a grassy pasture (green), and a mud puddle (brown).

Toy farm animals.

A toy fence to surround part of the pasture (optional).

Group size: One to four children.

Procedure: Ask a child to place a toy animal inside or outside the pond, pasture or mud on your direction or that of a child. Say, "Put the duck in the pond." "Put the pig outside the mud." "Put the horse inside the pasture, but outside the fence." As an independent activity, have the child place the animals. Later, ask the child to name where each animal was placed.

Questions: Where is the fish? Can it be anywhere else? Why is the pig in the mud? What can we put the pig in to get it clean?

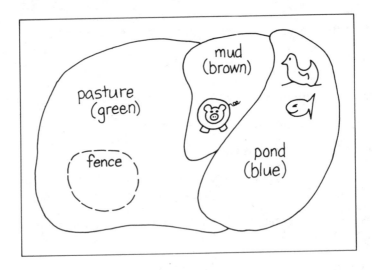

FARM FENCES

Concept: Place objects inside, outside, or on a shape.

Materials: Yarn or string.

Toy animals.

Table or desk.

Group size: Four to six children.

Procedure: Place on the table a simple closed curve made of yarn. Have each child place a toy animal by your direction inside, outside, or on the boundary of the shape. Say, "Put the dog on the fence, the cow inside the fence, and the horse outside of the fence." Give directions one at a time at first. Some children should be able to remember three directions at a time.

Variations: (1) Do this activity with flannelboard and flannelboard animals. (2) Use a worksheet with a closed shape. Have the child draw objects inside, outside, and on the boundary of the shape given directions.

Questions: Can you put the horse inside and outside at the same time?

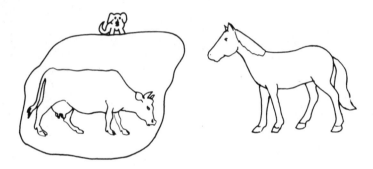

HUNGRY MONSTER

Concept: Describe when an object is inside or outside another object.

Materials: Yarn or string.

Flannelboard.

Felt picture cutouts.

Group size: Four to six children.

Procedure: Place the string or yarn on the flannelboard in the shape of a monster. Place various animals or fruits and vegetables on the board. Show the children that, when the monster eats something, it goes inside the outline of the monster. If something gets away from the monster or it does not like it and won't eat it, then the object or animal stays outside the monster. Let the children decide whether the monster will eat each object and then tell you whether the object is inside or outside the monster.

Variation: The monster can eat shapes instead of objects or animals.

INSIDE-OUTSIDE CONCENTRATION

Concept: Match enclosed shapes and nonenclosed shapes.

Materials: Deck of 40 cards, each containing two shapes. On 20 cards one shape is enclosed in the other; on the other 20 cards neither shape is enclosed.

Group size: Two to six children.

Procedure   Shuffle the cards and place them facedown in five rows of eight cards each. First, have the child select two cards. If one card shows "inside" and the other shows "outside," the child returns the cards to their original facedown position and the next child takes a turn.

If both cards show the same relation, the child must name that relation, "inside" or "outside." If correct, the child keeps both cards.

The winner is the player with the most cards.

In an easier variation that has no winners or losers, let each child turn over two cards at a time until a match is found.

Inside

Outside

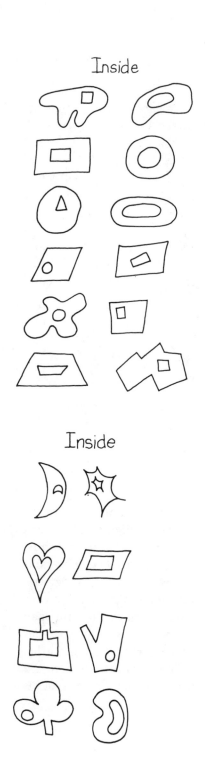

Inside

Outside

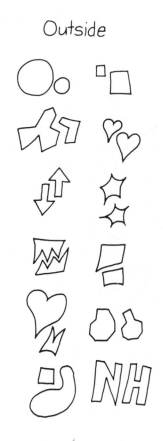

2.7   Surrounding on a line (betweenness)

Given a line and three points, *a, b, c* on line *abc, betweenness* means that point *b* will always remain between points *a* and *c* regardless of whether the line is a straight line or has been bent into a curved or angular form. An example from the child's physical world is the child's arm. When the arm is straight, the elbow is between the hand and shoulder. Change the form of the arm by bending at the elbow: the arm is in a different position, yet along the arm the body parts remain in the identical relationship. The elbow remains between the hand and the shoulder regardless of the position of the arm.

Until the topological concept of betweenness is understood, the child will rely on earlier stages of perception. In Figure 2.4, the dark dots represent points on a path, and the circle represents an object the child is directed to place on the path.

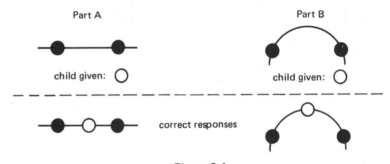

Figure 2.4

As shown in Figure 2.4A, the child will have little trouble placing the object on the path between the given points. However, in Figure 2.4B, when asked to place the object on the line so that it is between the given points, the child will place the object as shown in Figure 2.5 (incorrect). The child giving the incorrect response is making a judgment based on horizontal alignment (proximity). Given the strategy of following the curved line with a finger or shown where the object should be placed, the child still may doubt the solution. The child correctly responding to betweenness activities understands the order of objects in space. As in understanding other mathematical concepts, there is a period of transition. During this transition, the child can see the appropriate relationship part of the time or can correct his or her perceptions by applying some strategy.

Figure 2.5

YOU'RE AMONG FRIENDS

Concept: Identify position of between given seats around a table or blanket.

Materials: A table or a blanket for children to sit around for eating or working.

A picture or a name card for each child (optional).

Group size: Class.

Procedure: Prepare for a snack or lunch by having one child assign seats.

Begin with two children sitting apart on one side. Ask the child to choose someone to sit between *Sam* and *Sue.* The child sits in a chair between *Sam* and *Sue.* Ask the chosen child to state that he/she is sitting between *Sam* and *Sue.*

Variation: Put pictures or name cards on the table. One child is asked to find the person who will sit between *Holly* and *Paul.*

Questions: Is there a space between *Perry* and *Tammie*? Who's sitting between *Cheryl* and *Darren*?

BETWEEN YOU AND ME

Concept: Name object between self and another person.

Materials: Various objects: a ball, pencil, chair, piece of paper, and scissors.

String to mark the circle to walk (optional).

Group size: Small group or class.

Procedure: Have yourself or a child stand in the middle of a large string circle with objects scattered between you and the circle boundary.

Direct a child to walk around the circle and on the command of "between" the child stops and identifies the object or objects between him or her and the person in the center of the circle.

Have the child walk in different directions or move at different paces such as hopping or running.

Questions: Which object between us is the nearest/farthest? Name an object which is *not* between us. Can you move so that the pencil is between us? Can you make it so that it is not between us?

BETWEEN THE PUDDLES

Concept: Mark points on lines that are between (surrounded by) two other points.

Materials: Newspaper.

Brown bags.

Group size: Small group or class.

Procedure: Lay out paths as illustrated below using pieces of brown bag to represent puddles and pieces of newspaper to represent rocks. Tape the path and obstacles to the floor.

Say, "You have gone out to play on a wet day and must cross a street by jumping to the rocks between the puddles." Point to some of the rocks as the child lands on them and ask, "Is that rock between two puddles?" "Point to the puddles that you are between."

Questions: Which rocks have more puddles between them? Are there any rocks that do *not* have puddles between them?

*puddles

BABY BEAR

Concept: Place objects so that they lie between given points along a pathway.

Materials: Drawings of pathways each of which has two pictures—a mama bear and a papa bear (see diagram). Make the pathways thick and dark.

Small lids or thick round objects with a picture of a baby bear on each.

Group size: One or two children.

Procedure: Show a child one of the baby bears and the diagram that looks like this: ———☺————☺——— . Tell the child that this is a family of bears. Point out mama and papa, the bears on the line, and the baby bear on the marker. Say, "The bears are going for a walk along the sidewalk." (Point to the "sidewalk," which is the heavy black line.) "Baby bear needs to stay between mama and papa on the sidewalk so that it doesn't get lost." Put the baby bear between mama and papa on the sidewalk. Have the child tell you the story before you present other pathways. Next, present another pathway design. Ask the child, "Can you place baby bear between papa bear and mama bear?" Begin with simple paths and move to more complex paths as the child gets the idea.

Accept the child's choices the first time through. Notice where the child places baby bear. This will indicate the child's level of perception.

See the next activity, "Bears' Return", for another set of variations.

Questions: Walk the sidewalk with your fingers. Who do you walk by on the sidewalk? Was baby bear between mama and papa?

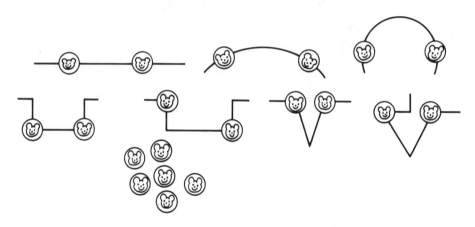

BEARS' RETURN

Concept: Place objects so that they lie between given points along the pathway.

Materials: Drawings of pathways each with two pictures—mama bear and papa bear. Also on the pathways include blank circles as alternatives for placement of the baby bear markers (see diagram).

Group size: One or two children.

Procedure: Show a child the simple pathway: ⌣—☺—◯—◯—☺—. Tell the child the story, as in the previous activity, that the baby bear is on a walk with mama and papa and must stay between mama and papa *on the sidewalk.* Ask the child to put a baby bear marker on a space between mama and papa. Let the child place baby bear on the other pathways proceeding from simple to more complex.

Variation: As alternative story themes, use a mama dog who must stay between two puppies or a car stuck on the highway between two trucks.

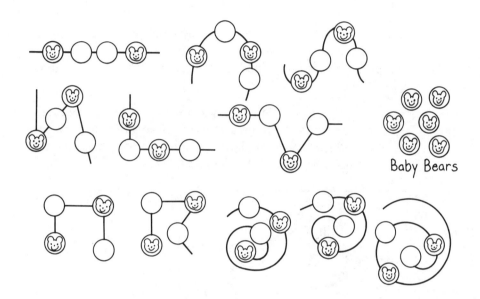

Baby Bears

HAUNTED HOUSE

Concept: Place an object between two other objects given a path to follow.

Materials: Cards showing differently shaped line segments, each segment having three or more circles or "points." Each line segment has a mother and a father animal on two of its circles, and between these two animals there is exactly one empty circle on the line segment.

Baby animal pictures, one for each adult pair.

Mask for child to wear (optional).

Group size: One to four children.

Procedure: Each card shows two animal parents in a room of the haunted house. Tell the child to find their baby and place it between its parents, in one of the circles along the path. The animal must stay in a circle on the path to avoid being caught by a monster. The baby animal must stay between its parents to avoid becoming scared and crying.

If placed correctly, the baby animal will enjoy the haunted house.

Variation: A mixture of easier paths (containing simple bends and only one or two empty circles) with more difficult paths (containing many bends and three or four empty circles) is desirable.

Variation: (1) Eliminate circles along the paths altogether. The child must put the animal marker any place along the line between its parents. (2) Have the child put on the mask to help the animals go through the haunted house.

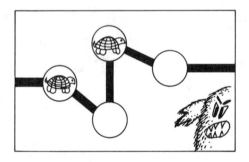

baby animal
marker

SKYSCRAPERS

Concept: Place an object physically between two given objects.

Materials: Snap-together cubes.

Group size: Four to six children.

Procedure: Give the child two or more differently colored cubes that are joined together. Tell the child a skyscraper will be built. At your direction, the child snaps more cubes between the ones he or she has. Continue directions to see who can make the longest row of cubes without an error. Stand up the blocks and admire the skyscrapers.

Note: The children must know colors to perform this activity.

Questions: Can you put a yellow cube between a green one and a yellow one? Who has the tallest one?

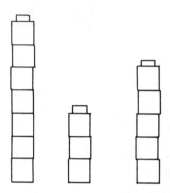

NECKLACES

Concept: Place an object between two others according to directions.

Materials: Beads in assorted colors.

String for beads.

Group size: Four to six children.

Procedure: Lay a string in front of the child with two beads set on it or just in front of it. Instruct the child to place another bead between these two beads. The beads will be strung once all of the beads have been placed.

Continue adding beads until the child has enough to be satisfied or until there is not any more space on the string. Make a necklace from the beads.

Questions: Look at your necklace and point to the bead between the red one and the yellow one.

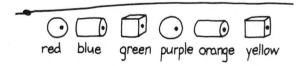

red   blue   green   purple   orange   yellow

JEWELRY WORKSHEET

Concept:　　Draw a point between two points marked on a line.

Materials:　　Duplicated worksheets, showing "beads" on "jewelry."

　　　　　　Crayons.

Group size:　Class.

Procedure:　Distribute worksheets and say, "Children, draw a bead between the beads on the first piece of jewelry." "Now do the same thing for the next piece."

　　　　　　(Special discussion should be given to the last piece of "jewelry" as it is connected.)

Questions:　Can you draw more beads between the ones that you have now?

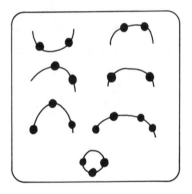

CHAPTER 3

Shape

3.1 Introduction

The child operating geometrically in the topological domain views circles and squares as being equivalent figures, both figures having closed boundaries. Children have difficulty differentiating one figure from the other until they begin to be aware of features of the boundaries of the figures themselves. At this time, work with shapes should be begun.

The shape chapter has been divided into four sections—readiness, naming shapes, drawing shapes, and constructing with shapes.

Readiness activities are designed to familiarize the child with basic shapes without naming or associating names with the shapes. In these activities the child is asked to match shapes that look alike or are the same. This assumes that the child understands the term "alike" or "same"; otherwise, time must be spent discussing these terms. Then the teacher should demonstrate how to match shapes to determine those that are like. In these activities, be certain that shape is the only dimension that is different in the material used; initially color and size variations should not be mixed in with shape differences.

The second section involves learning the names of the shapes. The child must learn to say the name when presented with a shape or choose the shape when the name is heard. At first the shape is associated with the symbolic representation as the concept of the shape is internalized. This involves linking visual and tactile perceptions to the symbols. During the process of learning a shape, the child should generalize his or her perceptions of, for example, one particular circle to other circles internalizing the concept of "roundness." A variety of materials should be used to encourage the child's generalization.

The child's ability to draw shapes may not develop at the same time or rate at which the child learns the names for the shapes. In fact, it is not necessary to be able to draw shapes to successfully learn their names. Fine motor skills, such as holding a crayon and controlling its direction, develop over time, but the sequence of activities used in teaching the names of shapes (circle, square, triangle) coincidé with the sequence of fine motor skills used when drawing these shapes. Circles are easiest to draw, squares next, and triangles (in which diagonals cross the child's midline) are last. Again, naming and drawing shapes may or may not occur at the same time.

The final section, constructing with shapes, contains general activities that provide opportunities to use the shape names either as a review or as extra exposure to tactile and perceptual features while names are being learned. This section on constructing with shapes will fit in well with art and cooking activities.

Shape and color

Studies show that shape perception precedes color perception. This fact is not always obvious when working with children. Some children know the names of colors and use them correctly before they can name and identify shapes. This is partly due to the fact that children are cued more often to color than shape when adults and peers talk about "red hat," "blue jeans," and "yellow door." These are cues to color. Shape cues are seldom used.

Preschoolers, in particular, confuse the words "shape" and "color." As an example, you might ask a child to tell you the name for a shape, and the child answers with its color. The child must associate the word "shape" with shape names, generalizing the perception of shapes to the linguistic symbol for that perception. Teach a unit on shape to completion before introducing the color concept, allowing the child to make the name distinctions.

Notice that children can and do learn color and shape associations in completely informal situations as may be found in the home. As a teacher, you do not have to exclude color descriptions in informal conversations with the children when they are learning shapes. The naturalness of your responses is preferable unless you perceive a problem with a particular child.

3.2   Shape readiness

Readiness activities do not require the use of shape names. The emphasis is on matching like figures through tactile and visual experiences. Activities vary from requiring a child simply to match figures when given a collection of shapes, to higher level activities that require retaining the visual image of one shape while finding its physical match.

Activities emphasize the definition of shape as what "goes around the outside." Have children trace the outside of shapes with their fingers when materials are available.

"How did you know it was a circle you felt?"

SHAPE GOES AROUND THE OUTSIDE

Concept: Identify meaning of the word "shape."

Materials: Assorted real objects which are relatively flat, i.e., jar lid, playing card, puzzle piece, 3″ × 5″ card, book, and shoe box lid.

Group size: Any size group.

Procedure: Introduce the word "shape" with the chant, "Shape goes around the outside." Have the children repeat this sentence with you.

Let the children take turns selecting an object from the collection and tracing around the shape with their fingers.

After practicing with real objects, the children may be given geometric forms to manipulate. Shape names (circle, square) should *not* be introduced at this point.

Trace around shapes to make a collage.

Questions: Does this piece of paper have a shape? Can you trace around it with your finger? Can you find something else in the room that has a shape?

SHAPE WALK

Concept: Identify meaning of the word "shape."

Materials: Masking tape, jump ropes, or chalk.

Group size: Any size group.

Procedure: Lay the shapes out on the floor of the room or out in the hall-way. Show the children the shapes on the floor that have been formed with masking tape, jump ropes, or chalk.

Have the child say, "Shape goes around the outside," while walk-ing along a shape.

Each child may be given a chance to "make a shape" for another child to walk along.

Variation: Slide along, march, or walk backward on the shapes.

Questions: Are there any shapes that look alike?

TRICKY SHAPES

Concept: Match similar shapes.

Materials: Geometric shapes with variable borders.

Group size: Any size group.

Procedure: Have each child sort shapes, grouping the same shapes together, despite the variability of the borders. Have them trace the shapes with their fingers.

SHAPEBOARD

Concept: Place a block on the playing board, matching the shape on the block with the shape drawn on the playing board.

Materials: Tagboard card with shapes drawn on it (see diagram). Shape blocks to match the drawn shapes.

Group size: One to three children.

Procedure: Distribute cards to the group and place blocks made from different geometric shapes in a pile in a center area. Each child takes a turn at choosing a block and placing it on the geometric shape whose side it matches. Say, "Can you choose a block and place it on the shape it matches?"

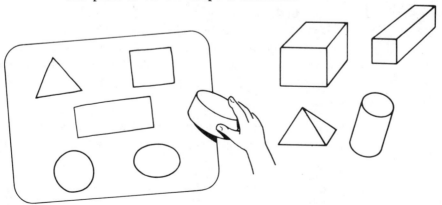

SHAPE BOX

Concept: Match shape with cutout of the shape.

Materials: Sorting box.

Shapes.

Group size: One to four children.

Procedure: Remove all shapes from the box. Let the child put them back, matching the shape to the cutout. Check the child by taking off the lid and seeing if all the shapes in each division are the same.

Variation: Blindfold the child and repeat the activity.

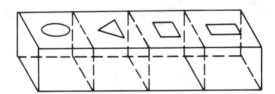

LOOK ALIKES

Concept: Match shapes through sight.

Materials: Cardboard puzzles like those in the diagram.

Group size: One to three children.

Procedure: Have each child sort the shapes into piles of those that look alike. Demonstrate with two like shapes. The child can work with one shape at a time or with two or more shapes whose pieces have been mixed. Have the child feel around the outside of the pieces. Next, demonstrate stacking the correctly sorted shapes.

The adult does not need to identify the shapes by name, although these may be used later when the child is learning the name.

Variation: Paint concentric circles and hang them concentrically as a mobile.

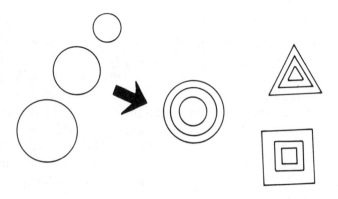

SHAPE HUNT

Concept: Match similar shapes. Choose shapes in immediate environment that match a given shape.

Materials: Chalkboard.

Chalk.

Dittos.

Items in room that have specific shape.

Group size: Class.

Procedure: Put the shape that you are going to hunt on chalkboard (or flannelboard). Say, "See the shape I made? Can you make one in the air with your finger?" "See how the lines go! Can you find something in the room with this shape?" Have children hunt for things in the room that match that shape. Objects found could be drawn under the shape on their papers.

3.3 Naming and discriminating shapes

This section provides activities for teaching the geometric concepts of circles, squares, ovals, rectangles, and triangles. Activities concentrate on emphasizing special features of each shape. Interaction with each particular shape is encouraged through physical and tactile experiences.

Once the names of the shapes have been introduced, activities are provided that require a discrimination between shapes. The initial activities utilize discrimination between one or two shapes and later activities involve discrimination using three or more shapes. The teacher must intersperse activities requiring discrimination with activities teaching shape names. For instance, once the child has been introduced to circle and square, it is appropriate to do some discrimination activities involving circles and squares. Then return to teaching the name of triangles and follow these activities with discrimination activities involving circles and triangles or squares and triangles. The teacher must decide on the timing of presentation of these activities based on the ability and progress of the children.

One could ask if repetition of shape names at this point will ensure each child's ability to name shapes correctly. Certainly not, as maturation in the ability to recall name symbols and figure images are both factors unique to each individual. Sensitivity on the part of the teacher to a child's limitations is most important.

The activities provide a forum of experiences for the child to sample or explore. The child's ability to recall a shape name or grasp a concept is not necessarily a reflection of the quality of teaching but, rather, an artifact of the range of time necessary for the child to internalize the concept.

"This one is next because it's the same shape
(color, size, thickness)."

Closing activities in this section provide some situations in which children can identify a shape when only part of the shape is visible. In the environment shapes are not always visible in a complete form—a circular tire is partially hidden by a mailbox or a square piece of toast is partially hidden in a toaster. The child's knowledge of shapes must be applied to partial forms to mentally complete the shape.

CIRCLE SONG

Concept: Associate song describing shape with circular motion.

Materials: None.

Group size: Any size group.

Procedure: While singing the tune, you and the children make large circles in the air with your arms.

Tune: *Farmer in the Dell*

> The circle goes a-round.
> The circle goes a-round.
> A great big wheel, it never stops,
> The circle goes a-round.

Variations: (1) Make different-sized circles. (2) You may wish to make a circle poster using the wheel.

Questions: How does it look when we make circles with our arms? Do we stop? Do we keep going? Do we make corners? Listen while I sing, and watch my finger make the shape. Can you trace the shape with your finger?

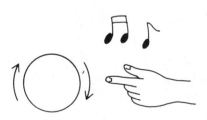

JUST A ROLLIN' ALONG

Concept: Identify circles in environment by the ability to roll the object.

Materials: Any circles in the room that can be rolled, i.e., lids, poker chips, wheels, cardboard circles, buttons. Place around the room in obvious locations.

Group size: Any size group.

Procedure: Show the child a circle and demonstrate how it rolls. Let everyone roll it, then either as a group or one at a time the children go around the room and bring back circles to share with the others.

    Variations: (1) Roll the circles as far as they can. Ask, "Which rolls the farthest?" Roll other shapes of different sizes. See if different sizes roll different speeds or distances. (2) Roll the circles up their legs. What does it feel like?

Questions: Will this circle roll? (Show a second circle.) Try it. Will all circles roll? Try some more. Can you roll a shape that is *not* a circle? Try it.

Just a Rollin' Along

CIRCLE STACKS

Concept: State the name of shape as circle.

Materials: Lids, same size preferably, but not necessarily. Lids from frozen juice cans stack well or coins or poker chips.

Group size: Two children or small group.

Procedure: Show the lids to the children. Talk about the shape. Trace inside the lid rim with a finger. Give five to ten lids to each child depending on the ease of stacking those particular lids. Have children make stacks of lids. Let children share in building a stack.

Questions: What shape is this lid? (Hold one up.) Is it the same shape as this lid? What happens to some of the circles when they fall? (Hold up another one.) Do the circles roll if they fall? If they are pushed?

SQUARE SONG

Concept: Associate song describing shape with motion of making a square.

Materials: None.

Group size: Any size group.

Procedure: You and the children trace large squares in the air with your arms, while singing. (Make one square per song line.)

Tune: *Farmer in the Dell*

Squares have straight sides,
Squares have straight sides,
Over, down, across and up,
The square has straight sides.

Variation: You may wish to make a square poster using a drawing of a block.

Questions: Can you trace a square with your finger?

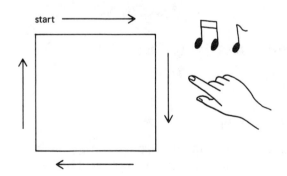

BODY SQUARES

Concept: Construct shape with physical involvement.

Materials: None.

Group size: Four or more children.

Procedure: Have the children make squares with their bodies on the floor. Four children of about the same height must be selected; emphasize that a square has four sides of equal length.

Select also a child supervisor to make sure the square has four sides and good corners.

Variation: With appropriate modifications, this approach can be used for the triangle (children of the same height) and the rectangle (two shorter children, and two taller children).

TRIANGLE SONG

Concept: Associate song describing shape with motion of making a triangle.

Materials: None.

Group size: Any size group.

Procedure: You and the children trace large triangles in the air with your arms, while singing. (Make one triangle per song line.)

Tune: *Farmer in the Dell*

> Triangles have three sides,
> Triangles have three sides,
> Up the hill, then down, and back,
> Triangles have three sides.

Variation: You may wish to make a triangle poster using a picture of a hill.

Questions: Listen while I sing, and watch my finger trace the shape. Can you sing with me? Can you trace a triangle with your finger?

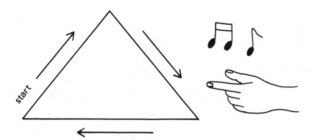

OVAL SONG

Concept: Associate song describing shape with motion of making an oval.

Materials: None.

Group size: Any size group.

Procedure: You and the children trace large ovals with your arms in the air, while singing. (Make one oval per line.)

Tune: *Farmer in the Dell*

> The oval is an egg,
> The oval is an egg,
> Around the top, then underneath,
> The oval is an egg.

Variation: You may wish to make an oval poster using a picture of an egg.

Questions: Can you trace an oval with your finger?

TURKEY EGGS

Concept: Find oval shapes.

Materials: Oval-shaped eggs (paper), oval-shaped rocks, or jelly beans.

Group size: Any size group.

Procedure: Hide "turkey" eggs around the room; let the class find eggs in a "turkey" egghunt.

Make some eggs very small or very large.

Questions: Are there any eggs that are not this size (size of most eggs)?

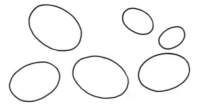

ROCKS

Concept: Sort ovals from other shapes.

Materials: Oval-shaped rocks (you may find smooth oval-shaped rocks in creeks, rivers and along oceans).

Round rocks or miscellaneous shaped rocks.

Sorting pans or a box.

Group size: One or two children.

Procedure: Child sorts oval rocks from other rocks.

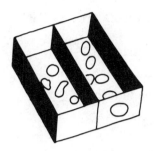

RECTANGLE SONG

Concept: Associate song describing shape with motion of making a rectangle.

Materials: None.

Group size: Any size group.

Procedure: You and the children trace a large rectangle with your arms in the air, while singing.

Tune: *Farmer in the Dell*

> Rectangles are like doors,
> Rectangles are like doors,
> Short side, long side, short and long,
> Rectangles are like doors.

Variation: You may wish to make a rectangle poster using a picture of a door.

Questions: Can you trace a rectangle with your finger?

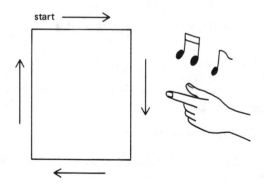

FEED THE RHINO

Concept: Discriminate rectangles.

Materials: Rhinoceros drawn or pasted on one side of a cardboard box, with a slit at the mouth.

Assorted shapes.

Group size: Any size group.

Procedure: Tell the children that they will feed the rhinoceros but that it likes to eat only rectangles.

If the child selects a rectangle, the child may feed it to the rhino, that is, insert it through the slit in the mouth.

(To make the game self-checking, cut the rhino's mouth carefully, then cut the shapes so that only the rectangles will fit through the slit.)

Variation: Other sides of the box can be decorated with animals for the other shapes: oval (orangutan, octopus), circle (centipede, cicada), square (squirrel, shark), triangle (turtle, toad).

Questions: What shape did you pick? Is it a rectangle? Does the rhino like triangles? Find a shape the rhino likes.

HUMPTY DUMPTY'S WALL

Concept: Stack rectangular "bricks" to build Humpty Dumpty's wall.

Materials: Small or large dominoes (blank side up), commercially made rectangular snap-together toy bricks, or other rectangular blocks.

Some nonrectangular blocks.

Plastic egg decorated with indelible marker to look like Humpty Dumpty.

Group size: Class.

Procedure: Introduce children to the rhyme, "Humpty Dumpty." Tell them that they will have a chance to build Humpty Dumpty's wall but that only bricks which look like rectangles can be used. Each child selects a brick and stacks it into place.

When the wall is finished, Humpty may be placed on top and the rhyme dramatized.

Variation: Paste paper rectangles onto dittoed outlines of a wall. Children take turns drawing rectangular bricks on the chalkboard to construct a wall. One child draws Humpty Dumpty.

Questions: What shape are the bricks? Can you find a brick shaped like a rectangle? Can you stack the brick onto the wall?

POSTCARDS

Concept: Discriminate rectangles.

Materials: Construction paper postcards, half of them rectangles, half of them other shapes.

Bag to hold postcards.

Group size: Any size group.

Procedure: Choose a child to be the letter carrier. Have the letter carrier pull out each postcard from the bag and deliver them to the other children. Have the child deliver only rectangular postcards.

Variation: Write a child's name on each postcard.

Questions: What shape is the postcard? Is it a rectangle? The letter carrier is delivering only rectangles today. Can you deliver that one?

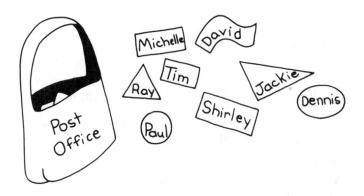

SHAPE MATCH

Concept: Identify shape that is the same as a given shape.

Materials: Geometric shapes cut from cardboard or paper.

Form board.

Shape sorting box.

Group size: Any size group.

Procedure: Show the children a circle and name it. Talk about its characteristics (round, no sides, it will roll, etc.). Repeat its name and have children repeat it. Now set out three or four shapes in front of the children (including a circle). Give one child a circle and ask that child to touch another circle. Tell the child to find one that looks just like the shape you are holding. Repeat the question using a square, triangle, and the remaining shapes. After you've covered basic shapes, have children sort all of them out at the same time.

Questions: What is this shape? Yes, it's a circle. Hold it. Now find another circle on the table. Put your circle on top of the first circle. Do they match? Are they the same shape? Are they both circles?

SHAPE MATCH-UPS

Concept: Match similar shapes.

Materials: Set of geometric domino cards, each with two shapes. Include circles, squares, triangles, ovals, and rectangles.

Group size: Two to four children.

Procedure: Dominoes are shuffled face up on a table. Have the first child select any domino to start. The next child must select a domino to match either shape on the first domino. Play continues with other children. A child who makes an incorrect play is "out." When dominoes are all used or when no more plays can be made, the remaining children are winners.

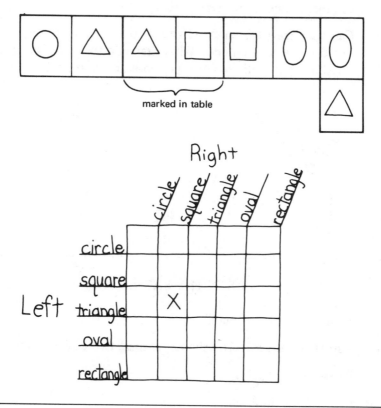

SHAPE SCOPES

Concept: Find and name shapes.

Materials: Five paper towel rolls.

Colored acetate (one color), clear contact paper or clear wrap.

Five shapes that are small enough to be fitted in end of towel roll.

Group size: One or two children, small group, or class.

Procedure: Have a child name a shape and find the cylinder that has that shape inside when viewed from the uncovered end. You might wish, at first, to put the cylinders in a box so that the child can only identify the shape inside by looking through the tube (scope) rather than seeing the tubes lying on edge.

Have a child next look through all of the cylinders and name each one.

Variation: Put the outlines of the shapes further inside. Use ten cylinders and have the child match like shapes. Children can make their own shape scopes.

Questions: Can you draw the shape in the air that you see in the cylinder? Look at the covered end. What shape do you see inside? Is that the shape you will see when you look in the scope?

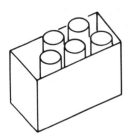 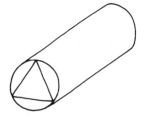

IT'S IN THE BAG

Concept: Identify shape by touch.

Materials: Assorted flat geometric shapes, at least two of each shape.

Paper bag.

Group size: Four to six children.

Procedure: Put two or three different shapes in a bag, then hold up a duplicate of one of those shapes for the child to see. Without looking, the child must feel in the bag for the shape to match yours.

The task can be made more difficult by (1) increasing the number of shapes concealed in the bag or (2) including several shapes of very similar shape, such as circles and ovals.

Questions: Is my shape round and smooth? Does it have bumps or corners?

AIKEN DRUM

Concept: Name and discriminate shapes.

Materials: Chalkboard.

Chalk.

Song to the tune of *Aiken Drum.*

Group size: Class.

Procedure: Ask the children to watch while you draw a person named Aiken Drum. Tell them that he is going to be made of shapes. "Now, listen while I sing . . .". Draw Aiken Drum on the chalkboard one body part per stanza as children name shapes to fit the song. Occasionally misdraw the shape named.

> His head was made of a triangle,
> A triangle, a triangle,
> His head was made of a triangle
> And his name was Aiken Drum.
>
> His feet were made of circles . . .
>
> His body made of an oval . . .

Variation: Make Aiken of all one shape. Draw a house and car to fit Aiken Drum. Let children draw in parts when possible.

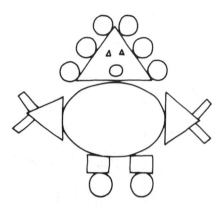

NAMESHAPES

Concept: Find and name shapes.

Materials: Chalk.

Chalkboard.

Design of shapes (see diagram).

Group size: One to four children.

Procedure: Draw numerous shapes on the chalkboard. Have each child take a turn pointing to and naming a shape. A child's name is printed in each shape named correctly. When a child responds incorrectly, state the correct answer and have the child repeat the name, then put his or her name in the shape. The idea is to have repeated successful experiences naming shapes, not who wins.

Variation: Ask a child to find a given shape.

Questions: Can you name all of the shapes and point to them as fast as you can? (Children who can recognize their names can name those shapes that have their name in them.)

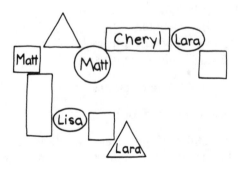

FINGER SHAPES

Concept: Discriminate square from circle using tactile sensation.

Materials: None.

Group size: One or two children, small group, or class.

Procedure: Using your finger, draw a figure (circle or square) on the child's back. Have the child then name the shape. The child who names a shape correctly draws a shape on the next child's back.

Also, you could let children in partners take turns drawing shapes on each other's backs. Let them draw shapes on your back!

If there is a child who cannot name the shape, give a visual clue by placing two or more different shapes in front of the child. Let the child point to the shape that he or she thinks is being drawn on his or her back.

Variation: Draw a shape in the air in front of the child either while or before drawing on his or her back. If drawing the shape in the air, ask the child if the shape you draw on his or her back is the same or different.

NOW YOU SEE IT, NOW YOU DON'T

Concept: Recall and name missing shape.

Materials: Shapes.

Group size: One to three children.

Procedure: Begin with only two shapes and progress to using three and then four shapes with this activity. The activity may be performed many times on many days.

Place the shapes in a row in front of the children. Name the shapes together. Have the children close their eyes while you remove one shape. Have them open their eyes and tell you which shape is missing.

CAN SHUFFLE

Concept: Find given shapes. Name and identify a shape from memory.

Materials: Three identical cans or milk cartons with one end taken off.

Wooden shapes which will move around easily underneath a can.

Group size: One to four children.

Procedure: Display the three shapes and then cover them up with the cans. Move the cans around, mixing them up. Have one child point to the can under which is the shape that he or she wants to try to name. Lift the other two cans and let the child guess the uncovered shape. If the child is right, give him or her a turn at shuffling the cans.

If this activity seems difficult for the child, use only two shapes and two cans.

Questions: How did you know which can had the triangle? What shape am I putting under this can?

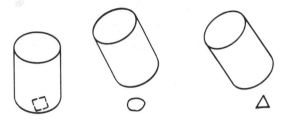

SHAPE RUN

Concept: Discriminate a square from a circle and take a course of action based on the discrimination.

Materials: Two circles and two squares; carpet scraps, paper, yarn, blocks, or anything that has these two shapes.

         Masking tape starting line.

Group size: Small group or class.

Procedure: Place one circle and one square about 6 feet apart from the other circle and square on the ground. Set each circle and square apart. Call two children up to the starting point. On the call of a shape both children run to the shape and run around the shape called out and return.

         Stress any good points. This is less a competitive game than a feedback game on their ability to recognize shapes.

Questions: What shape did I call? Where is it? Did you run around it? Do you both have a circle? Do you both have a square?

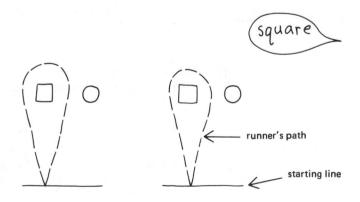

THE NOT GAME

Concept: Identify what is not a circle (square, rectangle, etc.)

Materials: Shapes.

Group size: Any size group.

Procedure: Have a child point to shapes or select shapes that are *not* circles.

Use with any shape; this is excellent as an introductory activity.

Say, "This is not a square." Take one object that is not a square. Now, have the child take one that is not a square.

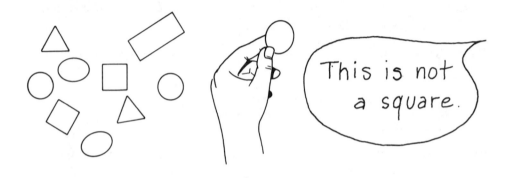

POP-UP SHAPES

Concept: Identify partially hidden shape from portion showing.

Materials: Paper with five slits that shapes will slide through.

Five paper shapes (same color).

Five popsicle sticks.

Group size: One child.

Procedure: Have a child identify shapes on the basis of the part that can be seen. Let the child confirm the guess by raising the popsicle stick, pushing the shape up through the hole.

Variation: Use a piece of paper with one slit. Put a shape part way through the slit and let the child guess which shape it will be. Pull that shape out and put in another for the child to guess. This activity can be used with a small group or a class.

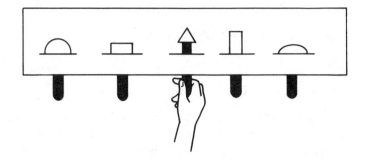

MATCH ME

Concept: Match parts of shapes to form wholes.

Materials: Five cards, each with one shape on the front and a different sized face on the back. Cut cards in half to make puzzles. (More cards are optional.)

Group size: One to two children.

Procedure: Place all of the cards with the shape parts up. The child or children match the shape parts and then turn each card set over to see if the face matches. If the face matches, then the child has correctly made a complete shape from each set.

                Variation: Make a design on back so that a picture is made using the shape on the front.

Questions: What shapes did you make?

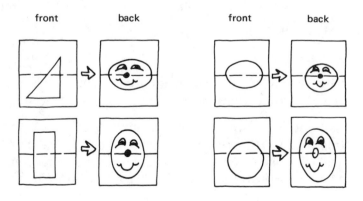

SHY SHAPES

Concept: Recognize partially hidden shapes and compare them.

Materials: Twenty cards of the designs below.

Group size: One or two children.

Procedure: Tell the children that the cards show "shy" shapes. The shapes are hiding because they are shy. Let the children know that they are going to try to find "shy" shapes that are the same shape.

Have two children deal the cards equally between them. At the same time, both children turn one card face up on the table. The children decide if the cards are the same, and, if they are, which shape is the "shy" shape.

Same shapes are left face up to one side. Different shapes are turned upside down. These may be used in later turns in an attempt to get a match.

Questions: What shape is this hiding "shy" shape? What shape will this be when it pops up out of the dark?

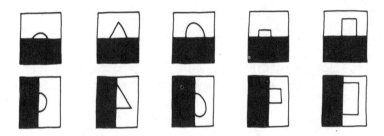

SHERLOCK SHAPES

Concept: Identify shape given descriptive clues.

Materials: Cutouts of shapes.

Group size: Any size group.

Procedure: Give hints to the children about a shape you are thinking about. Have them guess what shape it is.

Questions: Can you guess what shape I'm thinking of? It's a door shape (rectangle). It's a shape like a piece of pie (triangle). It's round and rolls like a ball (circle). It looks like a circle someone sat on and squashed (oval). It looks like a box (square or rectangle).

BEAT THE CLOCK

Concept: Name as many objects of a given shape as possible in a limited period of time.

Materials: Clock with second hand.

Group size: One or two children or small group.

Procedure: Give each child 30 seconds to name as many things as possible that have the shape of a circle (square, oval, triangle, or rectangle). The child may look around the room while naming objects.

Praise all attempts; it takes practice to develop the ability to think quickly of things of a particular shape or class. The child will not likely know how long 30 seconds is. The limit is for consistency and lets the children know that there is some structure guiding the activity.

Variation: You might wish to keep a record and have the child try to better his or her record (this encourages improvement). Have all children call out objects of a given shape during a timed period.

Questions: What made you think of saying plate?

SHAKE A SHAPE

Concept: Discriminate circles from squares.

Materials: A gameboard such as the one in the diagram.

                Markers for each child.

                Die with three circles and three squares. Make from wooden cube, box, or foam.

Group size: One to three children.

Procedure: Have one child take a turn rolling the die. Then the child is to move the marker to the next block on the board that has that shape. Encourage the child to name the shape that has been rolled. Give each child a turn until all of them have reached the end.

                Taking turns is often difficult for children 5 and under, so your help is needed in keeping the game going. Also you might talk about rolling the die only once in each turn.

                Variation: Include more shapes on the board and use a die with more shapes present.

Questions: Can you point to all of the circles on the board? Squares? Can you find the circles on the die?

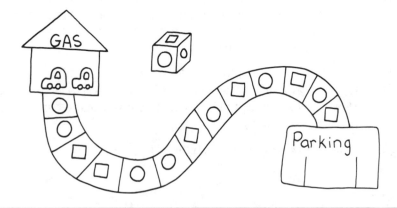

TREASURE HUNT

Concept: Discriminate and match shapes.

Materials: Gameboard with a path of triangles leading to a final space labeled "Treasure Chest."

                Spinner marked with circles, squares, and triangles or a deck of cards with these shapes.

Game marker for each player.

Small "Treasure Chest" box containing toy jewelry or other treasures.

Group size: Two to four children.

Procedure: All players begin at "go." Each child takes a turn spinning the spinner (or drawing a card). If a triangle turns up, the child may advance to the next space. If a different shape comes up, the child must wait for another turn.

The first child who gets to the Treasure Chest may open it and share the loot.

Variation: Use an old map to make the gameboard for an authentic look.

Questions: Trace around that shape with your finger. Is it a triangle? Is it a different shape?

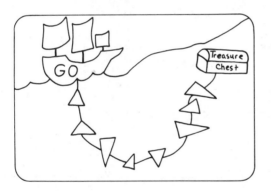 

FLOWER GARDEN

Concept: Identify and mark given shapes on worksheet.

Materials: Gameboard (or duplicated worksheets) showing "flowers" made of squares, circles, and other closed curves.

Game chips or other tokens (for gameboard).

Crayons (for worksheet).

Group size: Any size group.

Procedure: Direct child to select a bouquet of squares from the flower garden.

If the gameboard is used, a marker is placed on each square flower.

If worksheets are used, have the child color only the square flowers.

Variation: The gameboard can be covered with clear contact paper and the child directed to trace over the squares with crayon, grease pencil, or washable marker. The child can be directed to find all the circle flowers.

Questions: Can you trace the squares with your finger?

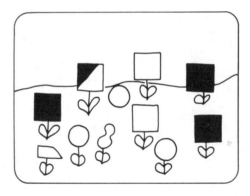

X MARKS THE SHAPE

Concept: Mark object of given shape.

Materials: Gameboard containing pictures of real objects, some of which are circle shaped, some of which are not. The basic shape of each picture can be outlined with marker.

Small X's of cardboard, or poker chips marked with X's.

Group size: One to four children.

Procedure: Have a child find all the shapes that are circles and place an X on each one.

Variation: This activity may be adapted for ditto work.

Questions: Trace around this box with your finger. Is it a circle?

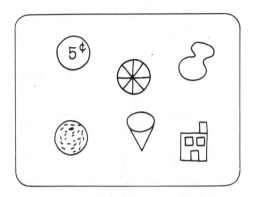

3.4 Drawing shapes

Children's first efforts at drawing shapes really begin with what appear as scribbles. Watch a young child scribbling. Some children use circular motions, others lines. Scribbling provides the foundation of drawing shapes as children experiment with motions and their impressions. Numerous freehand drawing and painting experiences are especially important and should be primary activities in a curriculum. Children universally draw circles and ovals, triangles, squares, and rectangles without guidance (Kellogg).

The activities collected extend the opportunities for a child to experiment with drawing motions. Later activities deal with copying shapes, a skill that requires slightly different abilities from those used in freehand drawing. When copying the child must translate a whole shape into the separate parts, retain their image, and reconstruct the whole (Gibson).

Some children show a reluctance to draw or paint. Often such a child has not yet developed adequate fine motor skills to hold a crayon and paintbrush or to apply appropriate pressure on the paper. Offer these children experiences that help develop fine motor skills such as stringing beads, stacking blocks, or using tools.

Kellogg, Rhode. *Analyzing Children's Art.* Palo Alto: National Press Books, 1970, 32.
Gibson, Eleanor J. "Perceptual Learning and the Total Cognitive Process." In J. Sants and H. Butcher, *Developmental Psychology: Selected Readings.* Maryland: Penguin, 1975, 218.

SCRIBBLE

Concept: Draw scribbles.

Materials: Paper.

Tape.

Large crayons.

Group size: One or two children, small group, or class.

Procedure: Tape a paper to the table for each child so that he or she can concentrate on scribble motion rather than on both moving a crayon and holding the paper down.

Observe how each child prefers to scribble. Some children scribble in circles, others in lines. You can use the information to concentrate on either lines or circles with each individual child.

You are going to try in future activities to encourage drawing one line or one circle instead of the multiple lines and circles that appear in scribbling.

Plenty of free expression is important. Allow time for this among scattered planned drawing activities. Note also how children hold a pencil and the pressure that they put on the paper.

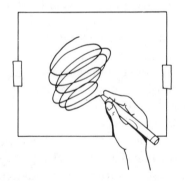 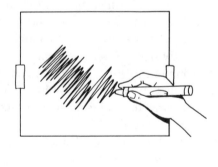

SIZE SCRIBBLES

Concept: Draw scribbles in circular or linear directions.

Materials: Paper in three sizes: large, medium, small.

Crayons or pencils.

Group size: One or two children or a small group.

Procedure: Each child is given one of the three pieces of paper to draw on. They choose which to start with.

Observe which children can vary the size of the scribble to fit the paper size. Some children will scribble off of the paper.

In combining circles and lines in later drawings, the child will need to develop the ability to control the size of the drawing motion.

Variation: Encourage children to draw small circles or zigzag lines to stay on a piece of paper or expand drawing to fill a large sheet of paper.

Questions: If a child has unsuccessfully drawn within the paper's boundaries, ask, Can you keep the scribbles on the paper and not go onto the table? Try it.

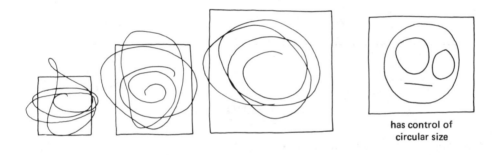

has control of
circular size

STIR A CIRCLE

Concept: Draw circles.

Materials: Bowl.

Instant pudding and ingredients.

Spoon.

Cups (optional) and spoons.

Group size: Small group or class.

Procedure: Combine the pudding ingredients in a bowl. Have the children stir the pudding in the bowl or stir the pudding in individual cups. Encourage stirring circles in the pudding. Cool for 5 to 10 minutes and eat.

Variation: Make any food that can be stirred. Mud pies are fine.

Questions: Can you stir another shape? What shape is easy to stir?

CLEAN SCRIBBLES

Concept: Draw circular or linear scribbles.

Materials: Chalkboard.

Tables.

Sponges (wet).

Group size: One or two children or a small group.

Procedure: Have the children clean flat surfaces in the room with sponges. They will develop motions that resemble circular or linear scribbles.

Variation: Draw lines or circles on the chalkboard. Have a child erase following the chalk lines (images). Give a child two sponges, one for each hand. Let the child make circles with both hands at the same time.

Questions: Can you make circles with your sponge, round and round? Can you make lines with your sponge, back and forth? Are you making circles or lines?

COORDINATED CIRCLES

Concept: Draw circles with both hands, each moving in same direction and then opposite.

Materials: None.

    Poi balls (ball tied to a string, optional).

Group size: Any size group.

Procedure: Ask children to watch you while you move your hands or arms in circles as in the drawing below. Let them try to imitate you. Now draw air circles in the other direction and have them try to do the same.

    Variation: This variation requires the same coordination. Twirl small hoops on the arms or swing poi balls made from taped newspaper balls on the end of a string.

HEADBANDS

Concept: Draw lines along a strip of narrow paper as readiness for drawing shapes.

Materials: Paper long enough for a headband.

Crayons or magic markers.

Tape.

Group size: Any size group.

Procedure: Have each child color or draw lines along a band of paper. The shape of the strip of paper often encourages children to draw long straight lines, although, if a child does not, that is okay. This is just an opportunity that *usually* encourages line drawing, although the ultimate goal is to have a neat headband!

Add feathers, hat brims, or sunglasses for variety.

Variation: Make bracelets.

Questions: What are we going to make with this long thin paper? Yes, headbands. Can you decorate your headband? Start at one end and draw a decoration. Did your line go all the way down to the other end?

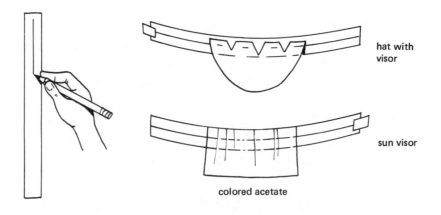

hat with visor

sun visor

colored acetate

WAVE NOTES

Concept: Draw line scribbles as readiness for drawing shapes.

Materials: Chalk.

Chalkboard.

Group size: One or two children.

Procedure: Stand a child at a chalkboard with chalk in hand. Have the child wave "hello" or "goodbye," making marks on the chalkboard at each up and down motion.

These marks are "wave notes." They may be lines, short dashes, or dots. Write the child's name below marks.

Questions: Can you see me waving "hello?" Who would you like to wave to? Are you waving "hello" or "goodbye"?

RAIN

Concept: Draw line scribbles as readiness for drawing shapes.

Materials: Magazine pictures of outdoor scenes.

Crayons.

Group size: Small group or class.

Procedure: Talk about the pictures; tell the children that a rainstorm is coming. Ask them to make the motion of rain coming down with their hands.

Next, ask them to draw rain on their pictures. Have them start at the top of the picture making lines down.

This activity is good for a rainy day.

Play a recording of Grofé's "A Storm."

Questions: How would rain come down on a windy day?

STREETS

Concept: Draw lines as readiness for drawing shapes.

Materials: Chalk.

               Chalkboard or paper and pencil.

Group size: One to two children, small group, or class.

Procedure: Draw two houses, one on each end of the chalkboard or one above the other.

               Have a child draw a line from one house to the other and back again.

               Give hand direction to the child if help is needed.

               Move houses closer together or farther apart, depending on how well the child is doing.

Questions: Whose house would you like this one to be? Whose house would you like this one to be? Would you like another house to go to? Put your chalk on this house. Can you draw a line over to this house? Can you go back again?

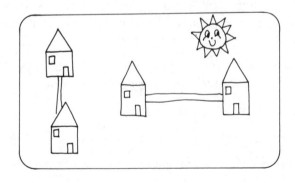

CLAY PLAY

Concept: Draw shapes with templates.

Materials: Templates of shapes.

Clay or sand.

Pencil or stick.

Group size: One or two children or small group.

Procedure: Let each child choose a template. Have the child draw inside the template in the clay or sand with a pencil or pointed stick.

Questions: What shape are you tracing? What shape does the edge of the template make?

GLUE TEMPLATES

Concept: Draw a shape and identify positions.

Materials: Glue in squeeze bottles.

Strong paper.

Crayons.

Group size: Small group or class.

Procedure: Draw shapes on paper with a pencil. Have each child follow shape outlines with glue. Make sure that the glue line is continuous around the shape. Set aside to dry.

When dry, the child can draw inside and outside of the glue outline as if it were a template. Use paint as a variation.

Variations: (1) Make a glue outline on wax paper. Make the outline thick and add a string to strengthen the outline. When dry, pull off and use as a template. (2) Have child make a collage by tracing circles of different sizes of glue outlines on the same page. (3) These activities can be and should be adapted to include the other shapes.

Questions: What shape would you like to make? After the shape is dry, ask if they can feel the shape. Can you trace around it with your finger?

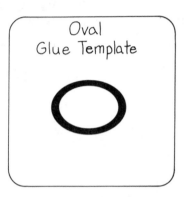

JAR LID AND MILK CARTON TEMPLATES

Concept: Draw with templates.

Materials: Paper.

Lids of jars or plastic lids cut out to leave the rim.

Boxes or milk cartons sliced into one inch squares.

Crayons.

Group size: Small group or class.

Procedure: Let the child choose a lid and draw around the inside of the template.

Children may attempt drawing around the outside.

Two children may work together. One holds the template steady while the other draws around the inside.

Variation: Use paper towel rolls cut down or toilet paper rolls to draw around on the outside or the inside. These are sometimes easier for a child to hold while drawing around.

Questions: Is it easier to draw around the inside or the outside? What shape can you draw if you squeeze the template while drawing?

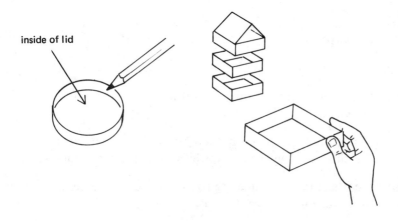

inside of lid

BOX AND CAN COLLAGES

Concept: Construct shapes using different media.

Materials: Empty boxes and cans of various shapes.

Construction paper.

Crayons.

Group size: Small group.

Procedure: Have each child choose one of the boxes or cans and draw around the edge to make a shape. Then choose a different box or can and continue, making a collage.

Have each child bring a small box or can from home to contribute to the cache for drawing.

FINGERPAINT SHAPES

Concept: Draw shapes using fingers.

Materials: Paper.

                Fingerpaint.

Group size: Any size group.

Procedure: Have the children put paint on their paper and draw shape designs with their fingers.

                Variation: Using a sandbox or cookie sheet with sand, have the children draw shapes in the sand using their fingers.

Questions: What shape are you going to draw? Can someone name a shape that everyone can try to draw?

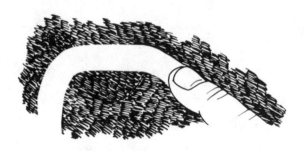

AIR SHAPES

Concept: Draw shapes in the air.

Materials: Bodies!

Group size: Small group or class.

Procedure: Use different body parts to draw a shape in the air. Let children choose the body part to use.

                Foot, leg, elbow, head, thumb, knee, back, . . .

                Variation: Rub tummy in circles with one hand. Draw shape in the air with the other.

Questions: Which body part is the hardest to draw with? Can you draw with two body parts at the same time in the air?

GUESS THE SHAPE

Concept: Identify and draw shapes in the air.

Materials: None.

Group size: Small group or class.

Procedure: Draw shape in the air with a finger. Have the children guess which shape it is.

Let one child draw a shape while the other children guess what it is.

Variation: Draw a shape as large as you can, as small as you can. Draw a shape as fast as you can. As slow as you can.

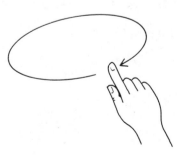

CURVES AND ZIGZAGS

Concept: Trace curves and zigzags.

Materials: Dittos.

Pencils and crayons.

Group size: Small group or class.

Procedure: Have each child trace curves or zigzags as in the diagram.

Questions: What do these lines look like? Put your finger on the end dot. Can you trace the line with your finger?

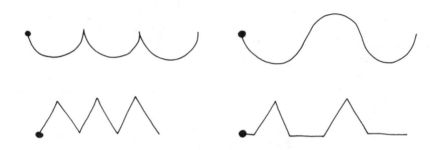

DON'T FALL OFF THE SIDEWALK

Concept: Copy shapes within decreasing sizes of lines.

Materials: Chalk.

Chalkboard.

Group size: Any size group.

Procedure: Have each child trace shapes on the board trying to keep within the borders or lines. Decrease the width of the lines.

Questions: Which is the hardest to stay inside? The easiest? Why?

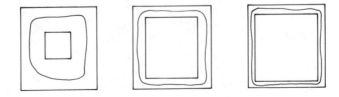

COPYCAT

Concept: Trace images for readiness in drawing shapes.

Materials: Dittos.

Crayons or pencils.

Group size: Small group or class.

Procedure: First, have the child trace lines. The child should complete the series of drawings involving curved lines at a separate time from the series of drawings with straight lines. Some children will have little difficulty with curved and straight lines. In this case they may complete both types of drawings in the same activity period.

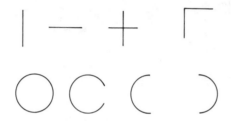

Common errors:

DOT TO DOT

Concept: Connect dots with lines to form shapes.

Materials: Chalk.

Chalkboard.

Group size: One child.

Procedure: Dots are drawn on the board one at a time. After the teacher draws the second dot, the child connects the dots using chalk.

Then the teacher places a third dot and the child continues the line to the third dot, etc. The teacher controls the shape formed and the pace of the activity.

Variations: (1) Draw dots that when connected with lines will form a shape. Draw all the dots before the child connects them. (2) Let the child make dots and allow another child or yourself to connect the dots.

Questions: What shape are you drawing? What shape do you think these dots will make?

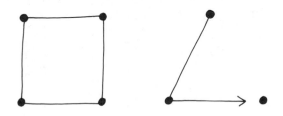

LISTEN AND DO

Concept: Draw shapes inside, outside, and around by direction.

Materials: Paper.

Pencils.

Group size: Any size group.

Procedure: Have the child draw shapes changing sizes and locating shapes correctly by your verbal direction.

For example, say "Draw a big circle." "Now draw a little circle inside, but do not let the little circle touch the big circle." "Draw another big circle." "Now draw another little circle outside and touching the big circle."

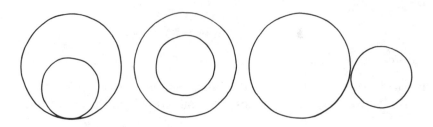

TRANSPARENCIES

Concept: Draw shapes.

Materials: Overhead projector (optional).

Transparencies of shapes.

Paper.

Pencils.

Group size: Class.

Procedure: Show the first transparency to the class. Have all the children name the shape and copy it. Then place another transparency on top of the first. Have the children copy again to match the projection. You can make a picture of something and have the children guess what it is before they are finished. Other transparencies can be added to make it more difficult.

For those children who cannot draw, have them place paper shapes or block shapes in position to make the pictures.

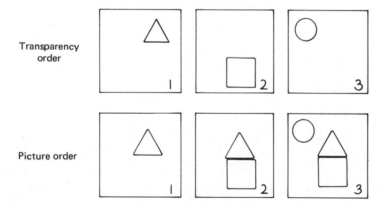

SHAPE MEMORY

Concept: Recall and draw shapes.

Materials: Shape cards.

Paper.

Pencils.

Group size: Any size group.

Procedure: Show a shape card to the children for approximately 10 seconds; then have them draw a picture of the shape. Cut down the time as the children progress. You can show a pair of cards to the children and then have them reproduce or arrange shapes to match the picture. Then show them the card(s) so that they can check themselves.

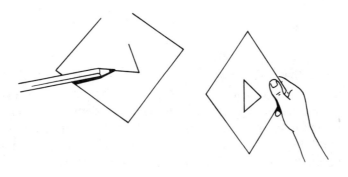

BADGES

Concept: Draw and cut freehand shapes.

Materials: Paper.

Scissors.

Pencils, crayons, or magic markers.

Pins or masking tape.

Group size: Any size group.

Procedure: Let children draw and cut shapes to be used as badges. You or another child can print the words if the child who makes the badge cannot write. Some badges can just have pictures.

These are great for

Imaginative play: hairdresser, doctor, grocer and others.
Awards: The Greatest, Tallest, Happiest, Funniest, . . .
Identifying tags: Todd H.—Children's School
Sayings: "I'm lovable, Hug me," "Sing a song," . . .

Questions: What shape do you want for your badge? What shape is this badge? Can you cut out a badge that looks like an oval?

SIGNS

Concept: Draw and cut freehand shapes.

Materials: Paper.

Pencils.

Crayons or colored markers.

Scissors.

Group size: One or two children, small group, or class.

Procedure: Put to use the children's skills in drawing and cutting shapes in making signs.

The signs can announce an event, identify where objects are to be stored in an area of the classroom, identify a campaign issue, or give directions.

If unable to write the words, the child can dictate them to another child or the teacher.

Questions: To encourage thinking of shapes in connection with some event: What shapes do you think of in baseball?

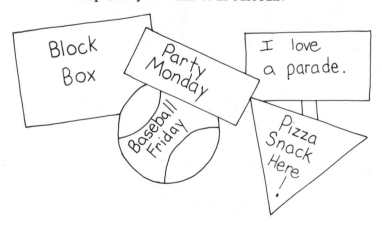

3.5   Constructing with shapes

Constructing with shapes excludes activities in which the ability to draw shapes is necessary. Regardless of whether children can or cannot draw (copy) shapes, they can participate in creative activities using premade shapes. The activities also extend opportunities to discriminate and label shapes.

GREETING CARDS

Concept: Construct and recognize whole shapes from seeing only parts.

Materials: Construction paper or ditto paper.

Crayons or colored markers.

Group size: Class.

Procedure: Demonstrate folding a piece of paper in half. Let the children try it. Then cut a design (making sure not to cut off all of the folded edge). Open the fold and talk with the class about the sides looking alike.

Have the children try to cut their own designs or draw a line on their paper for them to cut along. You might ask them what shape they want to appear when they open the folded, cut paper.

Cut pieces can be used to write invitations, cards, or signs.

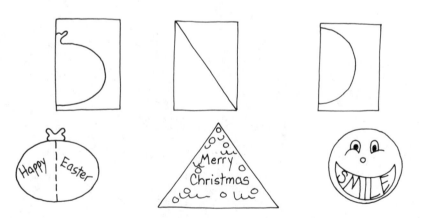

SHAPE MAN

Concept: Construct with shapes.

Materials: Cutout shapes and glue.

Group size: Class.

Procedure: Have cutouts of circles, squares, triangles, ovals, and rectangles. Allow the children to choose what "man" they're going to make—"square man," "circle man," "triangle man," "oval man," or "rectangle man." You can show samples of different men but put them away and let children make their own men. After they are all finished, talk about the different kinds of men they have. Display them on the bulletin board.

Children should be allowed/encouraged to make "square woman," "circle woman," "triangle woman," or "rectangle woman" if they choose to.

Questions: Who has the same-shaped man? Who has a shape woman?

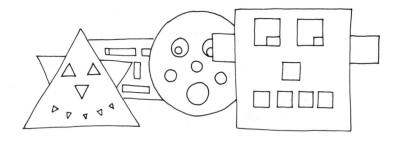

SHAPE MOBILES

Concept: Use shapes to construct a coat hanger mobile of basic shapes.

Materials: Metal coat hangers.

   Yarn or string of different lengths.

   Shape cutouts of construction paper, one set for each child.

   Tape, glue, or stapler.

Group size: Any size group.

Procedure: Each child is given a set of the shapes learned. The child tapes, glues, or staples each shape to a string end. Then you tie each string onto the hanger for the child.

Hangers may be hung for room decoration and used for rein-
forcement of shape concepts.

Variations: (1) If the children are advanced enough, they can
trace and cut out their own shapes. (2) Let each child distribute
shapes to different hangers so that triangles are on one hanger,
squares on another, etc.

SHAPE REFLECTORS

Concept:　　Use shapes to construct a shape reflector.

Materials:　Aluminum foil.

　　　　　　　Cardboard or heavy paper.

　　　　　　　Glue.

Group size: Any size group.

Procedure: Cut out shapes from the aluminum foil. Let the children name
　　　　　　　shapes one at a time and paste these shapes on the cardboard.
　　　　　　　Because the children can paste in different places, many unique
　　　　　　　reflector boards will result. You may wish to reflect the sun
　　　　　　　onto walls or the ground.

Questions: Name a shape that you would like to paste. Do you have any
　　　　　　　shapes that are alike? Does everyone's look different or the
　　　　　　　same?

SHAPE SCULPTURE

Concept: Construct shapes using different media.

Materials: Clay or play dough, taffy, cookie dough; cookie cutters or dull knives.

Group size: Small group.

Procedure: Using moldable materials, let the child make shapes freehand or make them with cookie cutters or a knife.

Variation: Sandwiches can also be cut into shapes, using cookie cutters or knives.

Questions: Can you make a clay rectangle? How would you cut a rectangular cookie?

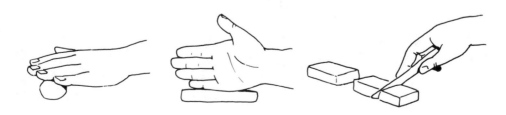

GLITTER SHAPES

Concept: Construct shapes using different media.

Materials: Glue in squeeze bottle.

Sand, birdseed, glitter, confetti, alphabet noodles, or other tiny macaroni.

Construction paper, tag, or cardboard.

Group size: Small group.

Procedure: Each child outlines a shape (it can be drawn ahead of time by an adult) with a thick bead of glue. Then glitter or other material is sprinkled on and the excess glitter is carefully poured off. Next the paper is allowed to dry on a flat surface.

Display the resulting glitter shapes in the room or hall.

Questions: What shape would you like to make? Where would you like to have it drawn on your paper?

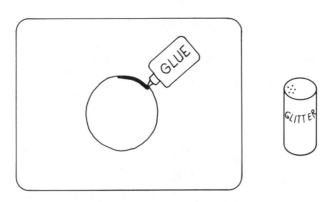

CHAPTER 4

Color

4.1 Introduction

Colors are ever present in the environment of infants and children. Colorful mobiles are hung above infants' cribs, and toys are designed in the brightest of colors. Studies indicate that infants begin discriminating color hues when they are as young as 4 to 6 months of age (Fagan). The basic colors of red, green, yellow, and blue (called focal colors) along with black and white are recognized more readily than the secondary colors of violet, pink, brown, etc. Occasionally you will find a child who will begin by recognizing a secondary color, naming it earlier than any other color. Some children seem to develop a preference for a certain color, recognizing and naming only that one color as if it were their "favorite" color. These children can be an asset in the class when teaching that one color to children, particularly if "their color" is one of the secondary colors. By the repetition of the favorite color name, the child reinforces the learning of the color name for the other children.

Color is included as a mathematical concept because colors lend themselves well to the mathematical functions of discriminating differences and using a visual phenomenon in classifying, sequencing, and patterning. Learning to discriminate different colors and giving them a name is similar to the use of names for shapes or numerals, that is, associating the name of a shape with the qualitative property of the object is analogous to associating the name of the color with the qualitative property of the object.

The ability to name colors seems to be a function of language development in the ability to link a visual image with a recalled name (E. G. Johnson). A stimulating environment with numerous language experiences will affect the child's ability to learn color names. As the child accumulates language experiences and matures in memory skills, formal teaching of color names will be successful. In other words, as a child encounters general language experiences and language skills develop, the ability to recall and link word names also increases, as in naming colors.

Fagan, J. E. Infant color perception. *Science,* 1974, **183,** 973–975.
Johnson, E. G. The development of color knowledge in preschool children. *Child Development,* 1977, **48,** 308–311.

Color is easier for parents and teachers to present than shape if only because on an average day color descriptions are used in more situations than shape descriptions. Red socks, blue room, yellow cat, green plate, and others are topics of daily discussion. The authors suggest that teachers do not mix teaching color names with shape names until one of them is well learned so as not to confuse shape names with color names.

4.2   Color readiness (matching without naming)

The activities in this section do not require a child to know the names of colors, although this does not mean that color names may not enter into the activities. Initially each child should be checked to see whether he or she can match the primary colors without the additional skill of naming them. A child who cannot match like colors may have difficulty discriminating the differences among colored objects or understanding the directions to find objects that are the "same" color.

Some activities can be presented so that the child could discover matched colors in the process of using the materials. Black, white, primary, and secondary colors can all be used in matching activities. If a new color stimulates a question about its name, be certain to respond, enhancing the child's knowledge and giving recognition to the inquisitiveness—even though the activites in this section do not emphasize names. Do not let the opportunity pass!

There is a step between matching colored objects and matching colored objects to their color names. The latter skill requires a child to recall a visual image of, for instance, "blue" to relate to the word blue. A child needs a visual image of a color. This color recall can be developed by having children match a blue color image to an object of the same color. An activity to accomplish this color imagery might include showing a child a blue block, then removing the block from sight, and displaying three beads of three different colors (one bead must be blue). Have the child find the bead that is the same color as the block removed from sight. The child must retain a visual image of the color of the block to select its color match. This activity can be extended to colors of clothes, home items, etc.

CANNED COLORS

Concept: Find object of matching color to a given object.

Materials: Four empty orange juice cans.

Blocks, buttons, or color chips in matched pairs of colors.

Bag

Group size: One child or small group.

Procedure: Under each can hide a block or object of a different color. Use the basic colors of red, blue, green, and yellow. Put the matching set of blocks in the bag. Let each child take a turn drawing a block from the bag and try to find its matching block by looking under the cans one at a time. Once the child finds the match, have him or her return that block to the bag for the next child's turn. Put the blocks under different cans in different positions once children begin to remember where the colors are hidden.

Note: Children enjoy the excitement of finding hidden objects. The element of surprise and the opportunity for you to "ah" and "oh" provide a stimulating simple game. Let children match secondary colors and also remember to include blocks that are black and white.

COLOR CARDS

Concept: Match objects of like colors.

Materials: 6″ x 12″ cards or a file folder divided as in the diagram.

Two sets of objects which can be matched by color (pencils, crayons, color chips, blocks).

Group size: One or two children.

Procedure: Place one set of objects in the spaces as shown in the diagram. Let the child place the second set in the spaces opposite your set by matching color. The children should take turns placing a block on the board.

Variations: (1) Let one child put the sets of objects on the card, then the other child places the matching blocks on the card. (2) Use a card with half of the spaces precolored. The child matches objects to both the precolored spaces and then places a block of corresponding color in the blank spaces.

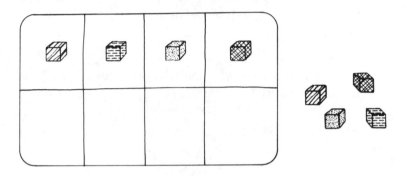

COLOR COLLECTIONS

Concept: Match objects of the same color with different hues.

Materials: Cards or objects of primary and secondary colors and black and white.

Group size: Any size group.

Procedure: Show one card and have the group find something in the room that is of the same color. Hues will often vary from the given color cue; children must generalize their concept of, for example, blue to blue shades.

Variation: Pass out color cards and let each child find something of that color to bring back to share with the group.

COLOR RECALL

Concept: Match color of an object from visual memory.

Materials: Color cards or paint strips.

    Objects of solid colors (coat, sweater, door, table, chair, glasses, rug, etc.).

Group size: One or two children.

Procedure: Have in mind an object in your classroom or a personal object of the children with whom you do this activity. The object should be a solid color and one that you can match by a color card.

    Show the child the chosen object and call attention to the color. (Do not use its name at this stage.) Remove the child from view of the object and have the child choose from two color cards the one that matches the object's color. Let the child check by comparing the object with the color card he or she has chosen in hand.

    Begin with the child choosing from only two color cards; then make the choice more difficult by using three to five color cards.

HOUSE FLOWERS

Concept: Match flowers to vases using color as the attribute.

Materials: Construction paper or plastic flowers, several of each color.

    Milk cartons for vases.

Group size: Two to four children.

Procedure: Have several flowers for each vase. Have all the flowers in a pile, unsorted. Begin by asking the children which flowers would go in one particular vase (point to one). Allow the children to sort the flowers into the vases. Ask how they decided to sort the flowers. Focus attention on grouping flowers of the same color together.

DOGS' SUBURB

Concept: Match objects of like colors.

Materials: Pint milk cartons covered with construction paper or adhesive paper in the colors black, brown, white, and gray.

Toy dogs or cardboard dog shapes in colors matching the dog houses.

Group size: One or two children.

Procedure: Select dogs and doghouses in colors of black, brown, gray, and white. These colors are used less often with children, although black and white are recognized early in a child's sensitivity to color.

Show the children the doghouses and the dogs. Ask them if they know how a dog (in this game) knows which house she lives in. Demonstrate how each dog lives in a house that is the same color as himself. Let the children match the dogs to the houses.

Use dogs with mixed colors and color patterns for a more complex variation.

Variation: Use color matched cars and garages.

FLASH A COLOR

Concept: Match color of an object from visual memory.

Materials: Blocks, buttons, or other identical objects in matching colored pairs.

Sheet of dark paper.

Group size: One or two children.

Procedure: Give each child a set of objects that are identical to yours. The set should include three to five different colors. Tell the children that you are going to show them a block. Select one of your blocks and place it behind the sheet of paper so that they cannot see it. Show them the block. When you cover it again, they are to find one of their blocks that matches the hidden one. Show them the block again so that they can check their responses.

Note: This activity precedes matching a visual color image and verbal color name. This activity helps a child hold a visual image of a color and recall it.

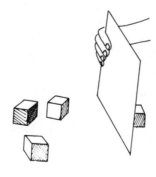

4.3 Naming colors

Repetition of color names in a variety of experiences may be the key to a fairly comprehensive knowledge of color names. The activities in this section provide experiences in which children can interact with numerous colors in one setting (as with a rainbow) or one color at a time (as with purple turtles). An attempt was made in many activities to rhyme the color names with object names to provide extra cues to the colors. Dramatic emphasis on the rhyming could enhance acquisition of the concept.

Again, utilize any "favorite" colors of individual children in the class both to teach these colors to others who may not know them and to provide positive rewarding experiences to those who can successfully identify their "favorite" color time and again.

HAT PARADE

Concept: Repeat name of a color. Identify color by name.

Materials: Bulletin board.

Different colored paper hat cutouts (enough so that there will be one for each child).

Paper faces, one for each hat.

Strips of paper with the names of each child.

Group size: Class.

Procedure: Put faces on a bulletin board with a child's name under each face. Tell the class that each child can have a hat. Have them either tell you the color that they want or point to the one they want. Always repeat or name the color that each child chooses. Say, "This is the green one. Do you want the green one?" Or, "Bob has the green one."

Change hats every day or so. Upon changing hats always talk about the color the child was wearing. Ask permission when a hat is taken from another child and then let that child choose another color if desired.

Variation: Use a clown holding balloons of different colors. Make slits in the balloons to insert interchangeable strips of paper with children's names on them.

Questions: Does anyone have a hat the same color as yours?

BOB   TIM   SUE   KAY

SAME NAME

Concept: Name color of an object.

Materials: Objects in sets of like colors.

Group size: One child.

Procedure: This activity is a bridge between matching like colors and naming colors of objects. The child uses his or her skill in matching objects of the same color to generalize that objects that look alike in color have the same color name.

Put two objects of the same color in front of the child. Point to one object and say, "What color is this?" If the child does not know the color, say, "This is blue." Then pointing to each object in turn, say, "This is the same color as this." Next, ask what color the second object is.

A child might not be able to give you a correct response. If the child is not ready to generalize a color name, have the child repeat after you the color names of the objects. Repeat the original activity at intervals until the child exhibits the ability to link colors and color names.

THE RED COAT

Concept: Relate a color to an object in frequent use.

Materials: Any object that has high visibility: coats, snack cups, paint smocks, etc.

Group size: One child.

Procedure: Take note of an object that the child enjoys using or wears often. Discuss the color of the object and label it frequently as, for instance, "red coat." Occasionally ask the child, "What color is that?" Ask this question with the object at hand. Later ask the question with the object removed. "What color is your coat?" Don't expect instant success. As the child's ability to label with colors develops the "red coat" may be one of the early successes in color naming.

COLOR FAVORITES

Concept: Name objects with a recognized color name.

Materials: None.

Group size: Any size group.

Procedure: Note any children who seem to have a "favorite" color. Often these children only recognize this one color. The color isn't always one of the primary colors; it may be orange, purple, or any other color.

Give the children opportunities to name and identify "their color." The opportunities fulfill two objectives. First, successful experiences in naming colors are provided for the child, and, second, other children are exposed to correct labeling by one of their peers.

THERE GOES MATT

Concept: Name color that a child is wearing.

Materials: None.

Group size: Small group or class.

Procedure: Choose one child to begin the activity. Have the child or the class name a color of a piece of clothing that the child is wearing. To the tune of *Here We Go Round the Mulberry Bush* the child walks or runs around a table or chair while the group sings the following song, substituting the child's name, clothing and color of the clothing:

> There goes *Matt* with *blue jeans* on,
> *Blue jeans* on, *Blue jeans* on.
> There goes *Matt* with *blue jeans* on,
> *Blue, blue, blue.*

Questions: Did anyone have the same color as you?

RED SLED

Concept: Discriminate and name the color red.

Materials: Small flat boxes or lids, such as jewelry or stationery boxes.

Cardboard or heavy paper "sled runners."

Staples or glue or tape.

Red tempera paint or felt-tipped markers.

Group size: Small group.

Procedure: Give each child a box and a pair of cardboard runners. Fasten the runners to the sides of the box and then paint the sled red. While work progresses discuss the color red and have the children repeat what they are making: red sleds.

Display the sleds and add one to the color display.

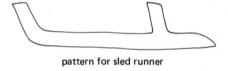

pattern for sled runner

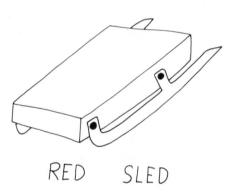

RED   SLED

YELLOW JELLO

Concept: Discriminate and name the color yellow.

Materials: Packaged yellow gelatin and the equipment necessary to make it.

Small paper cups for individual servings.

Spoons.

Tempera paint and paper.

Group size: Small group.

Procedure: Make yellow jello with the children's help. Follow package directions and pour the liquid jello into small cups. While work is proceeding, discuss the color yellow and have the children tell you what they are making: yellow jello.

When ready to eat, have each child tell you what he or she wants, yellow jello, before giving it to the child.

Let a volunteer paint a picture of the yellow jello to add to the color collage.

YELLOW JELLO

BLUE BREW

Concept: Discriminate and name the color blue.

Materials: Milk.

Blue food coloring.

Pitcher or bowl for mixing.

Spoon.

Cups.

Paper and paint.

Group size: Small group.

Procedure: Tell the children that you are going to make a blue brew. Let them watch as you pour blue food coloring into the milk; they can help stir. Or you can pour some milk into each child's cup, add a drop of blue, and let each child stir his or her own "blue brew." As work proceeds, discuss the color blue and have the children tell you what they are making: blue brew.

A volunteer can draw a picture of the blue brew for the color collage.

If the thought of drinking blue milk doesn't appeal to you, here are some other options:

Substitute water for the milk and feed the blue brew to the plants.

Locate some blueberry syrup and make "blue brew snow-cones."

Buy some "blue brew popsicles."

Take a field trip to a shop that sells slushy-type drinks and order blueberry.

Mix blue glue using paste and food coloring.

BLUE BREW

GREEN BEAN

Concept: Discriminate and name the color green.

Materials: Green beans (fresh is best).

Paper and green paint.

Knife (optional).

Group size: Small group.

Procedure: Give each child a green bean. If you wish, you may cut the beans open to let the children see what is inside. Let the children tell you what they have: green beans. Eat the beans. (Someone may want to plant one to see if it will grow.)

Have a volunteer paint a green bean to add to the color collage.

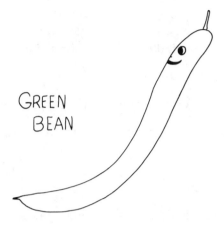

GREEN
BEAN

ORANGE ORANGE

Concept: Discriminate and name the color orange.

Materials: Fresh oranges (enough for each child to have at least a taste).

Paper and paint.

Group size: Small group.

Procedure: Have the children look at the orange. Point out that the name of the fruit and the name of the color is the same word. Cut or peel the orange and give everybody a piece. Ask the children what they are eating, and encourage them to call it an "orange orange." Ask what color the juice is.

A painting or drawing of an orange orange can be added to the color collage.

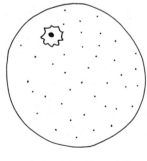

ORANGE   ORANGE

VIOLET PILOT

Concept: Discriminate and name the color violet.

Materials: Pattern for pilot's wings.

    Heavy violet paper or construction paper.

    Safety pins.

    Tape.

Group size: Small group.

Procedure: Help the children trace around the stencil and cut out their violet wings. Then pin a safety pin onto the back of each pair of wings, pin onto a shirt, and the children become "violet pilots."

    Before allowing each pilot to fly his or her airplane around the room, have them tell what they are: violet pilots.

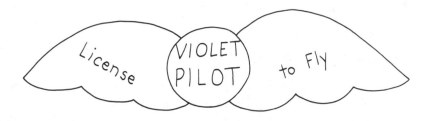

XYLOPHONE

Concept: Discriminate and name the primary and secondary colors.

Materials: Xylophone with notes of different colors.

Group size: Small group.

Procedure: Tell the children that, if they can name the colors on the xylophone, they can play the notes they name. Point to a note for each child to name, or let the child select a color.

    (This can be a powerful motivator for children who don't seem to care about learning the color names.)

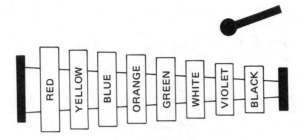

BROWN CLOWN

Concept: Discriminate and name the color brown.

Materials: Brown paper.

              Scissors.

              Hole puncher.

              String.

Group size: Any size group.

Procedure: Make a brown clown hat for each child by constructing a cutout that is similar to the diagram. Staple the back seam closed. Punch holes on sides for string ties.

              Talk about how a brown clown might act. Try making brown clown "faces," "walks," and "waves."

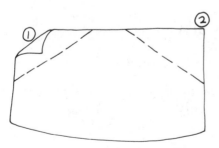

Fold ① and ②.
Staple together.
Trim base to fit child's head.

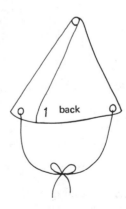

PURPLE TURTLE

Concept: Discriminate and name the color purple.

Materials: White paper cups.

                Purple cutouts for base of feet, head, and tail (see diagram).

                Glue.

                Purple paint.

Group size: Any size group.

Procedure: Give each child a cup and a base. Let each child paint the cup purple for the turtle's shell. Next have the children paste the shell on the turtle's back and draw a face on the turtle's head. Use the word "purple" often while the children work on their purple turtles.

WHITE KITE

Concept: Discriminate and name the color white.

Materials: White heavy paper *or* tinted paper and white tempera paint.

                Scissors.

                Yarn or string.

                Strips of paper to tie on the tail (optional).

Group size: Small group.

Procedure: Help each child cut out or paint a white kite. While the children are working, discuss the color white and have the children repeat what they are making: white kites. Punch a hole in the bottom of each kite and fasten a piece of yarn or string to make a tail. Pieces of fabric may also be tied onto the tail for a more authentic look.

Finished kites may be hung from the ceiling or walls. A white kite may be added to the class color collage or wall display.

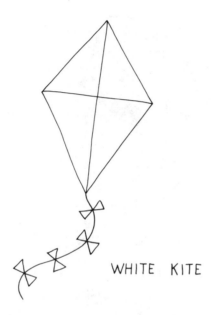

WHITE KITE

BLACK SACK

Concept: Discriminate and name the color black.

Materials: Black paint and brushes.

Sturdy paper sacks.

Old catalogs or magazines with pictures.

Group size: Small group.

Procedure: Introduce the color black by having each child make a black sack. While the children paint their sacks, discuss the color black and have the children repeat the color name and tell what they are making: black sacks.

While the sacks are drying (or at another time), have the children cut out pictures of black items from catalogs to put in their sacks. Or each child could take home his or her sack and bring back something black in it for show-and-tell (shoe, tie, pen, etc.).

You may wish to keep an extra black sack to begin a wall display or collage of colors.

BLACK SACK

HOP AND STOP

Concept: Discriminate between black and white.

Materials: One white and one black object (pieces of construction paper will do).

Group size: Small or large group.

Procedure: Have the children identify the colors black and white. When you hold up the black paper, the children are to hop with two feet. When you hold up the white paper, the children are to stop. After a little practice, you can eliminate the children who fail to respond correctly to a signal, one at a time, until a winner is left.

COLOR CREATIONS

Concept: Repeat color names of objects.

Materials: Depending on which activity you choose: colored construction paper, scissors, tissue paper, tape, green acetate.

Group size: Any size group.

Procedure: Introduce activities at the children's levels of ability. They can help cut, paste, color, tape or decorate the paper items as their skills allow. Do one of these activities a day.

The prime objective is to provide opportunities in which one color can be named and repeated in natural conversation with a great amount of repetition.

Red—cut and tape red apples to a paper tree.

Yellow—draw eyes and fold origami birds—hang as a mobile.

Blue—attach fish kites to string and run with them.

Green—make glasses or monocles using construction paper and green clear acetate

Black—attach black bears to popsicle sticks as puppets.

White—make tissue butterflies with tape to bunch the tissue in the middle. Let them float to the ground.

RAINBOW PUZZLE

Concept: Name colors.

Materials: Heavy cardboard cut into an interlocking rainbow puzzle (see diagram).

Colored markers.

Clear adhesive paper.

Group size: One or two children.

Procedure: Make a rainbow puzzle by coloring each arch a different color. Let children take it apart and put it back together. Have the children name the colors.

Variations: (1) Let children draw their own rainbows, naming the colors that they know. (2) Use a duplicate large rainbow to which the puzzle can be matched. (3) You might wish to use a prism and have the children look at the colors in the order that they occur.

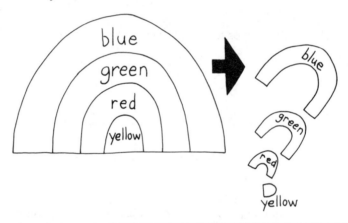

COLOR BOOK

Concept: Construct a color book.

Materials: Construction paper.

Blank paper for center pages.

Staples.

Scissors.

Paste.

Old magazines or catalogs.

Group size: Class.

Procedure: Staple construction paper for the cover of a book. The color of construction paper determines the color of the book. Use three or four pieces of blank note paper for pages. You may make enough books so that each child can choose a book of the color he or she wishes to have. Let the children look through old magazines and cut out pictures for their books. Children may want to add words to their books. Have each child describe his or her own book to the group.

COLOR TOWERS

Concept: Discriminate and name the primary colors.

Materials: Red-, yellow-, and blue-colored inch cubes.

Group size: Small group.

Procedure: Show the first child a cube and ask that child what color it is. If correct, the child may have the cube to begin building a tower. Proceed around the group, giving each child a chance to name the cube's color and earn the cube to build his or her own tower.

For an easier game, show the same color cube to a child for each of that child's turns, that is, one child may have a totally blue tower, another a red one, another a yellow. Or use only two colors instead of three.

COLOR LAND

Concept: Discriminate and name the primary colors.

Materials: Gameboard with spaces colored red, yellow, and blue.

Die or spinner marked with the primary colors *or* a brown bag containing blue, red, and yellow cubes.

Tokens.

Group size: Small group.

Procedure: Put the tokens, one for each player, at start. In turn, each child rolls the die, spins the spinner, or pulls a cube from the bag. After naming the color correctly, the child can move his or her marker to the next space of that color on the gameboard. If the answer is incorrect, the child loses a turn. Play continues until all players have reached the rainbow at the end.

Note: For primary and secondary colors, commercially made games are available.

FRAMED COLORS

Concept: Find and observe colors through frames.

Materials: Styrofoam meat trays.

Colored cellophane.

Stapler or tape.

Group size: Class.

Procedure: Cut the centers out of trays so that what is left is much like a frame. (You may have the children help in the construction.) Cut a piece of cellophane to fit, slightly overlapping. Either staple or tape the cellophane in the frame. Allow the children to look through the color trays. Have them find something of a given color while looking through their frames and "frame" the color with their trays.

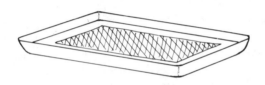

FISHING FOR COLORS

Concept: Catch a fish that matches a color on a spinner.

Materials: Construction paper fish.

Paper clips.

Fishing pole with magnet at end of string.

Paper plate and spinner attached with a brad.

Group size: Two to four children.

Procedure: Before beginning, discuss with the group that the spinner indicates which color of fish to catch. Spread the fish out on the floor and allow the children to begin spinning and fishing. If the fish caught is the wrong color, the child can toss it back and try again.

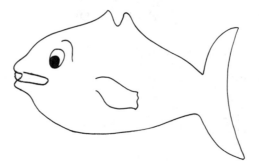

Place paper clips on mouth in order
for the magnet to pick up the fish.

COLLECTED COLORS

Concept: Name color of an object drawn from a box.

Materials: Box or can with lid.

Assorted items of different colors.

Group size: Class.

Procedure: Have the box filled with items and situated in the middle of the group. Allow each child to draw an object. As each one is drawn, discuss the attributes of each. Try to emphasize the color of it by repeating and having the children repeat the color name. Have each child take as many turns as possible. If a child doesn't name the color correctly, you may ask other children to help identify the color.

Use a reverse procedure by having one child describe an item using color cues and another child picking it out.

BLUE CAT?

Concept: Color items on a ditto following teacher directions.

Materials: Ditto worksheet (see diagram).

    Crayons.

Group size: Class.

Procedure: Give the children the worksheet. Have them find each picture so you are sure they know what it is. "Find a blue crayon and color the cat." "Find a red crayon and color the wagon." Also, let the children choose one color that everyone will use or let them color one item a color of their choice.

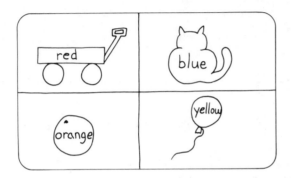

HOME SWEET HOME

Concept: Match like colors while taking turns in a game.

Materials: Gameboard (see diagram).

    Cards to go on the gameboard (see diagram). The cards represent slabs on sidewalks.

Group size: Four children.

Procedure: Show the gameboard to the children and discuss the following rules of the game. Each child chooses one of the game colors to be the color of his or her sidewalk. Next, have the children place a card of their color on the gameboard so that each child has a sidewalk with one section filled in. Now place the remaining cards upside down on the floor so that the colors are not showing. Children begin taking turns. Each child picks a card and turns it over. If the color on the card matches his or her sidewalk, then the child can lay it on his or her sidewalk; if not, the child lays it back down. Children play until they reach "home sweet home."

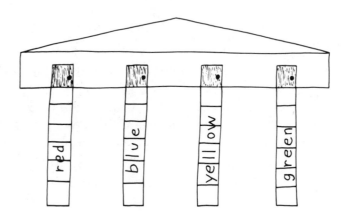

COLOR CALL

Concept: Recall color of an object that was viewed for five seconds and then removed from sight.

Materials: Blocks of different colors.

Group size: One to three children.

Procedure: Show the children a block and then take it away. After you take it away, they are to tell you what color it was. Show them the block again so that they can reaffirm their answer.

As the children get better at giving answers, have them look at two blocks and recall their colors in any order.

① Show block.

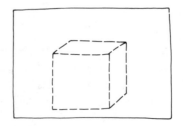

② Remove block from sight.

4.4 Recalling colors

This section on recalling colors is rather short, but one that is useful as a review of color names and colors of objects. Memory is the key to each of these activities. One activity requires the child to respond rapidly, pulling the information readily from memory. Another type of activity encourages the child to recall a place, an object, or a person and describe one of these in terms of its color. One activity might be as simple as asking children what color items they wore the day before, the teacher having recorded that information the previous day.

COLOR COMMENTARY

Concept: Point to object whose color is named.

Materials: Blocks or color cards in different colors. (Use three at a time.)

Group size: One or two children.

Procedure: Set three blocks in front of the child. Say, "I am going to name some colors." "Point to a block when I name its color." Demonstrate with the child once to see if he or she understands. Proceed to name colors, using colors that are in front of the child and colors that are not. Give the child enough time between each color name for deciding if the color is present or not. Do not indicate with your voice, eye movement, or body movement the answers.

            Discuss responses occasionally. Ask the child to name the color of the block that he or she is pointing to.

            Variation: Use two blocks and ask, "Which one is *not* blue?"

Questions: When a red block is not available and red has been named, ask, "Where is the red block?" "Name some colors that are *not* in front of you."

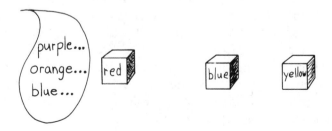

COLORS AWAY

Concept: Recall color of an object removed from sight.

Materials: Assorted colored cards.

Group size: Any size group.

Procedure: Determine from the parents the colors of objects around the home. A checklist might expedite this. Be sure to find out the child's favorite color. Ask the children to tell you the color of their rug at home, their house, car, or other object from home. A child may also point to a color card that matches an object at home and tell you what the object is.

You are encouraging a child to recall a visual image with color as the key element.

4.5   Shades and blends

Color recognition can be confusing when an object is, for instance, reddish-brown. Also, confusion can occur as, for example, in the shades from red to pink. One shade might be called red by one child and pink by another. These conflicts in recognizing colors may be resolved to an extent if children have opportunities to mix colors, change shades, or blend different colors in the process. The activities included in this section offer a variety of ways to use food coloring and paint in experimenting with color. It is also important that the children recognize that often the color of an object is not easily described, and group discussions can provide a forum that fosters children's creative use of their knowledge of colors.

SHADES

Concept: Sort by color given different shades of each color.

Materials: Paint samples with different shades of each color.

Group size: Two to four children.

Procedure: Place the color samples in the middle of the group. Make sure that the group understands the concept of shades. Discuss with them how a color can have different shades but is still the same color. Allow the children to sort out colors. All the greens go on one side, all the blues on another, etc.

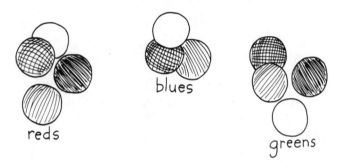

OFF COLORS

Concept: Identify which color strip does not belong among strips of like colors, different hues.

Materials: Paint strips in varying hues (get samples from a paint store).

Group size: One child or small group.

Procedure: Make sets of paint strips. Each set should include strips of varying hues of one color and one strip of another color.

Ask the child to find the color that does not belong. Should a child have difficulty, let that child put the strips of like colors together. This should leave the color that does not match to one side.

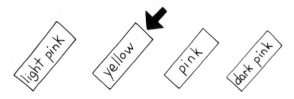

PAINTER'S DELIGHT

Concept: Discuss changes in the color white when other colors are added to it.

Materials: Cups or other containers.

White tempera paint.

Colored tempera paint.

Paintbrush to stir colors.

Paper for painting when activity is over.

Group size: One or two children.

Procedure: Begin with containers of white paint. Add color a drop at a time. Discuss with the children the results. "Is it still white?" "What is the color now?" "What will happen if we add more red?" "What will happen if we put yellow in it?" Allow the children to put in another color. Let the children use the blended colors for painting.

Questions: To generalize the experience ask, "What happens when any color is added to the color white?" "What happens when more of that color is added to the white?" "What happens when white is added to white?" "What happens when red is added to red or blue to blue?" Be sure to confirm the generalization by mixing the paints.

DROPS OF COLOR

Concept: Discuss color changes using water and food coloring.

Materials: Very large jar (at least one gallon, five gallons is best).

Eye droppers.

Food coloring.

Baby food jars.

Group size: Class.

Procedure: In a large jar of water, add red, yellow, or blue food color. Make sure that the color is dark. Allow the children to discuss what happened as you added the food color. Then add another primary color to it, one drop at a time. Discuss what happens. Allow the children to experiment with their own baby food jars talking about the colors as they change.

Variation: Use only one color, discussing the different shades of the same color.

MASTER MIXERS

Concept: Observes changes in colors as they mix.

Material: Clear baking dish.

Overhead projector.

Food colors.

Eye droppers.

Group size: Class.

Procedure: Place the baking dish on the overhead projector. Discuss with the class what they think will happen when you put one color in. Add color drop by drop. Discuss the results. Add subsequent colors in the same manner, asking whether the colors will mix, what will be the new color, etc. You may allow the children to add colors.

ICED COLORS

Concept: Observe changes in colors and ice, in the course of a day.

Materials: Large block of ice (25 pounds).

Food coloring.

Camera (optional).

Ice pick or similar tool.

Group size: Class.

Procedure: Place the block of ice in a deep tray. Punch holes in several places on the block of ice. Fill each hole with one color of food color. Have the children discuss several times during the day what is happening to the colors as the ice melts. You may want to take pictures of the block as it melts.

Variation: Make snowcones with shaved ice and different flavors (colors).

Size

5.1 Introduction

Beginning work with size should involve activities that allow the child to compare the items directly. The activities serve to build mathematical vocabulary that will be crucial to later work with seriation, classification, and general problem solving.

The initial size judgments should be made by directly comparing the items. The vocabulary should focus on positives not negations; that is, judgments such as tall–short, big–little, where a meaning becomes associated with both words. It would not be appropriate to work on tall–not tall, big–not big as negations are difficult for young children.

One must also be careful when making size judgments that the child is in fact judging on size, not spatial orientation. Often young children will respond that the item that is nearest is biggest when in fact the items are the same size. The teacher must remember to develop a strategy for the children that encourages direct comparison. Later, position the items and have the children judge which item satisfies the condition (big, tall, etc.); then confirm the judgments by direct comparison. This approach should systematically help the children develop their ability to make size judgments.

Drawing pictures in relative size sometimes reveals hidden talent.

The sections in this chapter are concerned with the more common size judgments. Should your curriculum require additional judgments, do not hesitate to use the lessons presented as models for developing additional lessons.

5.2 General size (big, little)

The judgments in this section are global discriminations of what is big and what is small. The teacher should be certain that the items used are very different in size. As the children become more and more proficient in judging, the relative size differences may be changed.

SIZE IT UP

Concept: Discriminate the sizes big and little.

Materials: Shapes in various sizes.

Group size: Small group of no more than five.

Procedure: Lay out two objects of the same shape but very different sizes. Then call on one of the children and ask that child to "pick up the big square" or "touch the small circle." If correct, the child gets to keep the shape. After three rounds, the child with the most shapes wins.

The children should be encouraged to pick up the shapes and physically compare them to check their responses.

ROLL–A–WAY

Concept: Identify objects by size.

Materials: Two balls, one small and one large (same color).

Group size: Small group.

Procedure: Have the children sit on the floor and spread their legs to receive rolled balls. One child at a time calls out the ball that
he or she wants. The child identifies the balls as the big ball
and the little ball. The size of the ball confirms that the name
the child uses fits that ball.

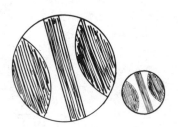

BINOCULAR WATCH

Concept: Identify relative body positions as big or little.

Materials: None.

Group size: Any size group.

Procedure: Show the children how to hold their hands as if they are looking
through binoculars. Have them look at you. Make yourself as
small as you can and say, "I am little." Make yourself as large
as you can and say, "I am big." Ask the children to watch you
through their binoculars and call out "big" or "little" describing
your size.

Let a child be the one who becomes big or little.

"little"

FIND A BIG ONE

Concept: Discriminate visually big and little sizes.

Materials: Common objects found in the room, for example, books, pencils, boxes, tables, toy animals, dolls, chairs, shoes, coats, hats.

Group Size: Class.

Procedure: Point to or hold up an object and say to the children, "Here is a little box. Can anyone find a big box in here?" Let the children (or just one child) locate the requested object. If possible, place the two objects side by side to compare them. If the child makes a mistake, let that child try again.

BIG AND LITTLE

Concept: Discriminate the sizes big and little.

Materials: Pairs of objects, one big and one little of each: spools, pencils, combs, toy horses, blocks, spice boxes, etc.

Two box lids, one big and one little.

Group size: Small group.

Procedure: Show the children the big box lid and tell them that the big things will go in it; then show them the little box lid and tell them that the little things will go in it.

Let the first child pick up a pair of objects (for example, the big block and the little block). Ask the child which block is the big one; have the child answer, "This is the big one." If the child is correct, he or she may put it in the big box lid. Repeat for the little block.

Let each child have at least one turn naming and placing a pair of objects.

Variation: To teach biggest and littlest, add a third object to each pair. Have the children sort only the biggest and littlest of each set into the box lids.

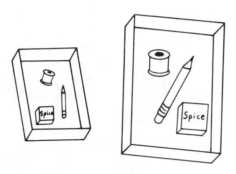

BIG SHAPE, LITTLE SHAPE

Concept:　Discriminate tactually the sizes big and little.

Materials:　Paper sack.

Wooden, plastic, or cardboard shapes, in pairs of big and little.

Group size:　Small group.

Procedure:　With the children either watching or not watching, place a big and a little shape in the bag. Shake it a bit, then ask the first child, "Can you pull out the little [circle]?" Don't let the child look in the bag; the object is to find the correct shape by feel.

Continue with other shapes, asking sometimes for the big shape and sometimes for the little shape.

FIT A POCKET

Concept:　Identify relative size of objects as big or little.

Materials:　Objects that will fit in a pocket and others that will not fit in the pocket.

Your pocket.

Group size:　Any size group.

Procedure:　Arrange the objects in front of the child. Begin trying to put the objects in your pocket. Let the child make observations about why the object will or will not fit in the pocket. Ask the child which objects are big—the ones in the pocket or the ones that did not go in the pocket.

NAILS AND SCREWS

Concept:　Sort nails or screws, matching all the same sizes together.

Materials:　Nails or screws of different sizes.

Muffin pan.

Group size:　One to three children.

Procedure:　Have the nails mixed. Ask the children if they can find all the ones like the one you have. Place them in one section of the pan. Continue with the other sizes until all are picked up. Discuss their reasons for placing particular nails in the sections. "Why did you do that? Are they the same? Do you see any others like it?" Get the children to discover that size is the attribute you are using. Be sure that there are obvious differences in size.

NUTS AND BOLTS

Concept: Match correct size of nut to corresponding bolt.

Materials: Different sizes of nuts and bolts.

Group size: One to three children.

Procedure: Have nuts in one pile and bolts in another. Begin by asking the children to help you put the nuts and bolts together. You may have to point out to the children to look at the hole of the nut and the diameter or end of the bolt. Again, you should begin with a few nuts and bolts and add more to increase the difficulty.

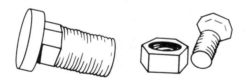

HOW BIG?

Concept: Illustrate with their bodies size of objects or animals as big or little.

Materials: None.

Group size: Small or large group.

Procedure: Talk about the objects below. Are they big or little? Ask the children to illustrate with their bodies how big or little they think those things would be.

house	penny
elephant	french fry
cow	bird
bed	pencil
car	cat

Questions: Is a house smaller than you? Bigger? Can you name anything as big as a house?

MAGNIFYING WONDER

Concept: Name objects as big or little.

Materials: Assorted junk.

Magnifying glass.

Group size: Class.

Procedure: Have the children seated around in a circle with the materials in the middle. Introduce the magnifying glass. Allow the children to experiment with it for awhile. One may discover that looking through one side increases size while the other side decreases size. Have children take turns looking through the glass at objects. Turn the glass around so that the two children may get opposing answers for the same object. Discuss with the class what happened.

Variation: You may cut out "play" magnifying glasses for the children from cardboard. Allow them to walk around the room naming large and small items.

GARDENERS

Concept: Compare sizes of plants.

Materials: Seeds.

Dirt.

Milk cartons.

Group size: Class.

Procedure: Allow the children to plant their own seeds. Every day have the children check on the progress of their seeds. As they grow compare the sizes of the children's plants. You also should discuss how the plants are changing. Young children will have difficulty doing this so you may want to take pictures of the seedlings that show their growth. You might also want to cut a piece of adding machine tape the same length as the plant and keep a graph of the growth on the bulletin board.

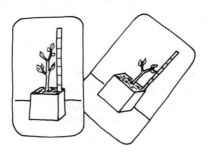

BIG PEOPLE, LITTLE PEOPLE

Concept: Represent big and little in drawing.

Materials: Paper.

Drawing or coloring crayons, pencils or paints.

Group size: Small group.

Procedure: Discuss with the children who are big people and who are little people. For example, adults—mommies and daddies—could be big people and children could be little people.

Have each child draw a picture with a big person and a little person in it. If a child doesn't get the sizes right the first time, allow the child to try again if he or she wishes. When the pictures are finished, label the people in them for the child.

ANIMAL SOUNDS

Concept: Discriminate big sounds and little sounds.

Materials: Pictures of animals, some of which make big sounds (lion, big dog, cow, crow) and some of which make little sounds (mouse, baby bird, kitten, rabbit).

Group size: Small group.

Procedure: Show the children an animal picture and ask them whether the animal makes a big sound or a little sound. Ask one child to make the animal's sound. (Help them, if necessary.) After you and the children have decided whether the sound should be big or little, have them imitate the sound as you make it.

BIG SOUNDS

little sounds

5.3 Length (short, long, tall)

Length judgments for the child are either in terms of height or horizontal length. The term short is used both in describing height (he is short) and length (she has the short train). These activities lend themselves to direct comparison for confirmation of judgments.

BUILDINGS

Concept: Discriminate tall and short.

Materials: Inch cubes, paper tubes or strips, or other building blocks.

Group size: Small group.

Procedure: Tell the children, "I am going to build a *short* building," then stack about two cubes. Then tell them, "Now I am going to build a *tall* building," and then stack about four or five blocks. Point to the short building and ask the children to tell you if it is short or tall. "Yes, it's a *short* building." "Can you build a short building?"

Have each child build a short and a tall building and then tell you which is the short one and which is the tall one.

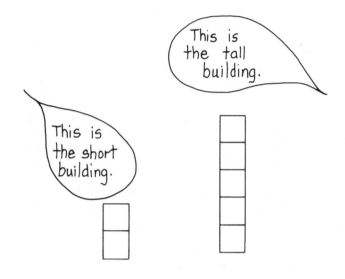

BACK TO BACK

Concept: Discriminate short and tall.

Materials: None.

Group size: Any size group.

Procedure: Divide the children into groups of three. Try to have all three children of each group of different heights. One child is designated the "referee;" the other two stand back to back. The referee decides which of the other two is short and which is tall. After children in the other groups have checked the referee's decision, another child in each group becomes the referee. Continue until all children have had a chance to be referee.

SUPERPERSON

Concept: Discriminate between short and tall.

Materials: Inch cubes or other building blocks, or short and tall toy buildings.

Doll to be "Superperson" (cape is optional).

Group size: Small group.

Procedure: Make some short buildings and some tall buildings with the blocks. Tell the children, "Watch Superperson jump over this tall building," and then have the doll do it. Next say, "Watch Superperson jump over this short building," moving the doll over the building. Give each child a chance to jump Superperson over a building, but first the child must tell you whether the building is short or tall.

WIGGLY WORMS

Concept: Discriminate between short and long.

Materials: Inch cubes or interlocking cubes.

Bits of clay to make "eyes."

Group size: Small group.

Procedure: Put two dots of clay on one block to make "eyes." (This is the head of the worm.) Then tell the class that you are going to make a short worm. Add about two blocks onto the head. Then repeat for a long worm, using about five blocks.

Ask the children if they can make both a short and a long worm. After they have finished, have them tell you which is the short worm and which is the long worm. They may wish to draw a picture of their worms, which you can label "long" and "short" for them.

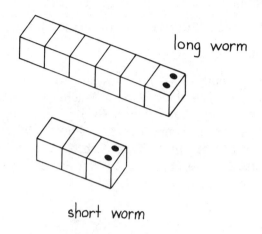

long worm

short worm

LINES

Concept: Identify lines as long or short through tactile identification.

Materials: None.

Group size: Any size group.

Procedure: Choose one child. Say to the child, "I am going to draw two lines on your back, one is short (demonstrate on child's back) and the other is long." "Erase" the child's back. Ask the child to raise the hand on the side you draw the *long* line. Repeat the comparison if the child has trouble.

RODS

Concept: Discriminate between longer and shorter.

Materials: Rods.

              Common objects in the room.

Group size: Small group.

Procedure: Give each of the children a rod. Ask, "Can you find something in this room that is longer than your rod?" Demonstrate with your rod, if necessary. After all the children have found something longer than their rods, ask them if they can find something shorter than their rods.

SNAKES 'N SNAILS

Concept: Name shortest and longest object.

Materials: Paper strips of different lengths.

              Magic markers.

              Tape.

Group size: Any size group.

Procedure: Lay one strip of each length in front of the children. Ask them to identify the longest, the shortest, and any sizes that are in between.

              Have each child take one or more strip sizes, identifying the longest and the shortest.

              Have the children draw designs. Make snails by having the children roll a strip and then tape the roll in place.

roll and tape

5.4 Width (wide, narrow)

Work with width is rather difficult for children because the judgments are made about a dimension that is not naturally used in the child's vocabulary. The activities presented should serve as a stimulus for using items around the room; the possibilities are only limited by the materials available about the school.

RIVERS

Concept: Discriminate wide and narrow.

Materials: Chalkboard and chalk or large paper and felt-tipped markers.

Group size: Small group.

Procedure: Tell the children a story about a river:

> "Once there was a little river. It was a very *narrow* little river. (Draw a narrow chalk line.) But as this river flowed on, it gathered more and more water and grew *wider* and *wider*. (Make chalk line wider.) Finally that little river grew so wide that by the time it reached the ocean it was very wide indeed. It wasn't a *narrow* little river any more."

> Give the children a chance to draw a river and tell its story. Have them show you the narrow parts and the wide parts.

narrow   wide

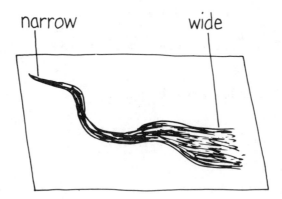

NOODLES

Concept: Discriminate between wide and narrow.

Materials: Clay.

Plastic knives or other utensils to cut the clay.

Group size: Small group.

Procedure: Roll the clay out flat and tell the children that you are going to make noodles. Cut some narrow noodles (as for spaghetti) and then some wide noodles (as for lasagna.)

Let the children take turns making noodles. Have them tell you whether they are making wide or narrow noodles.

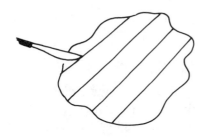

wide noodles

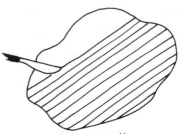

narrow noodles

DESIGNER STRIPES

Concept: Discriminate between wide and narrow.

Materials: Tempera paint.

Wide and narrow paint brushes.

Paper.

Felt-tipped marker (optional).

Group size: Small group.

Procedure: Tell the children that they are going to design some clothes with stripes. Draw a garment and show them how it can be painted with wide stripes or narrow stripes or both.

Let each child outline a garment (or you do it for them with a marker) and then paint stripes on it. Have each child tell you whether each of the stripes is narrow or wide.

When the garments are dry, cut them out and post them; have a fashion show on your wall or bulletin board.

wide stripes

narrow stripes

WIDE SPACE, NARROW SPACE

Concept: Discriminate between wide and narrow.

Materials: None.

Group size: Small or large group.

Procedure: One child is "It." The others form two lines, hands joined, facing each other. The two lines form a narrow corridor between them. "It" stands outside one end of the corridor and tries to walk, run, or crawl through the tunnel when you give the "go" signal.

As "It" is proceeding, call out "Wide space!" at which the two lines back apart, making "Its" progress easier, or "Narrow space!" at which the two lines quickly walk toward each other, stopping "It."

Before playing the game, stress that everyone is to move carefully so as not to bump into each other when making a narrow space. The child who is "It" should "freeze" when the corridor becomes too narrow.

5.5   Thickness (thick, thin)

One of the attributes of objects that children are often called to work with is thickness. A few activities directly related to this concept should help acquaint the child with the terminology.

THREAD AND ROPE

Concept: Discriminate between thick and thin.

Materials: Thread, string, and rope of different thicknesses.

Group size: Small group.

Procedure: Show the children two pieces of thread, string, or rope (use two different thicknesses); ask or tell the children which is thick and which is thin. Have then identify which is which. Then ask them, "If I wanted to sew on a button, which piece would I use, the thick one or the thin one?" Try to get them to tell you, "The thin one." Then ask, "If we were going to play tug-of-war, which piece would we use, the thick one or the thin one?" (If necessary, you can prove your logic to them by trying to thread a piece of rope through a needle and by trying to play tug-of-war with a piece of thread.)

Repeat with other pairs of thread, string and rope and using similar questions; or let the children ask the questions.

Thin piece

For sewing

Thick piece

For tug-of-war

CANDLES

Concept: Discriminate between thick and thin.

Materials: Clay.

Clay cutting tools (optional).

Group size: Small group.

Procedure: Tell the children that you are going to make some candles out of clay. Roll out the clay and show a thick candle and a thin candle. Let each child make at least one clay candle and tell you whether it is thick or thin.

Roll it out.

Extra lump for flame on wick

I made a thick candle.

I made a thin candle.

ANIMAL TAILS

Concept: Discriminate between thick and thin.

Materials: Chalk and chalkboard or paper and drawing or painting materials.

Group size: Small group.

Procedure: Draw some animals on the chalkboard or paper. Ask the children whether each animal has a thick or a thin tail. Let a child draw a tail on the animal to agree with the children's decision.

Some animals to be included might be squirrel, sheep dog, horse, raccoon, rabbit (thick tails); elephant, mouse, hippo, dachshund, cat (thin tails); lion (both!).

PENCIL–EATING PARROTS

Concept: Discriminate between thick and thin.

Materials: Thick and thin pencils (standard pencils and primary pencils will do).

Pictures of two parrots, Polly and Holly, drawn on a piece of cardboard, with a hole in their beaks; Polly's just big enough to put a thin pencil through, Holly's big enough for thick pencils.

Group size: Small group.

Procedure: Show the children the pictures and tell them that Polly the Pencil Eater likes to eat pencils but that she only eats thin pencils; she won't eat thick pencils. Holly eats both kinds, but only the thick ones belong to her. Give each child a pencil and ask her if Polly will eat this pencil. (Polly gets first choice since she is thinner.) Ask why and elicit from the child that the pencil is thin or that the pencil is thick. After the child has answered, let him try to feed Polly the pencil to prove it. If Polly can't eat it, let Holly have it.

Always have the child tell you whether the pencil is thick or thin.

5.6   Volume (empty, full)

Children must understand the terminology of empty versus full to be successful problem solvers in today's mathematics programs. They have encountered the terminology in everyday life: "drink all the milk, be sure the glass is empty"; "fill your bowl." This should make the task easier for the teacher.

RICE JARS

Concept: Discriminate between empty and full.

Materials: Baby food or other empty jars.

Dishpan of rice, beans, cornmeal, or puffed cereal.

Pouring cup or scoop.

Group size: Small group.

Procedure: Show the children an empty jar; tell them that it is called "empty" because it does not have any rice in it. Take another jar and tell them that you are going to fill it; let them tell you which jar is empty and which is full.

Give each child a chance to empty and fill jars and tell you which is empty and which is full.

Classification

6.1   Introduction

The ability to classify objects is based on the idea of a relation. Some common characteristic among the objects must be known to the child for them to be grouped together. Classification work, that of determining a relation that allows objects to be grouped as belonging or not belonging to the class, is the basis for later work with definitions.

Classification proceeds through at least three levels for the young child. First, simple classification is performed according to whether objects belong together; second, objects are classified into disjoint sets; and last, multiple classification takes place in which objects may belong to two or more of the classes. For example, if classifying objects as red–nonred, square–nonsquare, it is possible to have both red and square.

Each section contains an in-depth explanation of the type of classification involved.

6.2   Classifying objects that belong together

Sometimes called "simple" classification, this level of classification is the easiest and one of the earliest forms of classification used by children. Real world objects are grouped with something with which they actually belong. Simple classification can approach true classification—as in the request to put assorted animals together according to whether they live in a barn or a zoo. Each animal "belongs in" a habitat, and two distinct groups of animals are formed. Although the two groups are disjoint sets as with true classification, the child is making an association between each animal and its home, not an association on likenesses or differences between the types of animal groups formed. Simple classification draws on the child's associative experiences.

Another example of simple classification occurs when a child puts a circle and a triangle together to make an ice cream cone—the shapes represent things that belong together in the child's associative experience. If the task began as true classification—sorting objects according to shape—the child has changed rules and reverted back to simple classification by adopting a rule about how things belong together.

Many simple classification tasks appear to be similar to a one-to-one correspondence task. Given pictures of various hats and members of a family, the child gives each member a hat that might belong to that person. However, in one-to-one correspondence the concern is with pairing objects from different sets to determine which set has more or less, whereas, in simple classification, the concern is with constructing sets of objects that naturally "belong together."

Children with less–developed oral language abilities (those who are less verbal) appear to score as well in simple classification skills as their more verbal counterparts.

Simple classification is included in this chapter because certain classifying skills are involved. One skill involves utilizing a rule and consistently grouping according to that rule. Another is observing (discriminating) likenesses and differences to associate the correct groups, that is, noticing stripes on a baby zebra shows that that baby "belongs with" the striped mother zebra. Simple classification groupings can provide a beginning point for further discussion about groups that are formed into true classes.

COAT BOX

Concept: Classify objects by matching them to the person to whom they belong.

Materials: A large box (the size that paper towels come in is the most suitable) or a place where all coats are kept.

Children's coats.

Group size: Any size group.

Procedure: As children come in, have them put their coats into one large box. When it is time for the children to leave have one or two children pass the coats out to the persons to whom they belong. This simple classification encourages children to notice similarities and differences in the coats and the children to whom the coats belong.

The activity can be extended by having children find another child who has a coat in some way like theirs. Also group children with/without hats, gloves, and sweaters. Each time use only one dimension in judgment.

Variation: Do the same activity with paint smocks if each child has a distinctive one brought from home.

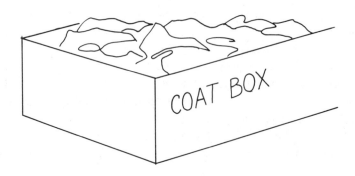

EMERGENCY VEHICLES

Concept: Classify objects by matching them to the place where they belong.

Materials: Toy fire engines, police cars, and ambulances.

Boxes decorated as firehouses, police stations, and hospitals.

Group size: Small group.

Procedure: Set out the three buildings. Have the children put each toy vehicle in or in front of the building where it belongs. At this point let the children play with the materials. The concept of matching the vehicles to the appropriate buildings will most likely occur again while play is in progress.

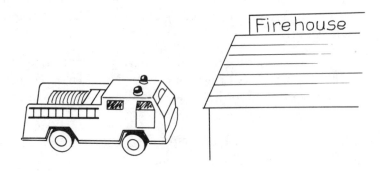

DOLL HOUSE

Concept: Classify pictures of items found in a home by the room in which they belong.

Materials: Pictures of items found in a home.

Pictures or drawings of different rooms in a home or a doll house.

Group size: Class.

Procedure: Display the pictures of the rooms. Discuss with the children the rooms and what you find in each. Show the pictures one at a time, discussing each. Ask where each belongs in the home. Allow the children to sort the pictures. Use as an individual activity after the children catch on.

Variations: (1) Play grocery store—children sort pictures of food into the correct department, e.g., steak/meat, milk/dairy, corn/vegetables, etc. (2) Play department store—children sort pictures of things found in department stores into their correct departments. (3) Play store—toy store, clothing store, food store, pet store. Children sort pictures into the correct store.

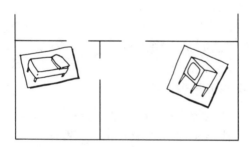

GO–TOGETHERS

Concept: Classify pictures of objects that belong together because of their use.

Materials: Pictures of items that are found together: toothbrush/toothpaste, salt/pepper, bacon/eggs, brush/comb, shoe/foot, knife/fork, bat/ball, soap/towel.

Group size: Any size group.

Procedure: Discuss with the class things that go together. Show pictures of items asking which ones would be put together. Allow the children to do this activity in small groups next.

Questions: Why did you put the comb and the brush together? The knife and the fork? etc.

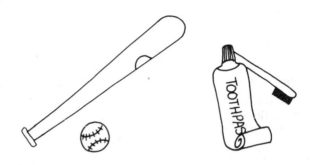

PAPA BEAR, MAMA BEAR, AND BABY BEAR

Concept: Classify objects by size.

Materials: Paper or felt cutouts of three bears and three each of bowls, spoons, chairs, beds (optional: cups, forks, knives, blankets, pillows, shoes). Papa Bear and his belongings should be the largest; Mama Bear's medium size; and Baby Bear's, the smallest.

Flannelboard (optional).

Group size: Small group.

Procedure: After reading or telling the story of *Goldilocks and the Three Bears,* display the three bears and ask the children to help give each bear its own things. Show the three bowls, and say, "Papa Bear had the biggest bowl. Which bowl is his?" Let a child match the largest bowl to Papa Bear. Do the same for Mama Bear's medium-sized bowl and Baby Bear's small bowl. When the children understand the task, give each child a group of three objects to match to the correct bears.

ANIMALS' HOMES

Concept: Classify by matching pictures of animals to the habitat in which they belong.

Materials: Pictures of animals: dog, bird, worm, monkey, squirrel, bee, cow, bear, rabbit, fish, mouse, pig, etc.

Pictures of habitats of these animals.

Group size: One or two children.

Procedure: Lay out the animals or their habitats. Have the children match the animal to its habitat. Demonstrate with the first animal. Use three animals during the first game and add more animals in later games.

Variation: Match baby animals to mother animals and both to their homes.

Questions: Many questions can be asked that provoke some thought with this activity: Why does a bird live in a nest? Why doesn't the dog live in a tree? Why does a mouse have a small hole?

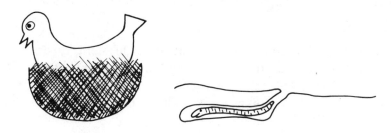

DRESS–UP

Concept: Classify pictures of clothing by matching them to family members to whom they might belong.

Materials: Pictures of clothes for babies, children, mothers, and fathers.

A picture of a baby, mother, father, and two children, one a boy and one a girl. Have sets of family members available to represent races present in the school.

This activity could be done with flannelboard objects.

Group size: Small group.

Procedure: Lay out the pictures of the family. Have the children match the pictures of the clothes to the person to whom they belong. Some clothes might fit into more than one group. Ask the children to explain their choices if they do not seem appropriate.

Questions: Is there someone in your family who wears [boots]? Who? Can you point to the clothes that look like they would fit you? Would not fit you?

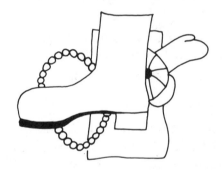

COOKIE SORT

Concept: Classify according to color.

Materials: Different color cookies, chocolate, vanilla, strawberry.

Group size: Class.

Procedure: At snack time, mix a number of different types of cookies together before placing them on the snack tray. Ask the children to sort the types of cookies (either by type, shape, chocolate topping, etc.). Then allow each child to select a favorite for snack.

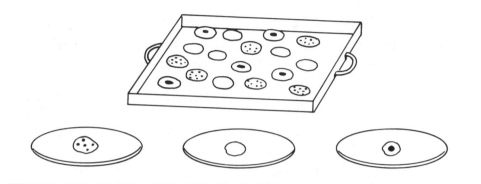

WHAT'S COOKING?

Concept: Classify food pictures according to time.

Materials: Pictures of food.

             Sorting board (breakfast, lunch, dinner).

Group size: Three children.

Procedure: Have pictures of meals that might be typical for breakfast, lunch, or dinner. Also, on your sorting boards, have a picture or drawing of people eating that particular meal. Give the children a clue to the meal that the board signifies.

             Discuss all the pictures with the children beforehand: when they would see this food, when they would eat it. Show them the boards and discuss those. Allow the children to sort.

             Variation: Include a few items (milk for instance) that could be eaten or drunk at more than one meal.

6.3 Classifying objects into disjoint (separate) sets

Activities involving classifying objects into disjoint sets (separate sets) occur frequently as a child begins to organize his world. The act of classifying focuses attention on factors that are similar. The task can be as easy as classifying objects into two groups or as difficult as multiple classification into numerous groups.

Classification into separate groups can begin by the teacher's identifying the criteria by which to separate the sets. As the child progresses (and this is most important), allow the child to discover or decide how objects can be grouped. There may be many variations in how some objects can be grouped. A young child may become distracted and switch classification rules in the middle of sorting; this often happens when the child changes from shapes (triangles and circles) to color (blue and green). Discuss changes in the classification rule with the child.

Classification into disjoint sets lends itself well to the use of concrete objects and to doing tasks in the classroom.

COLOR CLOTHES

Concept: Classify according to color.

Materials: None.

Group size: Class.

Procedure: Use this activity when you have the class together. Begin talking to all the children about all the colors that each is wearing. Decide on one piece of clothing, such as pants. Ask the children to find other children with their color of pants. They should end up in groups of the same color pants. Choose another piece of clothing and begin again. Continue for as long as time allows.

HOLIDAY CLEANUP

Concept: Classify according to color.

Materials: Holiday tree ornaments.

Group size: Class.

Procedure: As you are taking your holiday decorations down in your classroom make it a learning situation. Discuss the colors of the
decorations and how it is important to put the decorations in
the right box. Allow the children to put the decorations away,
talking about their colors as you do.

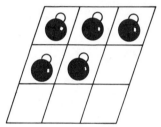   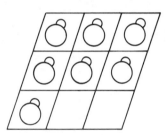

BIRD FAMILIES

Concept: Classify/sort objects by color.

Materials: Paper or felt cutouts of birds in different colors (all birds of
the same family must be the same color).

Paper, box, or pie pan nests of matching colors.

Group size: One child or a small group.

Procedure: Show the children the nests. Tell them that each bird family
has a nest of its own color so that all the family members know
which nest is theirs. The birds have been out hunting for food
all day, and now it is time for them to come home, each to its
own family. Give each child a turn to match a bird to its own
family nest.

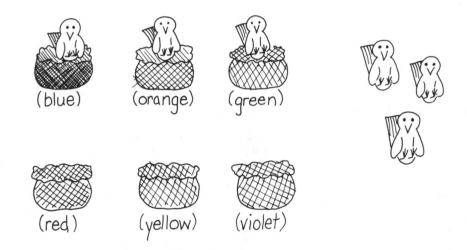

CRAYONS BEYOND REPAIR

Concept: Classify classroom objects into sets by those needing repair and those in good condition.

Materials: Crayons, some broken and some whole.

Pencils, some needing sharpening and some that do not.

Books, some that need tape and some that do not.

Scissors, some that work well and some that do not.

Group size: Any size group.

Procedure: Use the task of sorting broken or torn equipment as a classification activity. Let the children help in sorting the materials.

JOBS

Concept: Classify tools into sets according to who would use them.

Materials: Several tools used in each job category and an appropriate container for each set of tools; for example, *doctor:* "little black bag" (or old purse) with stethoscope, thermometer, bandages, tongue depressors; *repair worker:* tool box with hammer, screwdriver, nails, wrenches; *cook:* large pot with spoon, saucepan, bowl, measuring cups; *garment worker (sewer):* sewing basket with thread, pins, scissors, fabric scraps, thimble.

Group size: Four children (or one player for each category).

Procedure: Mix all the tools together in a box and let each child choose a job and its container. On a turn, each child chooses a tool belonging to that job and places it in the job container.

COLOR BASKETS

Concept: Classify/sort objects by color.

Materials: Jelly beans of different colors.

Small boxes or baskets, one of each color of jelly beans.

Large basket or box.

Group size: Small group.

Procedure: Mix all the jelly beans in the large basket. Give each child a turn to pick out one jelly bean, name its color, and place it in the basket of the corresponding color.

Variation: Instead of jelly beans, use plastic flowers, buttons, pegs, beads, blocks, or other small objects.

A THREE-RING CIRCUS

Concept: Classify objects into three separate sets as three circus acts.

Materials: Three felt circles about ten inches in diameter.

Toy objects that could be found in a circus—lions, elephants, horses, clowns, strongmen, monkeys, etc.

Group size: One or two children.

Procedure: Set out the three circles in a row and explain to the children that these are rings at a circus. Give the children the objects for classifying and ask them to put them in the rings so that each ring will have a different act. Have the children tell you about the acts (what the animals or people are doing) in each ring. The child might choose to sort by animals (elephants, lions, monkeys) or by actions (jumping, roaring, balancing).

  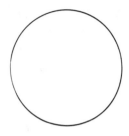

COLOR CARS

Concept: Classify according to color.

Materials: Cardboard or plywood box or small milk cartons.

Assorted color miniature cars, several of each color.

Group size: Two children.

Procedure: Color code each garage (box) to the colors of the cars. Ask the children if they can find the right garage for the cars. Tell them that the drivers need some help finding their garage. If the child does not understand where the cars should go, discuss with the child how one might decide where each car belongs.

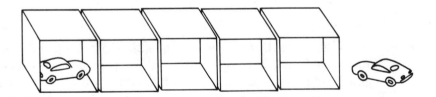

SORT THE OBJECTS

Concept: Classify objects into disjoint sets.

Materials: Empty margarine tubs, one for each category.

Several objects of each category used: blocks, pegs, crayons, beads; toy cars, people, dishes, furniture.

Group size: Small group.

Procedure: Mix all the objects together in a box. At first, use only two categories that are easy to distinguish, later add a third and then a fourth category.

Tell the children that, for this game, all the blocks must go into one tub, all the pegs into another tub, and so on.

To increase the difficulty of the activity, mix together objects with similar features, for example, forks and spoons.

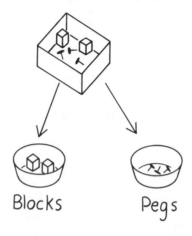

Blocks **Pegs**

BOTTLE CAPS

Concept: Classify bottle caps into separate sets.

Materials: Collection of bottle caps.

Sorting tray (may use TV dinner trays).

Group size: Four children.

Procedure: Show the collection of caps to the children and ask them how they could sort them out. Most will sort them out using color and brand of bottle cap. Most children will not need any assistance if given a sorting tray. The teacher should question the child's choices while the child is working. Many times a child might forget what the criteria for sorting were so simply say, "Does that belong there?" or "Is that (pointing at one set, the same as those?" (pointing at a different set). This reminder should be enough to focus the child to the task's direction.

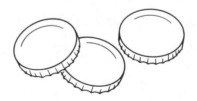

NUTS

Concept: Classify nuts into sets according to shape, color, size, or texture.

Materials: Bag of assorted nuts: walnuts, pecans, hazel, brazil, macadamia, cashews, pistachios, etc. Edible seeds could also be used.

Group size: Class.

Procedure: Seat the children around a table. Show them the nuts and discuss what they are, whether they are all the same, and what makes them different. Allow the children to sort using their own criteria. "Where does this one go?" "Do you see any that look like this one?" Keep the children on track using questions such as these if they begin changing criteria. At first, do not use all the different types of nuts but, rather, a few that are obviously different. Then rework the activity using all types.

How the nuts taste would be a good way to classify also. Make sure the children give reasons for their criteria. Do not let them say "because it tastes good." Ask them why it tastes good.

SUPER SEEDS

Concept: Classify according to shape and color.

Materials: Assorted seeds.

Muffin pans.

Group size: Two or three children.

Procedure: Every group should be given a muffin pan and the assortment of seeds. Tell the children to find the ones that belong together. A lot of direction should not be needed. If it is, questions should be used to get the children to observe the seeds closely by looking at the colors, shapes, and sizes. Help them decide on the attributes they will use for classifying. Afterward discuss the results of each group's work. You may find different results for each of the groups. Try to get them to verbalize exactly what attribute(s) they used.

ROCK HOUND COLLECTIONS

Concrete: Classify rocks into sets according to different attributes.

Materials: Collection of rocks with many different attributes. Have some large and small, rough and smooth, dark and light, etc.

Group size: Class.

Procedure: Have the children seated around a table. Place the rock collection in the middle. Allow the children to examine them. Ask them to place the rocks in groups. Two groups would be the easiest to begin with. Let the children decide on the attribute(s).

Variation: teacher gives the attribute used to classify. The children then will sort the rocks using those attributes.

SIZABLE GROUPS

Concept: Classify objects according to size.

Materials: Sets of matched objects, one big and one little, in each pair, such as spoons, books, blocks, cans, buttons, cups, etc. large–small monster boxes (see diagram).

Group size: Small group.

Procedure: Have the objects in their large and small pairs. The children should sort the objects into large and small. Give them one set at a time. Large items should be placed in the large section and small items in the small section. Items should be changed after the children have sorted several times.

            The large–small monster is made from a box cut on three sides. The fourth side makes the hinge. The box can be decorated like a monster.

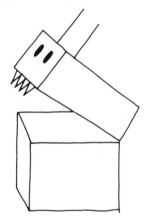

THE GREAT OUTDOORS

Concept: Classify collection of objects found on a walking trip.

Materials: Box in which to place found objects.

Group size: Class.

Procedure: Discuss with the children what kinds of things they might see on their trip. Set down rules before going, such as not breaking branches on people's trees. Ask the children to find things that they think are interesting. After the walk gather around a table and tell the children that you are going to sort the objects one at a time. Introduce a few found items. Let the children decide how they should be sorted. You should question the children's choices. "Why did you put the leaf in a different set from the pine cone?" "How are they alike?"

SUGAR AND SALT

Concept:　Sort foods into groups according to whether children put salt or sugar on them.

Materials:　Pictures of salt shaker and sugar bowl.

　　　　　　Pictures of foods.

Group size:　Two to four children.

Procedure:　Discuss with the children what foods you put sugar or salt on. Begin showing obvious pictures such as cereal–sugar, popcorn–salt. Have the children sort the pictures into two groups.

FLOAT OR SINK

Concept: Classify items according to their floating or sinking ability.

Materials: Container to hold water.

Items, some that float and some that sink; for example, cork, balloon, styrofoam, wood, button, clip, rock, marble, etc.

Two egg carton lids (one for floating objects and one for sinking objects). Put a sail on each illustrating floating or sinking.

Group size: Class.

Procedure: Begin by showing the items to the class. Question them on whether they think the items will float or sink. Ask how they can find out. Test out their predictions one at a time.

Variation: Have children draw pictures of objects that sank or objects that floated.

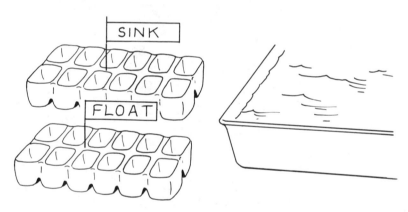

HOT AND COLD

Concept: Classify pictures of objects according to temperature: hot, cold, or neither.

Materials: Standup cardboard with three pictures on the divisions—sun/wood/ice—or any objects representing hot/cold/neither hot nor cold.

Pictures of objects ranging from hot to cold.

Group size: One or two children.

Procedure: Discuss the pictures on the stand with the child. Ask a child to point to something that is hot or cold. Sort the first few cards with the child placing them under hot (if hot) or cold (if cold). Objects that are usually not either hot or cold go in a stack in the middle. The stack in the middle may vary. One child might put spoon under hot because the child remembers that it was hot when he or she ate food. As long as the child can justify a selection, the classification choice is correct.

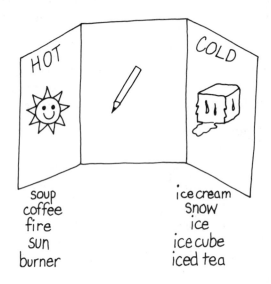

soup
coffee
fire
sun
burner

ice cream
snow
ice
ice cube
iced tea

ARE YOU ATTRACTED TO A MAGNET?

Concept: Classify objects according to a magnet's ability to pick them up.

Materials: Collection of materials, some magnetic—pins, coins, screws, nails, washers—and some nonmagnetic—buttons, blocks, paper, yarn, etc.

Group size: Class.

Procedure: If possible have enough magnets for every two children to use one. Different shapes and sizes would also be interesting for experimentation. Allow the children to experiment with their magnets, finding out what can be picked up and what cannot. Ask them to sort the materials into two groups, a group that can be picked up and a group that cannot be picked up. Discuss with the children their choices. Ask, "Why did you put the nail on that side?" Have them verbalize their reasoning.

HOUSE HUNT

Concept: Classify according to size.

Materials: Dolls and houses of different sizes.

Group size: Three to five children.

Procedure: Use cardboard boxes for the houses. Have the doors cut to the size of the dolls. Tell the children that the dolls are lost and need help to find their way home. Stress to the children that all the dolls do not live together, but live in the house with a door their size. Make sure that the children don't drop all the dolls into the large house.

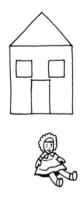  

NAILS

Concept: Classify by size.

Materials: Assorted nails.

Divided tray (lazy susan is very good for this).

Group size: Two to three children.

Procedure: With the children in their groups, discuss the terms of comparative size. Talk about what nails are and what they are used for. Tell the children that for the carpenter to use the nails they must be sorted in their respective sizes. Allow the children then to classify the nails, discussing what they are doing at the same time.

THE BUTTON BOX

Concept: Classify/sort objects by color.

Materials: Egg carton.

Buttons, several of each color being used.

Box or dish to hold all the buttons.

Group size: One child or small group.

Procedure: Show the children the box with all the buttons mixed together inside. Ask a child to help sort the buttons into the egg carton "button box," putting all the buttons of each color into one section. You can help them get started by guiding them to place one button into each section.

Variations: (1) Match buttons onto clothing cutouts of the same color. (2) Use bottle caps painted different colors instead of buttons.

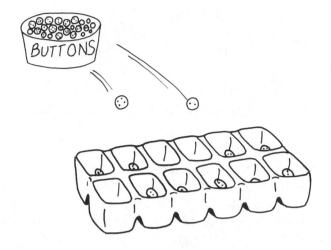

COIN CUTIES

Concept: Classify according to size.

Materials: Muffin pan.

Assorted coins.

Group size: Two or three children.

Procedure: Discuss the size differences of the coins with the group. Pass out coins and pans to groups. Tell the children to find the coins that belong together. Allow the children to sort the coins using questioning techniques rather than telling the children the attributes to use in classifying.

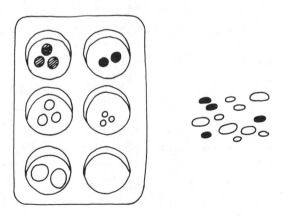

COLOR CUBES

Concept: Classify according to color.

Materials: Sorting box.

Assorted colored cubes (all the same size and shape).

Group size: Two children.

Procedure: Use only two color cubes to begin. Try to have the child decide
how the cubes should be sorted. Most likely the child will use
the only attribute that is not constant and that attribute is color.
Increase the number of colors as the child progresses. If the
child doesn't understand, use questions to allow the child to
discover the answer. If the child does classify by color, be sure
to ask why.

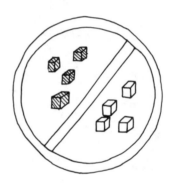

FIND-A-SHAPE

Concept: Classify according to shape.

Materials: Sorting box.

Shapes.

Group size: Two children.

Procedure: Begin using a box divided into two areas. Hang the shapes
above their respective trays. Try to give the child as few
verbal directions as possible by using questions to get started.
Begin with two shapes and expand as the children catch on.

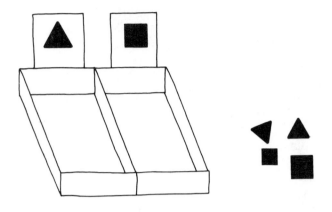

MAIL SHAPES

Concept: Classify/sort shapes into like sets.

Materials: Six shoe boxes for mailboxes.

Letter carrier's bag.

Letters or postcards, each marked with a circle, square, rectangle, oval, triangle, or a shape which is not one of these.

Group size: One child or small group.

Procedure: Label each of five mailboxes with one of these characters: Circle Sue, Square Stan, Oval Otis, Triangle Terry, and Rectangle Rex. Label the sixth box "Dead Letters."

Give each child a turn to pull a letter from the letter carrier's bag and deliver it to the correct mailbox. Any shape which is not a circle, square, triangle, oval, or rectangle goes into the Dead Letter box.

SHAPE FLOWERS

Concept: Classify/sort shapes into like sets.

Materials: Paper cutouts of circles, squares, triangles, rectangles, and ovals.

Pipe cleaners or popsicle sticks.

Tape.

Small cups or vases.

Group size: One child or small group.

Procedure: Tape each shape onto a pipe cleaner or popsicle stick to make a "shape flower." Mark each cup or vase with one of the five shapes.

To play, have the children sort the flowers into the corresponding vases.

SORT-A-SHAPE

Concept: Classify/sort shapes into like sets.

Materials: Five game cards on which to sort shapes, one card each for circle, square, triangle, rectangle, and oval.

Enough plastic or construction paper shapes to cover the spaces on the cards.

Paper bag or box.

Group size: Two to five children.

Procedure: Give each child a blank game card. Assign each child a different shape with which to fill up his or her card. (You can place the first shape on each child's card.) Mix the remaining shapes in the paper bag. As you pull each one out ask, "Who gets this [rectangle]?"

Variation: Place the game cards in a row before the group. Give each child a turn to pull a shape from the bag and place it on the correct card.

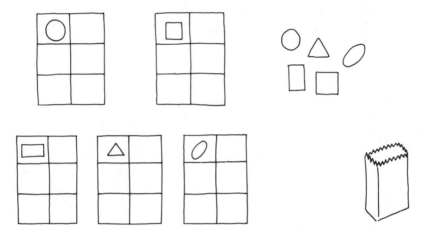

OFF TO SEE THE SHAPE WHIZ

Concept: Classify/sort shapes into like sets.

Materials: Chalkboard and chalk (yellow chalk is best).

Die marked with these shapes: circle, square, triangle, rectangle, oval, and star.

Group size: Small group.

Procedure: Draw the gameboard as pictured below. It should show five paths, all of which lead to the Shape Whiz. At the beginning of each path draw a different character: Circle Sue, Square Stan, Oval Otis, Triangle Terry, and Rectangle Rex.

To begin the game, ask the children to guess which character will make it to the Shape Whiz first. Then each child takes a turn rolling the die, identifying the shape rolled, and advancing the corresponding character one space along its path. For example, if a child rolls an oval, he or she says, "Oval Otis gets the oval" and marks the next space of Otis's path, either by coloring it in with chalk or by drawing an oval in the space. If the star turns up, the child rolls again. The first character whose path is completely filled has won the race to see the Shape Whiz.

Variations: (1) Let each of five children represent one of the shape characters. Each child can advance his or her character only when that child rolls the corresponding shape. (2) Make a gameboard. Instead of a die, make enough small shape cards to cover all the spaces on the paths. Let each child draw a shape card from a paper bag and place it on the correct path.

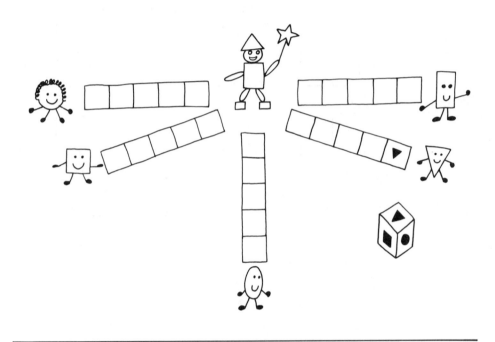

PLAIDS AND STRIPES AND SILLY DOTS

Concept: Classify cards according to patterns.

Materials: Cards made from different pattern materials or wallpaper samples with stripes, plaids, and dots.

Sorting box (see diagram).

Group size: Two to four children.

Procedure: Have several cards in each category of patterns. In a small group, without using the box, allow the children to sort the cards in different ways. The teacher might want to designate the number of groups. After the children have sorted in different ways, introduce the sorting box to them. One or two children can then sort using the box.

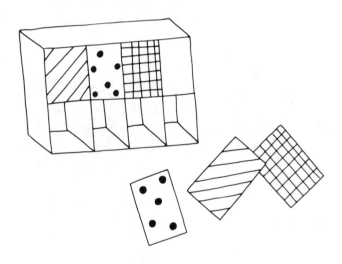

SAME AND DIFFERENT GAME

Concept: Classify pattern cards into those with the same designs and those with different designs.

Materials: Wallpaper or material samples.

               Posterboard and glue for mounting samples.

Group size: Class.

Procedure: Make a board with samples as in the diagram. Show the cards to the children. Ask them where they think each card should go. Let two or three children do the activity as an independent project. Pattern cards can be made at different levels of difficulty.

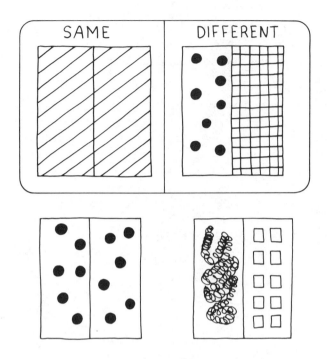

SLEEPERS AND CRAWLERS

Concept: Classify groups of children by the kind of activity in which they are participating.

Materials: String.

Group size: Any size group.

Procedure: Tell the children that you are going to play a game. Lay out the string into two large circles—large enough to hold ten children each.

Name two activities, animals, or objects. Designate one activity to each circle. Let the children choose the activity that they want, then they go to that circle, and perform the activity.

Questions: Are there as many in one circle as in the other? Is there a group that does not have anyone in it?

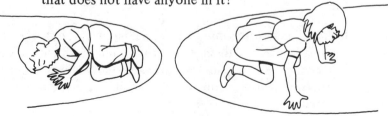

YOU ARE NOT . . .

Concept: Classify by telling what one is "not."

Materials: None.

Group size: Any size group.

Procedure: Have a child tell something that he or she is "not." "I am not _____." The child must name a characteristic of a group of which the child is not a member. You may give examples such as, "I am *not* a child. I am *not* a duck. I am *not* a dentist." This activity may be difficult for some children, so you might start with examples such as, "Are you a duck or a child?" When the child answers that he or she is a child, then say, "Then you are not a duck."

Questions: Why are you not a _____?

A TV SURVEY

Concept: Classify television shows by those which are watched and those not watched.

Materials: Chalk.

               Names of children's shows.

Group size: Class.

Procedure: Discuss with the class shows that they watch on TV. Ask about shows that are not mentioned. Make a list with the children helping you. After finishing, go over the list and the criteria.

               Variations: (1) Classify television characters either as bad or good, or by job. (2) Classify shows into types: comedy, cartoon, detective, cowboy, superhero, etc.

WATCH	DON'T WATCH

FOOD GROUPS

Concept: Classify foods in disjoint sets by their groups.

Materials: Pictures of different kinds of foods, for example, fruits, vegetables, meats, breads, dairy products.

Paper plates (one for each category).

Group size: Small group.

Procedure: Label one paper plate for each category. Mix all the food pictures together and tell the children that for this game all the fruits must go in this plate, all the meats in this plate, and so on. Let each child select a food picture and decide where it belongs.

Variations: (1) Give each child a labeled plate and say that for this game he or she can choose and eat only the type of food indicated on the plate. You might have to use a picture of the food group. (2) Have a child sort foods that come from a cow, a pig, and a chicken. This may be rather difficult for some children.

BY LAND, SEA, AND AIR

Concept: Classify transportation pictures according to type.

Materials: Pictures of water, street, air, and track vehicles.

Group size: Two to four children.

Procedure: Show the pictures to the children one at a time. Discuss each one, what they are, their use, etc. Display the pictures. Tell the children that you want to put the pictures in groups that go together. Have the children place the pictures in their respective categories.

Variation: Sort trucks, cars, vans, motorcycles, and bicycles into separate parking lots. Use posterboard sheets as parking lots marked with parking areas.

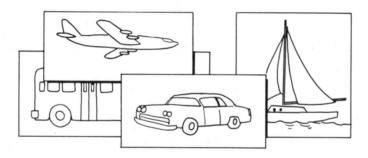

TO THE ZOO OR TO THE FARM

Concept: Classify animals into farm and zoo animals.

Materials: Pictures of farm and zoo animals or plastic toy animals.

Picture of a zoo and picture of a farm.

Group size: Two to four children.

Procedure: Give toy animals or pictures to the children. Ask them if they can put the animals into two groups. This may be difficult for children to do. Ask the children leading questions, "What kind of animals do we have?" "Where do they live?," etc. Introduce the pictures of the zoo and farm, and have the children sort again using the pictures.

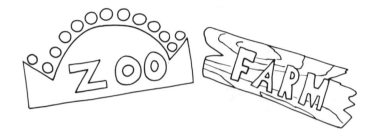

CATEGORIES GALORE

Concept: Classify pictures into categories of food, animal, transportation, people, etc.

Materials: Pictures for different categories.

Group size: Two to four children.

Procedure: Have the pictures in the top row placed so that the child will be able to subclassify. For example, animals could be farm animals, zoo animals, and house animals. Ask the children if they can find where the cards belong. While they are sorting, question the child regarding the column in which the picture should be placed.

You may wish to allow the child to first sort the cards by group. Then the cards in each group may be subclassified.

People			Transportation			Food			Animals		
🧍	🚶	🧍	🚐	🚁	⛵						

6.4   Classifying objects into intersecting sets (multiple factors)

Children can begin to classify objects into intersecting sets intuitively around the age of five.   Prior to this age children should classify with concrete objects so that they can readily verify the placement of the objects in the intersecting sets.   The use of Venn diagrams with yarn around objects will help the child visualize the relationships of the intersecting sets.

Matrices can also be used to help a child visualize classification by multiple characteristics.   Provide the child with a matrix that has some of the answers already filled in.   Remove more of the answers in successive activities as the child becomes adept at using matrices.   You may have the child use the same materials in both a matrix and a Venn diagram to show the intersection.

PEOPLE BLOCKS

Concept: Observe specific characteristics of the people blocks (sex, age, color and size) and sort them according to these characteristics.

Materials: People blocks (see diagram for instructions on making these).

Group size: Four to six children.

Procedure: Introduce the people blocks, one at a time, to the children. Have the children tell you as many things as they can about that block.   The attributes are color of clothes (blue or red), age (child or adult), size (fat or thin), and sex (male or female). Go through each block in this manner.   Allow the children to classify and sort the blocks using any of the above attributes.

Note: Use 1″ x 6″ board, cut 4″ sections numbering 16 pieces. Use permanent markers for figures, varnish the pieces to protect them.

Substitute index cards for wood if necessary.

ATTRIBUTE BLOCKS

Concept: Classify attribute blocks.

Materials: One set of attribute blocks including four shapes (circle, square, triangle, rectangle), each in four colors (red, blue, green, and yellow), and all in two sizes.

Group size: One to three children.

Procedure: Display the primary shapes. Ask the children to put the shapes in sets that belong together. Allow the child to decide on the attributes. Try to have the children verbalize their reasons for placing each shape. This should preclude the children's changing classification rules before finishing.

Variations: (1) Using the shapes play "Like Because." One person starts by placing one shape on the table. The next child has to place another shape next to it and tell why the shape is like the first one. "It is like because they are both blue." Then the next child places another shape and tells like because . . . . (2) Another variation would include shapes that share no attributes with the other shapes.

WHAT COLOR IS YOUR SHIRT?

Concept: Classify objects in intersecting sets.

Materials: Two ropes, each with ends taped together to form a circle and laid on the floor (or substitute two hula hoops).

Group size: Class.

Procedure: Choose one color for each circle and label the circles accordingly (determine color choice by the colors of the children's shirts). Ask each child, in turn, what color his or her shirt is. If the two colors chosen are blue and white and the child is wearing a blue shirt, the child may stand in the circle labeled "blue." If the shirt is white, the child may stand in the circle labeled "white."

If a child's shirt contains both blue and white, put the child in the blue circle, but lead the class to see that the child also belongs in the white circle. Let the child walk back and forth between circles until a solution can be found.

Introduce the "solution" by overlapping (intersecting) the circles and letting the child stand in the intersected space.

Each time you play the game, begin with two separate circles and intersect them only when a "solution" is needed.

Variation: Start with circles intersected and lead to a situation where there is not a person in the intersection. Discuss this with the children.

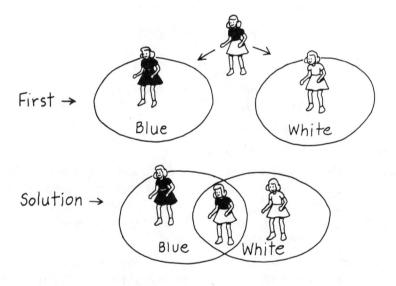

WHAT DO I LOOK LIKE?

Concept: Recognize single and multiple characteristics that divide children into groups.

Materials: None.

Group size: Class.

Procedure: This is a teacher-directed activity. Discuss with the children the different groups in the class. All the boys are one set, all the girls, everyone with brown eyes, etc. Any physical characteristic can be used. Pick a description of a group such as "all the children wearing boots." Have those children do an action. "Stand on your heads." Use one attribute to begin with; include more than one attribute as the children become more adept at recognizing multiple characteristics.

FIND A SECRET OBJECT

Concept: Discover a rule used in classifying an object.

Materials: Circle, triangle, square, and rectangle (use at least two colors and two sizes of each). Attribute blocks may be used.

A secret object.

Group size: One child or small group.

Procedure: Hide the secret object under one shape. Tell the child you have a rule for hiding the object under the shape and the child is to guess the rule. If you're hiding it under the yellow square, continue hiding it there until the child guesses the rule of "always under the yellow square."

Rules can vary using shape, color, size, and position or a combination of these. Other examples of rules include under circles, under large shapes, under the top row, under any shape, under large, blue shapes, etc.

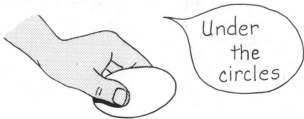

CLOTHES IN SEASON

Concept: Classify clothes into disjoint or intersecting sets according to the season in which they might be worn.

Materials: Pictures of clothes that might be worn in different seasons and ones that would be worn in more than one season.

                Pictures that depict the four seasons.

Group size: One child or small group.

Procedure: Show the children two season pictures. Discuss the seasons and the weather in each. Show the clothes one at a time asking, "When would you wear this?" Allow the children to decide. Some of the clothes can be worn in both seasons, so be prepared for some confusion by the children. Try to get the children to place these clothes in the middle between the two seasonal pictures. This is an example of intersecting sets.

MATRIX BOARD

Concept: Discover the correct pictures to complete matrices.

Materials: Matrix board (see diagram).

                Pictures.

Group size: Class.

Procedure: Show the matrix board to the children. The children should be asked questions about the pictures as you place them on the matrix. Begin by placing three pictures. Ask the children what they think should go in the empty space. Ask the reason for their choice. As the children gain experience, you may leave two pictures off the board and then three pictures.

Variation: Use attribute blocks instead of pictures.

WILD THINGS

Concept: Identify the attributes of the wild thing cards by sorting them into groups correctly.

Materials: Tag board for wild thing cards.

Magic markers.

File folder for a game board.

Group size: One child.

Procedure: Introduce one folder at a time. A single attribute is covered in each folder. Ask the child to look at both sides of the folder. Next, have the child tell you what the pictures on the left side of the card have in common. Next, discuss how the pictures on the right differ from those on the left.

Give the child one wild thing card at a time and ask on which side of the folder it might go. Allow the child to decide where the cards will go. Make sure that the child has a reason for each card that is placed; as long as the reasoning is sound, the child should be allowed to place the cards where he or she wishes. This is a game of observation, in which the cards are classified by the child according to attributes. The child must discover the attribute for there to be meaningful learning.

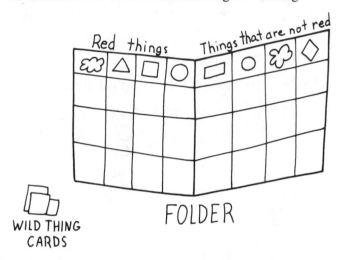

6.5   Classifying objects with an inclusion relationship

It is quite difficult for young children to work with classification activities that involve an inclusion relationship. As an example, consider classifying plastic objects as animals or horses. It is true that all horses are also animals, but this is difficult for the child to contend with until quite cognitively mature. Thus only a few activities of this type are included, and the teacher should generate additional activities, using these as models, should more be desired.

TOYS AND DOLLS

Concept: Classify toys using an inclusion relationship.

Materials: Toy shelf or closet or normal storage area for toys.

Toys, including some dolls and some nontoys (for example, some of the children's hats and coats).

Doll bed or box with a blanket.

Group size: Class.

Procedure: Mix the toys and nontoys together at clean-up time. Tell the children that they must put the toys up on the toy shelf, but that today they will also put the dolls in the doll bed.

Let each child select an object from the pile. First have the child tell you whether the selected object is a toy. If not, put it aside. If yes, put it on the shelf. Then ask the child if it is also a doll. If yes, take it from the shelf and put it in the doll bed.

Each child must tell first whether the object is a toy; if yes, then whether it is a doll.

Continue in turn until the room is cleaned up!

Variation: Have children put toys on the shelf and put the balls in a box.

BIRDS AND ANIMALS

Concept: Classify toy animals using an inclusion relationship.

Materials: Toy animals, including some birds.

Some toys that are not animals.

Fence made of toy fence sections or blocks.

Bird cage to fit inside the fence (an upsidedown berry basket will do).

Group size: Small group.

Procedure: Construct a fence and place the bird cage inside it. Tell the children that they are going to make a zoo for the animals. Mix all the objects (animals and nonanimals) in a box and let each child choose an object. After selecting an object, the child must first decide whether it is an animal. If not, it is discarded. If it is, let the child place it in the fence. Then ask the child if the animal is also a bird; if so, then it must be placed in the cage so that it won't fly away.

Be sure to have each child determine first whether the object is an animal (and, if so, place it within the fence) before allowing the child to name it a bird and put it in the cage.

Variation: "Children and Babies." The fence makes a play yard and a rightside-up berry basket becomes a playpen.

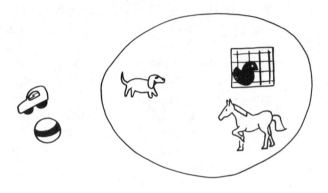

CHAPTER 7

Seriation

7.1 Introduction

Seriation is a skill that requires the child to be aware of certain differences between objects and to arrange those objects according to the differences. *Seriating* is a meaningful ordering of the elements of a set according to a given rule. To be meaningfully ordered, a set of objects must share an inherent property; objects may be ordered from "shortest to tallest" (objects share the property of height) or from "thickest to thinnest" (objects share the property of thickness).

Activities for teaching seriation begin with sets of no more than three objects. The child chooses two of the objects and utilizes the rule to determine the object satisfying the seriation rule. The identified object is then compared with the remaining object. This yields the first item in the seriation. The remaining items are then compared to complete the seriation. As an example, consider seriating the trees in Figure 7.1 from tallest to shortest.

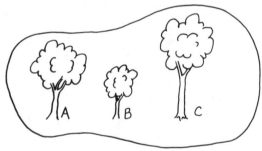

Figure 7.1

First the child compares tree A with tree B. Tree A is tallest and is retained for the next comparison. Then tree A is compared with tree C. Tree C is tallest and is the first object in the seriation. Then tree A is compared with tree B. Tree A is next tallest and leaves tree B last. Although the comparison of tree A with tree B was performed twice, children will often not remember the previous comparison. The important thing is that children need to learn a strategy for seriating a set of objects.

Later seriation activities should involve four or more objects. To seriate the set, two objects are chosen and compared. The object resulting from the first comparison is then compared with the next object in the set, etc. Once the first element in the seriation is identified, the procedure is repeated with the remaining objects in the set. The procedure seems simple for adults, but it is much more complicated for children because they do not have a strategy for attacking the task.

Readiness tasks involve identifying inherent differences between objects, selecting a starting comparison and making further systematic comparisons. The child should be allowed to discover a difference by which the objects could be seriated. A question such as "how are these objects different?" will guide the child to observe a difference that could be used in seriating. Begin with three objects and increase the number of objects as the child becomes proficient in identifying a seriation and a direction for laying out the objects. The direction for laying out the objects is difficult for the young child. There is no indication of whether a child will seriate from left to right or right to left. The teacher should encourage the child to order the objects from left to right as it correlates with correct reading direction.

Activities designed for learning seriation begin with seriations utilizing tactile qualities, then shape, color, and size. Many seriation activities are extensions of activities found in the chapters on shape, color, and size. Activities utilizing these concepts should be completed before attempting to seriate sets according to the number of objects in the set such as two balls, three balls, four balls (ordered from fewest to most). Recall that the child must conserve number before attempting this type of problem; that is, the child must recognize that "five" is invariant regardless of how the five blocks are arranged. A child who does not conserve might sequence sets from most apples to fewest apples as follows:

These apples are closer together and appear
as fewer than those in the set of four.

The teacher should take care not to utilize activities involving sequencing and mistake them for seriation activities. Not all objects or sets of objects can be seriated, although they may be ordered using a pattern. A few examples may clarify the difference between a seriation (utilizing an inherent property) and a sequence, or pattern (not utilizing an inherent ordering quality).

Seriation

Dark green, darker green, darkest green
Small circle, larger circle, largest circle
Tall tree, shorter tree, shortest tree

Sequence (or pattern)

blue, green, blue, green, blue, ...
circle, circle, square, circle, ...
3, 2, 1, 3, 2, 1, 3, ...

Pattern activities are found in the final chapter. In those activities the child (or teacher) will direct the order of the pattern, but the order is arbitrary with the sequence established at the discretion of the person directing the activity.

7.2 Size

Little, big

The seriation activities involving size have specific material suggestions for experiences accompanying each activity. Take time to find objects in your own setting that would be conducive to seriation. Each environment will provide some unique materials, and many times children have some unique interests that can be capitalized on. Have at least three objects available for seriation in each set of objects.

BIG 'N LITTLE

Concept: Order objects from big to little.

Materials: Three or more different sized objects such as in the categories listed below:

dolls	socks	wood	pots	jars
trucks	necklaces	crayons	cups	cans
hats	pencils	books	spoons	cloth scraps
shoes	nails	coins	forks	stuffed animals

Group size: Small group.

Procedure: Collect three or more objects in one of the above categories. Have the children arrange them from largest to smallest, shuffle the objects and do the activity again. Let the child try to order the objects independent of assistance. Help the children having difficulty by comparing only two objects at a time.

After a few times, change the order and go from smallest to largest.

Variation: Collect a few of the objects in the categories given in one box. Let the children sort the objects into like groups and then arrange them in size order.

STACK IT UP

Concept: Order objects vertically from largest to smallest; then, reverse the order and stack from smallest to largest.

Materials: Four discs from a stacking toy of the type that has discs of various sizes that fit onto a central dowel or pole. (You will not need the dowel as the discs will be stacked to balance on their own.)

Group size: Small group.

Procedure: Lay the discs in a mixed order on the table. Have the child stack the discs on the table with the largest disc on the bottom to the smallest disc on top, balancing them so that they will not fall over. Once the child completes the ordering, lay the discs out on the table in the order indicated.

Shuffle the discs again and have the child stack them with the smallest disc on the bottom.

Variation: Do this activity with all the discs from the toy.

Questions: Is it easier to stack the discs from smallest to largest or largest to smallest?

FIT–TOGETHERS

Concept: Order three-dimensional objects in sequence by size, so that they will nest.

Materials: Nesting materials: boxes, measuring spoons, or measuring cups.

Group size: Small group.

Procedure: Ask child to arrange objects in correct order so that they will properly "nest" together, one object fitting inside the other. This will be self-checking.

Be sure to set the objects on the table in order from smallest to largest after ordering.

SIZING UP BEANBAGS

Concept: Order objects in three sizes. Match three objects to another three objects by relative size.

Materials: Three beanbags in three sizes.

Three sizes of cans.

Group size: One to three children.

Procedure: Arrange the cans from smallest to largest in a row. Ask the child to line the beanbags up next to the cans putting the smallest by the smallest, etc.

Next shuffle the cans and the beanbags. Let the child order the cans from smallest to largest this time and then match the beanbags to the cans.

As an extension in using the materials, have the child try to drop or throw the beanbag into the can which it matches.

PUPPETS

Concept: Discriminate three puppets by size and voice level.

Materials: Three puppets of three sizes (stick puppets, sock puppets, etc.).

Cardboard stage optional.

Group size: Any size.

Procedure: Choose three children to wear puppets. Talk about each puppet's size, the voice that it might have to go with its size, the sound of its feet walking, or the kind of motion it might have walking. "Tryouts" for best voice, walk, or dance can be conducted. (Everyone can have a turn acting.)

The Three Billy Goats' Gruff or *The Three Bears* would both be excellent as plays using three sizes of puppets with corresponding sound effects.

FOLLOW THE FISH

Concept: Order objects in sequence by size from largest to smallest.

Materials: Cutouts of fish (see diagram). To make activity self-checking, make each fish large enough to totally conceal the next smaller fish when placed over it.

Group size: Small group.

Procedure: Tell the children that the fish go in order, with the biggest fish first leading the others. Have them find the largest fish and then the fish that will follow. Check to see if the largest fish covers the fish that follows.

For self-checking, the child places each fish on top of the next to see if the next fish is smaller.

Variation: Order from the smallest fish to the largest.

PIE ANGLES

Concept: Order cutouts from smallest to largest or largest to smallest.

Materials: Picture of a pie cut into five slices of different sizes (use felt or cardboard cutouts as a variation).

Group size: One or two children.

Procedure: Arrange the pie slices so that they fit together as a whole pie. Tell the child that the pie has been cut into pieces. Take the pie slices and lay them in a mixed order in front of the child. Tell the child to lay the pie slices in a row on the table from the smallest to the largest.

Next have the child try to put the pie back together.

Questions: Which piece of pie would you like to have? Why? Which piece would you give to a friend? Your Mom? Your Dad?

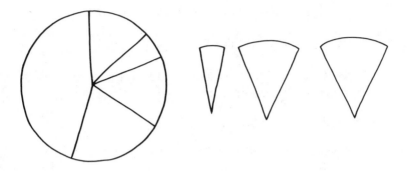

LOLLIPOPS

Concept: Seriate by stacking three circles from largest to smallest.

Materials: Circles cut into three sizes.

Popsicle sticks.

Paste or stapler.

Group size: Any size group.

Procedure: Have the children choose a circle of each size. Show the children a finished "lollipop" and ask them to tell you which shape is the largest, middle, and smallest. Have them stack and then paste their circles on top of each other. Paste or staple the "lollipops" onto the sticks.

Note: Use circles of all the same color so that size is the only variation, *or* like shades with unlike sizes/shapes for seriation by size or shape, *or* a variety of colors in each size with the color variables unrelated to the size.

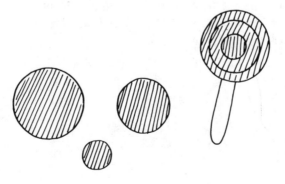

GROWING NEIGHBORHOODS

Concept: Order cutouts of objects by height.

Materials: Felt or cardboard cutouts in three or more sizes of different heights, for example, trees, houses, hats, etc.

Group size: One or two children.

Procedure: Select one set of cutouts and lay them in a mixed order in front of the child. Have the child arrange them in a given order beginning with shortest or tallest.

Variation: Have the child arrange trees in order of height. Next have the child match the houses to the trees in order of relative height.

BIGGER AND BIGGER

Concept: Order shapes from smallest to largest or the reverse.

Materials: Felt or cardboard hearts, stars, bows, apples, or other similar shapes in three or more size variations.

Group size: One or two children.

Procedure: Lay one set of objects in a mixed array in front of the child. Ask the child to lay them out from smallest to largest. Repeat with a second set of shapes.

Concept: Sequence circles from large to small.

Materials: Circles of different sizes cut from cardboard.

Group size: One to two children.

Procedure: Explain that the child should find the very largest circle; after finding that, find the next largest, and so forth. Most children will be able to do a comparison of two circles. Although this is not a true seriation, allow the child to attempt it alone. If unable to do a complete seriation, model the strategy of comparing the discs two at a time, then continue with the larger of the two discs and comparing it with the next disc, etc.

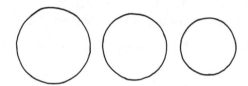

SQUARES

Concept: Order three or more squares by size from smallest to largest.

Materials: Squares in three sizes cut from cardboard or felt.

Group size: One or two children.

Procedure: Lay squares in a mixed array in front of child. Have the child order them from smallest to largest. Ask the child to find the smallest square first. Let the child order the others.

As a variation, after the child has ordered the three squares, mix them up again and hide one of them (preferably the largest or the smallest). Have the child tell you which one is missing.

Repeat the ordering with more than three squares.

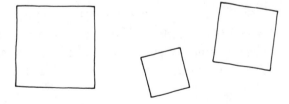

RANGING RECTANGLES

Concept: Order rectangles by differences in length, width, or a combination of these.

Materials: Rectangles cut from felt or cardboard as shown in the diagram: (1) same length/different widths, (2) same width/different lengths, and (3) different widths and lengths.

Group size: One or two children.

Procedure: Choose one set of rectangles that varies along one dimension. Have the children align them so that the order goes from shortest to tallest or narrowest to widest, whichever is appropriate. First, lay the rectangles so that the child will see the dimension that varies; next, lay them unordered so that the child must turn the rectangles to discover the dimension that varies.

Have the child order each of the sets of rectangles.

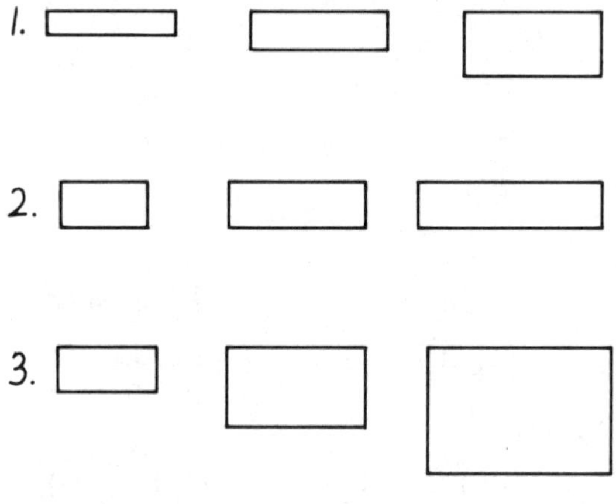

ANGLES

Concept: Order triangles by size differences from smallest to largest or largest to smallest.

Materials: Triangles cut from cardboard or felt as shown in the diagram: (1) base same length, vary height, and (2) right triangles (bases are the same length), vary height.

Group size: One or two children.

Procedure: Select one set of triangles that varies along one dimension. Lay them in front of the child in a mixed order, yet so that the child does not have to turn the triangles to discover the size variation. Have the child order them from smallest to largest (shortest to tallest) or largest to smallest.

When a child can order the triangles, lay them on the floor again, but this time shuffle the triangles so that the child must turn and compare the triangles to arrange them according to height or width.

ANIMAL KINGDOM

Concept: Recall size of three animals from largest to smallest.

Material: None.

Group size: Any size.

Procedure: Ask a child to name a large animal. Next, have the child name an animal that is smaller than the first one named, i.e., "Name an animal that is smaller than an elephant." Last, have the child name an animal smaller than the first two named.

Some children should be able to name three animals from largest to smallest or smallest to largest without help.

Have children who have the drawing skills draw a picture of the animals they named.

Questions: What is the smallest animal that you can think of? What is the largest animal you can think of?

Length

Length materials should vary only in length—excluding width variations. Provide a guideline for lining up objects of varying lengths. The ends should be even on one edge:

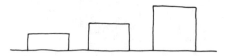

A child who cannot conserve length, that is, recognize that an object retains its length regardless of how it is arranged in space, will have special difficulty in identifying the longer of two objects when they are aligned:

For that matter, all children should be encouraged to utilize a guide line since this provides a strategy for seriating.

STRAWS

Concept: Arrange objects in sequence by length from longest to shortest.

Materials: Drinking straws, pipe cleaners, or paper towel tubes—cut into different lengths.

Group size: Small group.

Procedure: Ask a child to arrange the straws in order from longest to shortest or vice versa. Try to let the child do as much as possible. If a mistake is made, use questions to try to get the child to observe the error. Be sure also to ask questions when a correct response is given.

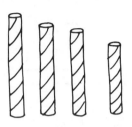

SHOES IN A ROW

Concept: Arrange objects in sequence from longest to shortest.

Materials: Three or more pairs of shoes of varied sizes.

You might have each child bring one old pair of shoes from home belonging to parents, brothers, or sisters, or their own.

Group size: Class.

Procedure: Lay out three or four pairs of shoes of different sizes. Have the class determine the correct order for arranging the shoes from longest to shortest or vice versa.

HOT DOGS AND BUNS

Concept: Arrange two sets of objects in order of length from smallest to largest.

Materials: Cardboard cutouts of hot dogs and buns, in different lengths. Each hot dog fits exactly into its own bun.

Group size: Small group.

Procedure: Have the child arrange the hot dogs in order of length. Then instruct the child to sequence the buns in the same order, so that each hot dog matches its own bun.

To check, have the child put the hot dogs in the buns. Be sure to check beforehand to be certain the dogs match the buns exactly.

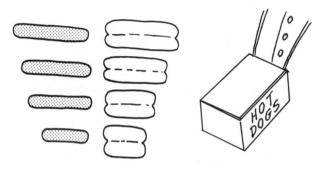

RECORD A JUMP

Concept: Order lengths of string that are records of jumps.

Materials: Long string.

Scissors.

Masking tape and pen.

Group size: Small group or class.

Procedure: Lay the string out on the floor in a straight line. Have each child take a turn jumping as far as possible (specify jumping with feet together or apart) along the string. Record the jump by cutting that length of string and mark it with child's name on masking tape.

When the jumping is over, let small groups of children compare their lengths of string and order them from longest to shortest. The whole class may order their strings from shortest to longest.

Save the strings and repeat at a later time in the year. Compare the old jump with the new one.

ROCKETS

Concept: Order three to four objects from short to long.

Materials: Cardboard tubes in three sizes.

            Magic marker.

            Paper circles for cones.

            Glue.

Group size: Any size group.

Procedure: Set out cardboard tubes, circles, and magic markers. Allow each child to choose a "rocket" and begin decoration and construction.

            Discuss sizes of rockets during and after construction. Rockets may be placed on display from smallest to largest.

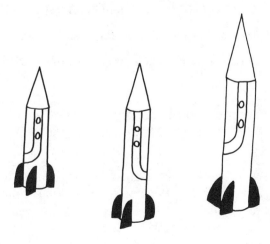

STAIR STEPS

Concept: Seriate three children in a row according to height.

Materials: None.

Group size: Small group or class.

Procedure: Ask for three children to come up and compare how tall they are. Have the remaining members of the class choose the tallest person first, then shorter and shortest. Show the class how two children can be compared by standing back to back or *even better* have the class find a way to compare two children.

Questions: How can we find out who is the tallest? Show me how much taller one child is than another.

HEIGHTS

Concept: Compare heights of people, naming tallest and shortest.

Materials: Roll of calculator paper, approximately two inches wide.

    Marking pen to write names and dates of heights taken.

Group size: Class.

Procedure: Tape strips of calculator tape on a wall or door. Make each strip the same length, a few inches taller than the tallest child in the class.

    Have each child stand against a strip. Mark the child's height with a line across the top. Write the child's name, date measured, and height (optional). Ask the children to find the tallest child and shortest.

Mark again later in the year and compare who grew the most and the least.

Variation: Cut the strips in order of heights and place from tallest to shortest.

GUESS MY RULE

Concept: Seriate objects in an order while another child identifies the rule of the seriated objects.

Materials: Three objects of varied length.

Three objects of varied width.

Three objects of varied size.

Group size: Two to three children.

Procedure: Have one child select and place three objects in an order. A second guesses the rule that the first child used in making the order, i.e., smallest to largest, tallest to shortest, etc.

Let the children take turns making an order of objects.

LONGER AND LONGER

Concept: Order pictures or cutouts of objects that vary in length.

Materials: Felt or paper cutouts of three or more sizes (see diagram): for example, dogs, pants, cars, pickles, cats' whiskers, etc.

Group size: One to two children.

Procedure: Lay one set of cutouts on the floor. Ask the child how the objects are different. Have the child then arrange the cutouts in order from shortest to longest or longest to shortest. Begin with three cutout sizes, mix the arranged order, and add one or two more sizes, having the child then reorder the cutouts.

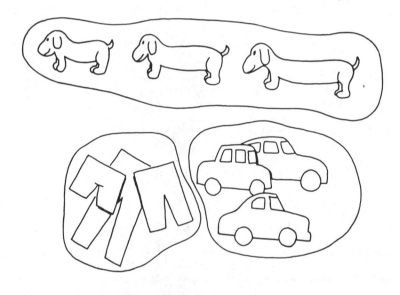

Width

Width activities are rarely used in everyday experiences. The similarity in the words "thick" and "thin" also poses problems in this concept. Be sure to include at least a few width activities in a curriculum for exposure. At first use materials with similar lengths having variations in widths only. Later, a few activities may be included in which both length and width vary. This will yield information about children's understanding of the language used versus those children using visual cues to seriate.

RIBBONS

Concept: Arrange objects in sequence from widest to narrowest.

Materials: Ribbons—all the same length, but of different widths.

Group size: Small group.

Procedure: Have the child arrange the ribbons in order from the widest to the narrowest.

               Let the children try this by themselves once they get the idea of what to do.

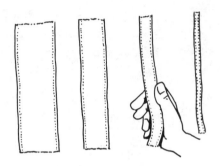

SKINNY PENCILS, FAT PENCILS

Concept: Arrange objects in sequence from fattest to thinnest.

Materials: Pencils of different thicknesses.

Group size: Small group.

Procedure: Have the child arrange the pencils in order from fattest to thinnest.

DOWELS

Concept: Seriate dowels according to width.

Materials: Board with four holes drilled.

                Four different diameter dowel rods to match the holes.

Group size: One or two children.

Procedure: Have the child fit the dowels into the proper holes. The board will be self-checking. The child must seriate correctly, or all of the dowels will not fit in the board.

                Variation: Drill a board with holes of the same diameter, then cut dowels of different lengths (all of the same diameter). Order the dowels from tallest to shortest.

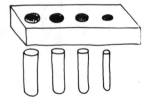

LINE DRAWING

Concept: Paint lines in order of length or width.

Materials: Paper.

                Paint.

                Paintbrushes.

Group size: Any size group.

Procedure: Begin by demonstrating how to make thin and wide lines with a paintbrush. Have the children paint a thin line from top to bottom or side to side on a sheet of paper. Now have the children try to paint a line that is wider than the line that they had just painted. Next, the children try to paint a very wide line.

Note that an activity that has length as the objective may be easier than width for some children. Have each child draw a line on their paper. Stop and have the children find the person who has drawn the longest line. Continue on as in the example above with width.

Variations: Paint wiggly lines or ones with shades from light to dark.

Questions: Who has the widest line? The thinnest?

7.3 Color shades

Experiences with color shades can be enhanced by the effort to equip the environment with materials in varying shades. Paints should be supplied in shades rather than in just the stock colors of red, green, blue, and yellow. Mix paints to provide the shades, having white paint or base available to lighten the stock colors. Crayons and paper should also be supplied in varying shades.

MATCHING PAINT CHIPS

Concept: Match a sequence of paint chips from dark to light.

Materials: Two duplicate sets of paint samples with three or more shades of red, green, blue, yellow, and others.

Cards or strips of paper on which to paste one set of shaded paint chips (one card for each color, i.e., shades of red).

Paste and scissors used in making the strips.

Group size: One to two children.

Procedure: Paste one set of shades (i.e., shades of red) on a card from darkest to lightest. Cut out the second set of red shades for the child to use in matching the card.

Begin with one card and its matching shade chips. Let the child match the shades to the card. Talk about the darkest and the lightest. Ask the child questions about his or her choices or ask the child to find "the darkest" if help in getting started is needed.

PAINT CHIPS

Concept: Sequence paint chips from dark to light or vice versa.

Materials: Paint samples in shades of red, green, blue, yellow, and others from the paint store.

Group size: One to three children.

Procedure: Have the children find the very darkest sample. Begin with gross differences in shade and become more subtle as the children become better at it. Move from the darkest to the next darkest. If child is unable to order samples from darkest to lightest, then start with only two shades of paint in the sequence and build upon that. Make sure the children understand the vocabulary before beginning. Also, seriate from light to dark.

SHADY EGGS

Concept: Order shades from light to dark.

Materials: Paint chips cut into the shapes of eggs, plastic eggs in shades, *or* hardboiled eggs shaded with food coloring.

               Egg carton.

Group size: One or two children.

Procedure: Show the child the eggs and the egg carton. Tell the child the eggs will be ordered from light to dark. Ask the child to find the lightest green egg and put it in the first egg slot. Next have the child find the next darkest egg; have the child finish the sequence independently.

               Variation: Have the child match shades arranged in one row of the carton.

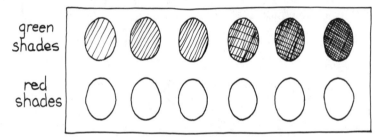

SHADE COLLECTORS

Concept: Match shades of dark, lighter, and lightest of mixed colors.

Materials: A card deck made from paint samples glued to cards: color three shades each of the colors red, green, blue, yellow, orange, and purple.

Group size: Two or three children.

Procedure: Deal each child three cards. Then children take a card one at a time, and, when the child obtains three of the same shade, the child lays down the "book." When all the cards are drawn, the child with the most books wins. Shuffle and play again.

7.4   Tactile

Tactile experiences encourage children to become physically involved; materials require manipulation. Children need not experience the materials solely as a formal seriation situation; rather, you can involve children in putting the materials together. Tactile discrimination can begin as the child contributes to selecting and preparing materials.

JARS

Concept: Seriate heaviest to lightest jars.

Materials: Plastic jars filled from full to empty with plaster or sand.

Group size: Small group.

Procedure: Introduce the jars and talk about heavy, heavier, heaviest. Allow the children to feel different jars and decide which is heaviest. Have the children go on finding the next heaviest until finished. Allow the children to do the ordering on their own.

Variation: Order the jars from fullest to empty.

WATER

Concept: Seriate from hot to cold.

Materials: Water in leak-proof containers of varying temperatures.

Group size: Any size group.

Procedure: Talk about hot and cold with the class. Allow the children to feel the water or container while they talk about each temperature. Have them find the hot, warm, cool, and cold container.

FABRIC SQUARES

Concept: Arrange objects in order by touch, from smoothest to roughest.

Materials: Fabric squares of different textures. Satin, muslin, nubby polyester, corduroy are good choices.

Group size: Small group.

Procedure: Give each child three or four squares of cloth of varying textures. Have them feel the cloth. Talk about rough and smooth and let the children hold up samples or pass them around for others to feel. Next, have the children arrange the squares in order from smoothest to roughest.

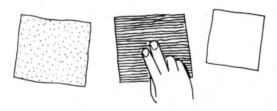

TOOTHBRUSHES

Concept: Order objects from rough to smooth.

Materials: Cardboard cutouts of toothbrushes, with bristles of different roughnesses (see diagram) or real toothbrushes.

Blindfold (optional).

Group size: Small group.

Procedure: Have a child arrange toothbrushes in order from smoothest to roughest.

If a child does not know what smooth and rough are, say, "Which toothbrush has the smoothest bristles? Which one would feel the smoothest on your finger? Put it over here. Now which toothbrush is the next smoothest? Which would be the roughest on your finger?"

For greater difficulty and to encourage the use of touch, a blindfold can be used.

SANDPAPER

Concept: Seriate textures from roughest to smoothest.

Materials: Sandpaper of different textures (mount on blocks to use as sandblocks during music).

Group size: Small group.

Procedure: Have class discuss terms of roughness and smoothness. Make sure they understand. Allow children to feel the different types of sandpaper. While doing this, talk with them about how each feels. After discussion, have the children find roughest sandpaper, then the next roughest, and so on. Place the sandpaper in the sequence that the children designate. Use the sandpaper for ordering individually after the small group work.

WATER JARS

Concept: Arrange objects in sequence by volume, from fullest to emptiest.

Materials: Identical transparent jars, filled to different levels with colored water or dry rice.

Group size: Small group.

Procedure: Have the child arrange the jars in order, from fullest to emptiest.

As a variation, remove one of the jars and have the child order the remaining ones. Then let the child find where the missing jar should be and place it there.

HARD AND SOFT

Concept: Seriate materials from hard to soft.

Materials: Piece of metal, styrofoam, clay, foam rubber, and any materials having different degrees of hardness. (Try to have the size of the objects similar so that the child does not try to discriminate by size.)

Group size: Small group or class.

Procedure: Make sure that the children have a solid grasp of the vocabulary before beginning. Allow the children to feel the materials deciding which is the hardest, next hardest, and so on. Question the children as they do the ordering.

Variation: Set one or two materials aside while the children are ordering the others. Have the children then fit the missing ones into the sequence.

Questions: Why is this one the hardest? How did you decide that this is the hardest one?

Soft   Hard

CHAPTER

Numerals

8.1   Introduction

The mathematical symbols used to express numbers are called *numerals*. The numerals take three forms:

spoken	"six"
abstract symbol	6
written	SIX

The spoken form is the first encountered by children. Often, one of the earliest interactions that a child has with numerals is chanting them from one to ten. It is important that the child learn to state the name as correctly as that individual child's verbal abilities allow. As early as 20 months, some children can repeat the word stated by the adult or parent. With children under age three, it is important to chant the number names in order, but only using two or three number names at one time. That is, ONE (pause), TWO (pause), THREE and those are all the names used at this session. Be sure to repeat the activity five or six times—jubilantly reinforcing each attempt by the child. At a later time during the day, or on other days, the activity should be repeated. Later, the activity is altered to include FOUR, FIVE, and, maybe, SIX. After some work with ONE, TWO, THREE, you might instead work on TWO, THREE, FOUR. Rhyming activities such as ONE, TWO, BUCKLE MY SHOE, might also be included and reinforced throughout the complete days.

It often seems a milestone to parents when their child can successfully count to ten. It is quite possible for a child to be able to count (chant) and have no concept of what the numerals mean. However, the chanting is *very* important in the cognitive development of the child.

Work with recognition of the abstract symbol (such as 6, 4, or 7) can be undertaken with most three year olds. The concept developed here is simple recognition of the abstract symbol (7) and the spoken name of the symbol (seven). Activities should focus on giving one of the stimuli and having the child provide the other of the pair. As an example,

clue	child responds
four	points to 4
2	states "two"

After learning to recognize the abstract symbol, children can learn to draw (or copy) the symbol. Initial work should involve tactile involvement with the symbols leading to learning to draw the symbol. Some rhyming jingles for each symbol have been included to aid in learning to draw the symbols.

Understanding the concept of quantity is developmental and most three-year-olds exhibit some understanding of number quantity. Often two-year-olds understand how many one and two are. They hand one of something on request or (touching both ears) say "two ears," "two shoes," etc. Their knowledge is dependent on the presence of the concrete materials; that is, they have no concept of the abstract twoness but, rather, respond to a stimuli of two objects with the correct response for how many. Working with one 21-month toddler on twoness led to the following interaction:

(as a dog walked past the class window)

Teacher: "Look, Drew, it is a dog. Can you say "dog"?
Child: "Dog!"

(a second dog joins the first in front of the window)

Child: (unprompted) *"Two* dogs!"

The point is that the terminology of two had been used in enough different situations so that as the second dog joined the first, the child responded to the concrete twoness. Three-year-olds can extend this ability to the numbers three and four. Quantities up to five are the easiest for the child to recognize without having to have prerequisite ordering or counting skills.

8.2   Chanting numerals

Chanting or counting numerals is a memorization task. Listen to children as they learn to count; they may skip numbers—an indication that the numbers do not yet have meaning. At the onset of learning to count up to ten, the child probably does not have a mental image of the quantities associated with every number name. The names "one," "two," and "three" begin to have meaning as children have such experiences as with "one" glass of milk, "two" socks, "three" cookies. The comprehension of these quantities is partly a factor of language experiences. If the child encounters frequent situations in which people talk about quantities of everyday objects, it is more likely that some numbers will have meaning by the time the child is three years old.

A child may be able to count to ten but may not differentiate one numeral name from another. Ask a child to count to a number other than ten. There is a stage in which children will count on to ten, passing the number that you requested. The chant appears to be one word written: "onetwothree-fourfivesixseveneightnineten." Activities have been included that allow children to count to numbers other than ten to begin having them differentiate the number names. Eventually the idea is to have the child count only to the number requested; this becomes important in combining chanting with counting objects in which the child must stop the chant when all the objects have been counted. Nursery rhymes that include number chanting are excellent for counting both to ten and to numbers less than ten.

Chanting with objects entails pacing the chant to the motion of touching or making eye contact with the objects being counted. Initially children will often count in one of the following ways:

X   X   X X   X X X X X X X X X X   X X   X X

"1 2 3 4 5 6 7"   "1   2   3   4   5   6   7"

counting too fast   **counting too slowly**

Some of the activities included have the child physically move each object as it is counted as in placing one object at a time in your hand. Others have the child pace the motion of touching objects with counting them. Align objects in a row. Have the child point with one finger. Carefully guide the child's hand while you show the child how to touch each object and count. With practice children readily acquire pacing skills. Mistakes are then only made when the objects are grouped randomly and the child forgets where counting the objects began.

At this stage the child should be combining skills in useful situations to recognize some grouped quantities (as a group of two blocks placed in any relationship to each other) and to use paced counting. The child can begin to bring objects as needed—cups to the table, pencils to share, etc. Success in organizing one's own world should be a positive experience.

PANTOMINE COUNTING

Concept: Chant number names in sequence while pantomining an action.

Materials: None (pictures or story to relate to the action are optional).

Group size: Any size group.

Procedure: Choose an action to pantomine. Repeat the action on the count of each number. The action can be chosen to correspond with an event in the classroom, a holiday, a weather phenomenon, an everyday occurrence—see examples following:

Take bites of food	Pet an animal	Put on hats
Pick fruit	Comb hair	Climb ladder rungs
Lay out plates	Pull up socks	Touch clouds
Stir a cake	Wipe hands	Catch bugs
Roll a pie crust	Shake hands	Paddle a boat
Shine apples	Hug a bear	Shake rugs
Sweep the floor	Shake off water	Blow up balloons

CARNIVAL COUNTING

Concept: Chant to ten with objects.

Materials: Ten open boxes or coffee cans, each containing a different amount of objects (blocks, beads, pencils, crayons, checkers, toy animals).

Tally card for each child (optional).

Gummed stars or stickers (optional).

Nerf ball.

Group size: Small group.

Procedure: Line up the boxes of objects in a row either on the floor or on a table. (A table just high enough so the children can't see inside the boxes is best. Having the boxes against the wall helps too.)

Taking turns, each child stands a short distance from the boxes and tosses the ball. After removing the objects from the box in which the ball landed, the teacher should count the objects with the children chanting along. If the ball misses the boxes, give the child another chance.

You may paste a star or sticker on the child's "carnival card" for each correct turn.

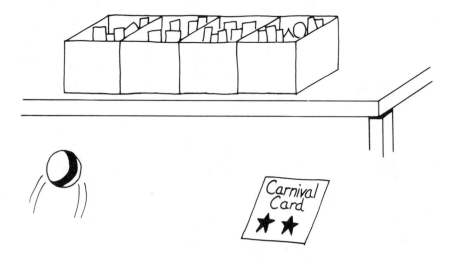

TEN LITTLE INDIANS

Concept:　　Chant number names 1 through 10.

Materials:　　None.

Group size:　Any size group.

Procedure:　Teach the children to sing or recite *Ten Little Indians.*

> One little, two little, three little Indians;
> Four little, five little, six little Indians;
> Seven little, eight little, nine little Indians;
> Ten little Indian (children).

Hold up one finger for each Indian as you sing and encourage the children to imitate you.

This activity can be used for "chanting with objects" by having ten children crouch and pop up one at a time as you sing.

For numeral recognition, "feathered" (construction paper) headbands numbered 1 to 10 may be worn.

A PIG ALIVE

Concept:　　Chant numerals 1 to 10.

Materials:　　None.

Group size:　Any size group.

Procedure:　Recite the following rhyme and have the children repeat it with you:

> One, two, three, four, five,
> I caught a pig alive.
> Six, seven, eight, nine, ten,
> I let it go again.

1-2-3-4-5...

I caught a pig alive...

6-7-8-9-10...

I let it go again.

TWO EARS, TWO EYES

Concept: Chant with body parts to the numeral 2.

Materials: None.

Group size: Small group.

Procedure: Ask the child to count his or her ears. Show the child how to touch each ear in turn, saying, "One, two. I have two ears." Repeat with other body parts—legs, feet, arms, hands, knees, elbows, ankles, hips, etc.

                Variation: Following the above activity, ask the children to touch two ears, three legs, four eyes, two feet, etc. Each time you ask them to touch more of their body parts than they have (three legs), they are to tell you that they can't.

WHAT YOU COUNT IS WHAT YOU GET

Concept: Chant with objects up to 10.

Materials: Small bits of food, i.e., popped corn, dry cereal, bread or cracker crumbs, pieces of apple.

Group size: Small group.

Procedure: Put ten food bits in a row in front of each child. Help each one point to each bit while "counting" them aloud. The child can then eat what has been counted.

BUILD A TOWER

Concept: Chant to different numbers up to 10.

Materials: Blocks for stacking, paper clips or beads for stringing.

Numeral cards.

Group size: Small group.

Procedure: Select a numeral card at random. Read the numeral to the child. If the child recites the number names correctly to the numeral on the card, provide that many blocks. The teacher should slowly count out the blocks and give them to the child as a reward.

If a child seems to have difficulty, be sure the numeral card drawn for that child is 5 or less to enhance success.

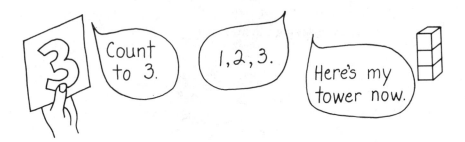

NUMBER ECHO

Concept: Repeat the names of numbers in sequence.

Materials: None.

Group size: Any size group.

Procedure: Have children repeat the names of numerals after you, one at a time. Vary the tone and speed of your voice with each echo sequence. When children echo the numbers one at a time well, have them echo two or three numbers, i.e., "1 — 2 — 3" or "1–2–3."

A MOVING CHANT

Concept: Chant numbers in sequence while moving in rhythm with the body.

Materials: None.

Group size: Any size group.

Procedure: Choose a body motion that can be done with a sequenced counting chant. You can clap, sway, stamp feet, jump, tap body parts, clap hands with a friend, or nod the head, one motion to a chanted number.

The rhythm of the body helps to set a counting pace. Each motion helps to single out the separate names of the numbers. The use of body pacing will help later when the child uses self-pacing in counting objects.

Variation: Whisper the chants or move the mouth without any sound in saying the numbers.

CHANT A RHYTHM

Concept: Chant numbers with a rhythm.

Materials: None.

Group size: Any size group.

Procedure: Choose a counting rhythm such as 1, 2, 3–4, 5–6, 7, 8–9, 10. Emphasize the rhythm by either speed of counting or voice loudness. Say the chant and let the children join you when they are ready. Add body motions or direct with the hand to emphasize the rhythm.

$$(1-2-3) \quad (4-5) \quad (6-7-8) \quad (9-10)$$

$$\text{slow} \quad \text{fast} \quad \text{slow} \quad \text{fast}$$

PARADE MARCH

Concept: Chant to numbers less than 10 and combine the chant with body motion.

Materials: None.

             String for variation.

Group size: Any size group.

Procedure: Counting and marching is a common activity of young children, so this activity may occur spontaneously!

             Let children march without music or instruments so that the rhythm is given by the chant. Use the chant, "1–2–3–4." Try chants with other numbers.

             Variation: Lay a string on the floor around a table. Have the children straddle the string and at each step count 1–2, or 1–2–3–4, or other number chant.

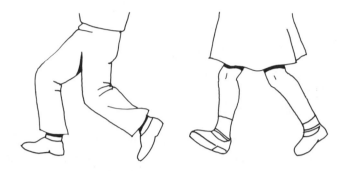

CHANT AND FREEZE

Concept: Chant to numbers less than 10 stopping at a number given prior to the chant.

Materials: None.

Group size: Any size group.

Procedure: Let the children space themselves out so that each has room to move. Tell the group that you are going to play a game. Everyone can move about while there is counting. As soon as the counting stops, everyone must freeze or stop moving. Choose a number with which to end the counting and have the group count with you. Ask the children to show ways that they could be moving about in their area. Demonstrate how to freeze and call attention to the quiet when the counting stops. Repeat the chant alternating with periods of "freezing." Change the ending number of the chant only after the children understand to stop when the counting stops.

NUMERAL TRAIN

Concept: Chant to different numerals up to 10.

Materials: Chairs, one per child.

Number cards from 1 to 10.

Group size: Small group.

Procedure: Line up the chairs in a row or column to make a "train." Ask each child to count to a number up to 10; if successful, the child may sit in the train. Give each child on the train a number card. Tell the group that when you call a number, the child or children with that number on their cards must get off the train, count to their number, and then get back on the train.

STUBBORN DONKEYS

Concept: Chant to numbers less than 10.

Materials: None.

Group size: Any size group.

Procedure: Describe a situation in which a group of children could help move an animal, person, or object. Stress that to move the animal, such as a stubborn donkey, everyone must push or pull at the same time. Show where the imaginary donkey is standing. Gather the children around and have them get ready to push or pull. Tell them that together you are going to count to "5" and on "5" everyone push or pull. Repeat, changing the number with which you end the chant.

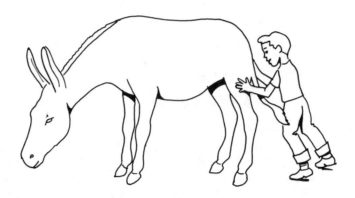

HELPERS

Concept: Chant numbers while counting objects up to 3.

Materials: Objects commonly used in the class.

Group size: One child or any size group.

Procedure: Have the children help collect materials for activities in the class. Many occasions should arise when a child can use a chant up to 3 to count out objects. Let the child choose two pieces of paper, bring one doll, get three blocks, put away one pencil, etc. To reinforce the chant and the pacing used to count objects, occasionally have a child count the objects to show you how many there are.

SNACK SERVER

Concept: Chant numerals while touching up to three objects.

Materials: Food selected for snack time such as

pretzels	nuts	fruit slices
oyster crackers	celery sticks	

Group size: Any size group.

Procedure: Have the children help distribute the snack. If each child is to get one of an item, ask a child to pass out enough for each child to have one. Let the server figure out how many items are needed.

When two or three items are being passed out, most children over age 3½ can count these out. Demonstrate how to take one item at a time and count as items are placed on a napkin or in front of the child.

8.3   Numeral recognition

Recognizing numerals is a visual perception and memory task. The visual perception ability plays a role in discriminating the numerals from each other. Often children confuse 2–3–5, 1–7, or 6–9. Have the children match identical sets of numerals placing the one's together, the two's together, etc.

Giving names to the numerals is both a perceptual and a memory task. Much like linking color names to colors, naming numerals develops as the child's memorization abilities mature.

Repetition in identifying numerals provides the child with reinforcing and correcting experiences. Those children who do not seem developmentally ready to recognize numerals easily can be given periodic trials to test their development. Make recognition experiences as positive as possible for the children by allowing them to point to (and name) those numerals that they know.   Another low stress strategy in recognition activities is to allow children to respond in small groups in a noncompetitive manner. The likelihood that numerals are recognized by any one child is increased in a small group and the response provided by the child who recognizes the numeral answers for those who are still learning the names. Numeral naming serves as a stimulus-response bond for those children still learning the names.

PALMED NUMBER

Concept: Recognize a number drawn on the hand.

Materials: None.

Group size: Any size group.

Procedure: Draw a number on a child's palm. First draw it so that the child can see the number. Have the child tell you what number you have drawn. Next draw the number so that the child cannot see, but only feel the number. Let him or her name the numeral.

Variation: Draw a number on the hand with a watercolor marker.

AGE NECKLACE

Concept: Trace a number through tactile sense.

Materials: White glue.

Wax paper.

Colored markers.

Thread and needle.

Prepare the glue numbers on the waxed paper one or two days in advance.

Group size: Any size group.

Procedure: Write the ages of all the children in white glue on the waxed paper. Be sure that the paper is in a place that it can lie flat for a day or two. Make a few extra numbers should any not turn out well or break. Make the numbers about two inches with ¼- to ½-inch thick lines. Let the glue dry for about one or two days. Peel the numbers off the waxed paper.

Let the children color the numbers with colored markers. Using the thread and needle make a hole in the top of the number, pull the thread through, and tie as a necklace.

Variation: Dip yarn in wheat paste, shape it into a number on waxed paper. Let the child choose a yarn number when it dries. Tie, with strings, as a necklace.

GLITTER NUMBERS

Concept: Recognize numerals by touch.

Materials: 5″ x 8″ index cards.

White glue.

Colored glitter (rice, sandpaper, or yarn may be substituted).

Blindfold.

Group size: Small group.

Procedure: On each index card draw a numeral, fill it in with glue, then sprinkle it with glitter. When dry, it will be pretty to look at as well as easy to feel.

Blindfold a child and hand him or her a numeral card. Help the child trace over the numeral with a finger and identify it.

HIDE–A–NUMBER

Concept: Find and name numerals.

Materials: Numerals written on paper or large cutout numerals.

Group size: Any size group.

Procedure: Hide numerals around the room. Put some numerals in places that a child would delight in crawling to reach, as on the underside of a chair or table. Put other numerals at the child's eye level or an extra large one on the ceiling.

Let the children find the numbers; give plenty of hints so that all are found.

To extend the repetition of matching the number game to the written symbol, play games such as asking a child to tell you where the 3 is as you have lost it, or tell the 4 under the table that you will visit it tomorrow. The idea seems silly, but the children delight in the humor of it.

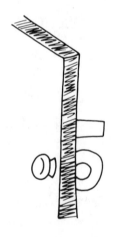

OVER AND OVER

Concept: Name numeral given written symbol.

Materials: Flash cards with numerals. Use numerals 1 to 3, then 1 to 5, and finally 1 to 10.

Group size: Two to four children.

Procedure: Have the children as a group or one at a time name the numerals on flash cards. If a child is just learning to recognize two or three numbers, include many flash cards with those numbers, even repeating the same number on different flash cards so that the children will have repeated successes.

NUMBER PUZZLE

Concept: Match and identify numerals 1 to 10.

Materials: Heavy paper or cardboard.

Felt-tipped markers.

Knife or razor blade.

Clear contact paper.

Group size: Small group.

Procedure: With a felt-tipped marker draw the numerals 1 to 10 on heavy paper and cover with contact paper. Cut out the numerals with a knife, leaving the background intact.

As an independent activity, have the child match the numerals into the corresponding spaces.

As a numeral recognition activity, ask the child to name each numeral before allowing him or her to place the piece into the puzzle.

NUMBER TRAIN

Concept: Recognize visually the numerals 1 to 10 *or* sequence numerals 1 to 10.

Materials: Cardboard train cars, numbered 1 to 10, cut so that they will join properly only if correctly sequenced.

Group size: Small group.

Procedure: Place the engine at the left of the work space. Tell the children that you are going to put the train together but that the cars have to be put on in a certain way or they won't fit.

Ask the first child to find the car with the "1." After a car is chosen, ask the child to check to see if it is correct by trying to fit it to the engine. Continue by asking the second child to find the car with the "2" and so on.

Note: This may be used as an independent activity for sequencing the numerals 1 to 10.

NUMBER CONCENTRATION

Concept: Recognize visually the numerals 1 to 10.

Materials: Deck of cards numbered in pairs from 1 to 10 (total of 20 cards, two of each numeral).

Group size: Small group.

Procedure: Shuffle the cards and place them face down in four rows of five cards each. The first child turns over two cards. If they do not match, the child turns them over again and play proceeds to the next child. If the cards match, the child may keep the cards. To get another turn, the child must name the numeral. If the child cannot name it, play proceeds to the next child.

A match— so you may keep the cards. Now can you name the number? That's right! Take another turn.

NUMBER WALK

Concept: Recognize visually the numerals 1 to 10.

Materials: 9″ x 12″ pieces of paper numbered from 1 to 10 and covered with clear contact paper.

          Music.

Group size: Small group.

Procedure: Place the numbered rectangles in random order in a circle on the floor. When the music begins the children walk around the path of the numbered pieces. When the music stops, each child stops on a card. Each child must say the name of the numeral on which he or she is standing to remain in the game for the next round.

NUMBER NECKLACES

Concept: Recognize visually the numerals 1 to 10.

Materials: Pieces of brightly colored construction paper.

            Yarn or string.

            Hole punch.

            Felt-tipped marker.

Group size: Small group.

Procedure: Ask each child what number he or she would like to wear on a necklace. Draw the numeral on a piece of colored paper. Let the child punch two holes in the paper and string a piece of yarn through to make a "necklace." While wearing the necklace, the child must name the numeral whenever someone asks what it is.

Note: The numeral can be worn around the wrist as a bracelet. This is especially helpful for teaching a numeral with which a child is having difficulty.

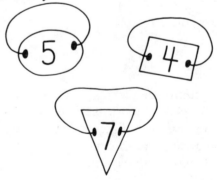

GROCERY STORE

Concept: Recognize visually the numerals 1 to 10.

Materials: Empty food containers (cereal boxes, milk cartons, candy bar wrappers, cans).

Masking tape or blank stickers.

Marking pen.

Group size: Small group.

Procedure: Place a sticker or piece of masking tape on each food container and mark each with a "price" of 1¢ to 10¢.

To play, ask a child to go to the store to buy something for 3¢. See if the child can find an item marked with the price you specify. Or tell the child that he or she can "buy" any item if the child can tell you the price.

Variation: Mark "prices" on the toys in the room. The child must tell you the price on a toy before he or she may play with it.

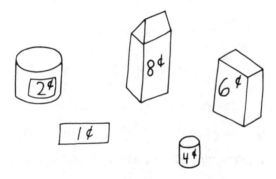

NUMERAL WINDOWS

Concept: Name numeral given written symbol.

Materials: One piece of construction paper cut as in the diagram.

One piece of paper, same size as construction paper, for the backing.

Group size: Small group.

Procedure: Construct a house with windows that open as shown in the diagram. Write a number in each window. Let the children play with the house, discovering the numbers they know. The children are involved physically in opening the shutters. This element of surprise adds interest.

FISH IN A BUCKET

Concept: Match like numbers and name numerals.

Materials: Lightweight cardboard fish numbered 1 to 10 on both sides.

Ten paper cups (buckets) numbered 1 to 10.

Stick with string attached.

Magnet to attach to the string and pole.

Ten paper clips, one for each fish.

Group size: One to three children or a small group.

Procedure: Attach the paper clip to the fish. Tie the magnet to the end of the string.

Let each child catch a fish with the pole and match the numeral on the fish to the bucket with the same number.

Variation: Name a numeral and have a child try to catch a fish with that value. Also, take away two "buckets" and let the children find out which buckets are missing.

STAND-UP MATCH

Concept: Match numeral name to written number.

Materials: Number cards.

Group size: Small group or class.

Procedure: Hand out number cards, one to each child. Call out a number and ask the children to stand up if they have that number.

          Variation: Give other activities to do when each number is called; for example, "If you have a 5, jump up." "If you have a 3, turn around."

NUMBER POCKETS

Concept: Match like numbers.

Materials: One large piece of cardboard.

3″ x 5″ rectangles numbered 1 to 10.

Tape.

3″ x 5″ cards with duplicate numbers.

Group size: One to three children.

Procedure: Arrange one set of numbered rectangles on the cardboard and tape or staple these down to make pockets.

Lay the second set of numbered rectangles out on the floor in front of the board. Have the children match the numbers, putting the matched number in the pocket.

WHO HAS MY NUMBER?

Concept: Match like numbers.

Materials: Two sets of numbers, one number on each slip of paper.

Group size: Class.

Procedure: Tell the children that you are going to play a game. Each child will get a piece of paper with a number on it. They can look at their numbers, but they are not to show it to anyone or call it out loud. Pass out the numbers. Ask the children to find the other children in the room who have a number like theirs. Have each pair tell what number they had.

Variation: Cut each number in half. Match number halves.

NUMERAL CHARACTERS

Concept: Name numeral given written number.

Materials: Numeral characters on construction paper (see diagram).

Crayons.

Group size: Any size group.

Procedure: Cut out numeral characters. Let children choose the character that they want and color it. Use the names of the numerals throughout the activity to provide repetition. Help the children recognize the numerals that they have chosen. Keep extra numerals available in case some children want to do more than one.

NUMERALS IN A SHOE

Concept: Name written numerals.

Materials: Twenty or more pieces of paper, each with a number written on it.

           A place to put the names for handing them out—in your shoe, a pocket, a glove, a hat, or up a sleeve.

Group size: Any size group.

Procedure: Place the papers in your pocket, shoe, or other hidden place without the children seeing you do it. During the day "find" the numbers and begin passing them out. Say, "Oh, here is a 5, would someone like to have a 5?" Your excitement about finding this cache of numerals should carry over to the children. Also, most children enjoy "surprises." Give them choices of numerals or give them the numerals that they request. Ask them to name the numbers that they received.

MATCH A HATCHED NUMERAL

Concept: Match like written numerals.

Materials: Egg carton with numbers on paper pasted in each pouch.

           Small discs or chips with numbers corresponding to those in the egg carton.

Group size: One to three children.

Procedure: Have children place the numbered discs in the egg carton, matching like numerals. Should children only recognize a few numerals, use only those numerals in the egg carton.

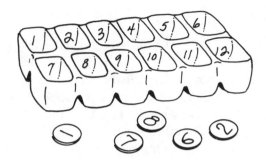

---

6 and 9

Concept: Differentiate a 6 from a 9.

Materials: 6 and 9 each drawn with a face in the enclosed section (see diagram).

Group size: One or two children or a small group.

Procedure: Show the children the six and the nine. Tell them what they are. Say, "The nine stands up, can you find the nine?" "The six stands on its head, can you find the six?" Mix the cards up and repeat. Have the children point to a number and tell you if it is a 6 or a 9.

Variation: Place 6's and 9's around the room. Have children find all the number 9's standing up or 6's standing on their heads.

MAGIC NUMERALS

Concept: Differentiate the 6 from the 9 by naming.

Materials: One card with a 9 written so that it will look like a 6 when turned upside down.

One scarf.

Group size: Small group.

Procedure: Tell the children that you have a magic trick. You are going to turn a 6 into a 9. Show the card to the children as a 6. Cover the card in your hand with the scarf and chant a magic chant. Turn the card around and remove the scarf with fanfare. The children will guess what you are doing, which is fine. The main idea is to get repetitious labeling of the numerals. Let the children take turns trying the trick.

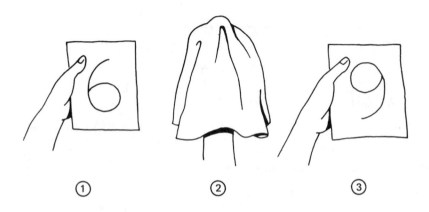

PICK A 3, 5, OR 8

Concept: Differentiate by naming a 3, a 5, and an 8.

Materials: Chalkboard.

Chalk.

Group size: One to three children.

Procedure: Draw a tree and three large baskets. Put the numerals 3, 5, and 8 on the tree in many places. Have one child at a time name and point to a number. Erase the number and rewrite it in one of the baskets. Put all 3's in one basket, 5's in another, etc. The object is to provide repetition in recognizing numbers. Help a child having problems by labeling a number that is already in a basket. Have the child find one like that one on the tree.

(Be sure to take time to draw the numerals carefully as you reproduce them in the baskets. This provides a visual stimulus for later work with drawing numerals.)

FLOORED NUMERALS

Concept: Differentiate the numerals 3, 5, and 8.

Materials: 3's, 5's, and 8's written on slips of paper with colored marker.

               Tape.

Group size: Any size group.

Procedure: Let each child choose two numbers (may be the same number twice). Tape the numbers to the soles of their shoes. Let the children compare numerals or just show them off to one another throughout the day.

               Variation: After all children have chosen their numerals and have them pasted on in private, gather the children in a group. Have them take turns guessing which number is underneath a shoe.

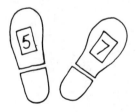

SHOW AND TELL A NUMERAL

Concept: Differentiate a 3, a 5, and an 8.

Materials: Each child brings a numeral to school. It can be any material or size the child chooses and either a 3, 5, or 8.

Group size: Class.

Procedure: Have each child bring in a 3, 5, or an 8. Let each child show his or her number and tell about how it was made or who helped make the number. Display the numbers to promote further repetition of identification of these three numerals.

NUMBER PATTERNS

Concept: Match a sequence of objects.

Materials: Felt or paper cutouts of numerals 1 to 9, two of each numeral.

Group size: Small group.

Procedure: Arrange a row of numerals in order. Have the child try to arrange the remaining numerals in the same order.

It is *not* necessary for the child to know or name the numerals.

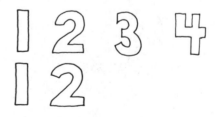

ORDERED NUMBERS

Concept: Seriate numerals in correct order.

Materials: Numerals that can be ordered; these may be wooden, plastic, paper, felt.

Group size: Two to three children.

Procedure: Spread the numerals in front of the children out of order. Have the children talk about which number is the first one, which the second. Let the children place the numerals in the correct order.

NEXT NUMERAL

Concept: Sequence numerals in the correct order.

Materials: Chalk.

               Chalkboard.

Group size: One to three children.

Procedure: Write a number on the chalkboard. Have a child tell you which number comes after the one written on the board. Write it. Repeat with other numerals. As a variation also ask which numeral should precede the one written.

               Variations: (1) Write numerals in sequence 1 to 10 leaving out a few numerals. Have the child tell you which numerals are missing. (2) Write the numerals on rungs of a ladder. Let a child tell you which numerals you have left out. Be sure to verify the answers by counting.

$$3 \; \underline{4} \; , \; \underline{\quad} \; 5, \underline{\quad} \; 9 \underline{\quad}$$

8.4   Numeral writing

A child's recognition of written numerals may or may not correspond with the child's ability to write numerals. The writing skill depends on the child's fine motor abilities including eye–hand coordination. We have included chants that may aid a child in remembering how to make the numerals. Guide the child's hand while saying the chants until you feel that the child is taking the initiative in writing. When the child senses the symbol, you will feel the child's hand pulling in the appropriate direction. Dittos could be made available on which the children can trace numerals and complete the drawing when given the beginning parts of the numeral, such as:

Once children begin to write numerals successfully., a wide range of activities becomes available in which children can write numerals in playing games, making props, sending notes, or making graphs and calendars. Utilize their writing skills in making the materials.

Numerals from 1 to 9 (and 0) need not necessarily be taught in sequence. A few numerals are easier to write than others. A few activities in teaching those numerals that are easily confused in recognition and writing are provided in this section.

FRAMES

Concept: Draw numerals in a numeral frame.

Materials: Numerals drawn as in the diagram.

Crayons.

Group size: Any size group.

Procedure: Allow each child to choose the numeral that he or she wants to draw. Demonstrate how to write a numeral within the frame of the numeral.

FUN WITH 1, THEN TO 9

Concept: Draw numeral while chanting rhyme.

Materials: Pencil and paper.

Group size: One child or small group.

Procedure: Model the drawing of the numeral while saying the rhyme:

A straight line one
It is fun.

Around and back
on the railroad track
makes two, two, two.

Around the tree
and around the tree;
this is the way
you make a three.

Down and over
and down some more.
This is the way
you make a four.

With a long neck
and a round little tummy,
Then put his hat on,
five sure looks funny.

Down to a loop,
the six rolls a hoop.

Across the sky
and down from heaven,
this is the way
you make a seven.

Make an S
and do not wait.
Climb back up
to make an eight.

A loop and a line
makes a nine.

I. D. CARDS

Concept: Draw numerals freehand.

Materials: Paper or 3" x 5" file cards.

Crayons or markers.

Group size: Any size group.

Procedure: Allow the children to design their own I.D. cards and choose an I.D. number. The cards can be used in make-believe games. Children can draw pictures of themselves or of characters they want to portray on their I.D.'s.

USING NUMERALS

Concept: Draw numerals freehand.

Materials: Paper.

Scissors.

Pencils and crayons.

Magazine pictures.

Group size: Any size group.

Procedure: Encourage children to use their ability to draw numbers in making

badges	telephone dials
numbered airplanes	play money
race cars	tickets
envelopes	instrument dials and knobs

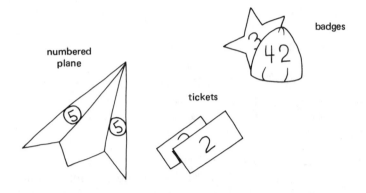

numbered
plane

badges

tickets

PLACE AND TIME

Concept: Draw numerals freehand.

Materials: Calendar without numbers.

Construction paper.

Crayons.

Group size: Any size group.

Procedure: Two situations lend themselves to drawing numbers—calendars and placemats. Allow the children to write the dates on calendars or on number placemats made of construction paper to use at snack or lunch. Have the children cut a fringe around the placemat.

CHAPTER 9

Numberness

9.1 Introduction

This chapter contains a strand that sequentially develops numberness. It includes sections on sets, one-to-one correspondence, equivalence, numerals for numbers, and ordering the numbers.

The concept of numberness, as referred to in this book, is the cardinal number of the set. The cardinal number of a set is the quantitative property of the set answering the question, "How many objects in the set?" Numberness has been defined in the preceding chapters as attempts were made at delineating a "prenumber" curriculum. The introductory chapter discussed the preconserving child and how that child is misled by the position of objects when asked to make judgments about quantity. The numeral chapter also contains a discussion of how children develop some concept of small quantities.

In the chapter on classification the child made sets of objects according to whether objects "belonged together" or met the multiple criteria for membership. In this chapter the child again makes sets; however, the objective is now placed on utilizing the set for some purpose. The focus is on the structure of the sets: defining boundaries.

The next section introduces techniques for using one-to-one correspondence in comparing two sets. The subsequent section utilizes one-to-one correspondence when making judgments of equality or inequality regarding two sets.

Then the numerals are associated with how many objects are in the set. The difference between this and the previous chapter is that no activity in the previous chapter required the child to conserve numberness, whereas this chapter does. The ordering of the first ten numbers in the last section serves to give meaning to the chants of number names and to get a notion that although the symbols are of the same physical size, the numbers they represent are not. Covering these topics in order should enhance the understanding of numberness and maximize children's learning of the numbers. Coupled with textual material available in most elementary school series, the teacher should be able to provide the child a stimulating, well-conceived development of number.

9.2 Sets

Some specific work with sets is necessary to working with numberness. Although work in chapters on shape, size, and classification involved forming sets, the sets were formed as a means for performing the activity. In this section the focus is on making sets as the primary objective of the activity. This does not preclude redoing many of the previous activities but, rather, alters the focus for the teacher and child. It may even be advisable to redo many of the previous activities to maintain those concept skills while recognizing that a secondary focus on the constitution of sets is now advisable.

ROPED SETS

Concept: Construct sets of objects.

Materials: Jump ropes, one per child.

Common objects in the room, for example, chairs, puzzles, toy trucks, books, dolls, etc.

Group size: Small group.

Procedure: Give each child a rope and have each one outline a set on the floor. On direction, each child collects a set of objects within his or her set. If necessary, tell each child what to find: "Susie, make a set of lunch boxes." After they have made their sets, have each child tell the others about his or her set.

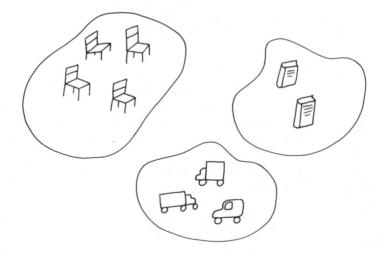

MAKING SETS

Concept: Construct sets of objects.

Materials: Large box or tray containing at least five of several different objects: bottlecaps, beads, blocks, pencils, erasers, beans, cotton balls, hairpins, toothpicks.

Piece of construction paper with a set boundary line—one for each child. Draw the boundary line on the paper.

Group size: Small group.

Procedure: Give each child a piece of construction paper and place the box of mixed objects where all can reach it. Direct each child to make a set: "Andrew, make a set of bottlecaps." "Cindy, a set of pencils," and so on. Be sure that each child places all objects within the boundary on the paper.

Questions: (As you place an object outside the boundary), Is this pencil in your set? Where should it go? (Showing a cotton ball to a child with a set of bottlecaps), Does this belong to your set? Why not?

FLANNEL SETS

Concept: Construct sets of pictures.

Materials: Flannelboard.

Felt cutouts representing real objects, i.e., rabbits, birds, ducks, apples, pears, trees, hearts.

Yarn or sting.

Group size: Small group.

Procedure: Make a set boundary of yarn on the flannelboard. Give a child some felt cutouts and ask the child to make a set of ducks. Then have another child make a set of something else, and so on, until all children have had a chance to make a set.

At first, give the child only the correct cutouts; later on, mix in other cutouts, i.e., apples with birds, so that the child must select only the correct members.

Variation: Two children can work side by side in a race.

Questions: Hold a tree next to a set of rabbits. Ask, "does this belong in your set of rabbits? Why not?"

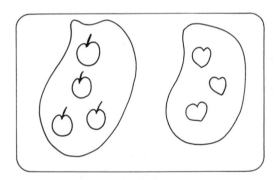

SHAPE SETS

Concept: Construct sets of mathematical objects.

Materials: Attribute blocks or a collection of shapes.

Yarn or masking tape.

Group size: Small group.

Procedure: Make a set boundary of yarn or tape for each child. Mix the shape blocks together and have each child make a set using a particular shape. Direct one child to make a set of squares, another a set of circles, another a set of triangles, and so on. Other alternatives include having one make a set of big shapes, another a set of little shapes; one make a set of fat shapes, another a set of thin shapes; or one make a set of blue shapes, another a set of red shapes.

Variation: Make shape sets on the flannelboard.

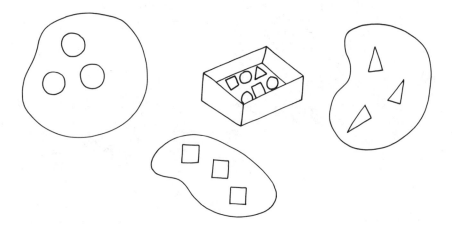

9.3   One-to-one correspondence

Activities in this section provide the child with a systematic development of the concept of pairing objects from different sets. Initially the pairing occurs between objects that the child should have experienced in the environment. A physical bonding (using yarn or other material) helps organize the structure of the pairing for the child and utilizes the tactile mode in developing the construct of "one-to-one"-ness. These objects should be recognized as naturally paired from past experience. Later activities involve more mathematical-looking objects that do not have "natural partners" in the sets.

WHAT'S MINE IS MINE

Concept: Associate naturally related sets in one-to-one correspondence.

Materials: Children in the class.

Children's own lunches, coats, shoes, chairs, or other belongings.

Group size: Class.

Procedure: Make a set of children. Then make a set of their belongings, using one item from each child in the set. Select another child to match each item, for example, each shoe, to its proper owner.

Be sure that the sets being matched are equal.

SNACK MATCH

Concept: Associate logically related sets in one-to-one correspondence.

Materials: Children seated at table or desks.

Snack materials, exactly one for each child: cups, cookies, etc.

Group size: Class.

Procedure: Ask one of the children to give each child a cup. Ask another to give each child a cookie. After the items have been distributed, help the children check to see that everyone has each of the items passed out.

ANIMAL TAG

Concept: Construct one-to-one correspondence between nonrelated sets of objects.

Materials: Flannelboard.

Felt cutouts of at least two different kinds of animals, i.e., rabbits, ducks, birds.

Yarn.

Group size: Small group.

Procedure: Make two equivalent sets of animals on the flannelboard. Tell the children that the animals are going to play tag: each rabbit will chase a duck. Let each child come to the flannelboard, take a rabbit in one hand and a duck in the other, and show the rabbit chasing the duck.

Variation: Pair each bird with a tree, each rabbit with a pear, and so on.

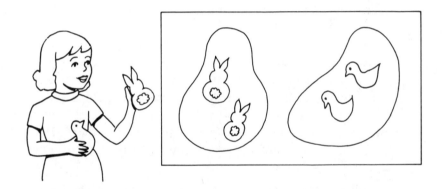

CIRCLE SETS

Concept: Construct one-to-one correspondence between physical and mathematical objects.

Materials: Attribute blocks or other shapes.

Group size: Small group.

Procedure: Make a set of circles equivalent to the number of children in the group. Ask one child to give everyone a circle. Repeat with other shapes.

Variation: On the flannelboard, match sets of rabbits to squares, ducks to triangles, and so on.

SHAPE PARTNERS

Concept: Construct one-to-one correspondence with mapping between sets of mathematical symbols.

Materials: Flannelboard.

Felt shapes.

Yarn, cut in pieces for mapping.

Group size: Small group.

Procedure: Make a set of four circles and another set of four squares on the flannelboard. Ask a child to match each circle to a square, pointing to indicate the pairs. Continue matching sets in this way until confusion occurs; then show the children how a piece of yarn can show which shapes go together. Have the children practice using yarn to show one-to-one correspondence between sets of shapes.

Variation: Using dittoed worksheets that duplicate the sets on the flannelboard, have the children draw lines to show one-to-one matching.

First:

Later:

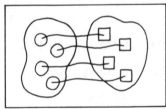

Matching sets is understandable when using concrete materials.

9.4 Equivalent sets

Before making judgments regarding equivalence, the child must construct (or be given) two sets and utilize skills in establishing a one-to-one correspondence between the sets. At first, the sets chosen by the teacher should be equivalent, which helps the child understand the terminology "same as." After experience with equivalence, the child should encounter sets of unequal number. This allows definition of "more than" and "less than." Many activities could be correlated with estimates about the equivalence, then performing the activity to confirm the judgment. Be sure to vary the question, sometimes asking which set has "more" and at other times, which set has "less."

MUSICAL CHAIRS

Concept: Determine whether two sets are equivalent or nonequivalent.

Materials: Chairs, one per child.

Music.

Group size: Class.

Procedure: Play this game as you would regularly play musical chairs, with a few added steps.

To begin, line up as many chairs as you have children playing. Have each child matched to a chair (i.e., sit down). Say, "Do we have more chairs, or more children, or are they the same?" Ask what happens when we play with the same number of chairs as children. Play a round or two to see. Try to lead the children to recognize that we need fewer chairs than children to play.

Before each round with music, ask the children to sit to determine which set is bigger, the chairs or the children. Sometimes use more chairs, sometimes more children, sometimes the same number. Before each round, ask the children to guess what will happen.

IS THERE ENOUGH?

Concept: Determine whether two sets are equivalent or nonequivalent.

Materials: Children seated at table for snack or lunch.

Crackers, cookies, sandwiches, or cups of juice.

Group size: Class.

Procedure: Show the children a set of snack items and ask them if there are enough cups of juice for everyone. Help them see that we can pass out the cups to find out. Assign one child this task. When completed, ask the children if there is enough juice. "Are there any cups of juice left over?" "Are there any children left over?" "Which set has more, the set of children or the set of juice cups?"

On some days, have too many snacks, on others have just enough, and on others have not enough. (On "not enough" days, keep the extras out of sight until the size of the set has been determined, then find the extras.)

HATS AND WORKERS

Concept: Determine whether two sets are equivalent or which one is larger.

Materials: Yarn.

Pictures of workers and their hats (look in old workbooks): firefighters, police officers, nurses, letter carriers.

Group size: Small group.

Procedure: Make the two sets of boundaries with yarn. In one set place pictures of the workers; in the other their hats. Sometimes have more workers, sometimes more hats, sometimes the same number. Have the children match each worker to a hat using yarn pieces and state which set is larger.

Variation: Match a set of party hats to a set of children.

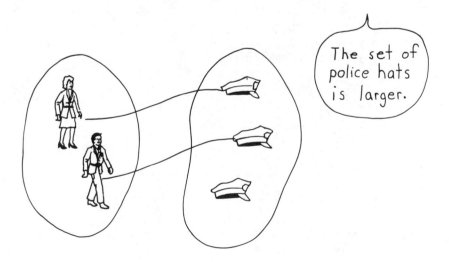

FEED THE ANIMALS

Concept: Determine whether two sets are equivalent or nonequivalent; which is the larger set.

Materials: Yarn.

Paper, felt, or toy animals.

"Food" for the animals.

Examples: Turtles and rubber bugs, felt rabbits and paper carrots, paper fish and pipe-cleaner worms, squirrels and peanuts, rubber ducks and popcorn.

Group size: Small group.

Procedure: On a table, outline two sets with yarn; put some animals in one and their food in the other. Ask the children if there is enough food for each animal to get exactly one piece. Have a child match each animal to a piece of food using yarn to map. Ask whether there are more animals or more food. Guide the children to see that the set with something left over is the larger set. Sometimes make the set of animals larger, sometimes the set of food larger, and sometimes make the sets equal.

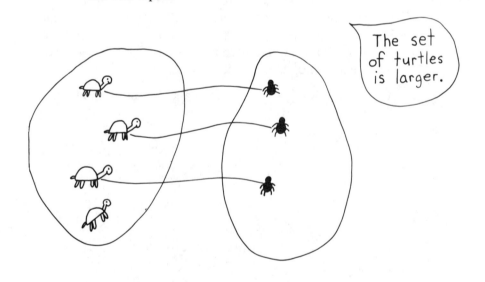

MORE SHAPES, FEWER SHAPES

Concept: Determine whether two sets are equivalent or which one is larger.

Materials: Attribute blocks or other shapes.

Yarn.

Group size: Small group.

Procedure: Make boundaries for two sets on a table. Place some shapes in each set. Ask a child which set has more; let the child match the shapes with yarn to find out. Sometimes make the sets equal and sometimes unequal.

Variation: Use the felt shapes on the flannelboard.

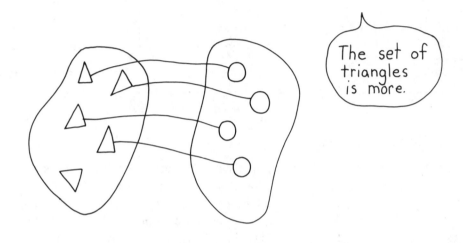

STRIPED SHOES

Concept: Match equivalent sets.

Materials: Shoe holder with pockets, unnumbered.

Five pairs of tagboard shoe cutouts.

Felt-tipped marker.

Five shoelaces, pieces of yarn, or string.

Group size: Two or three children.

Procedure: With the felt-tipped marker, mark each pair of shoe cutouts with one, two, three, four, or five stripes.

Mix the left shoes in one pile and the right in another. Each child selects a shoe from the left pile and then must find its mate from the right pile. The shoelaces can be laid between stripes in one-to-one correspondence for the child to determine whether two shoes are mates.

Each correctly matched pair can be placed in a shoe pocket.

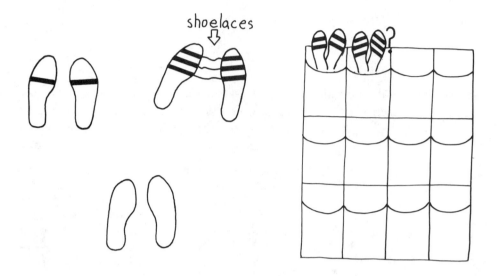

9.5   Numerals for numbers

This section provides some sample activities in which the child is asked to associate a number name with the cardinal number of the set. The *cardinal* number is the quantitative property of the set answering the question, "how many in the set?" Numerous informal situations will present themselves during the day in which the teacher can direct the child to (1) state how many in the set or (2) write the number for how many in the set. Prior to these activities it is assumed that the child can recognize and write the numerals; otherwise, the teacher should complete Section 8.5.

Meaningfully counting the objects in the set to determine the number associated with the set should be encouraged by the teacher. Later, the teacher might wish to have the child respond first "less than 5" or "more than 5" and then count to find the exact number.

WORN OUT SHOES, HOLEY SHOES

Concept: Match number of objects to corresponding numeral.

Materials: Shoe holder, with pockets numbered from 1 to 10.

Tagboard shoe cutouts, each punched or marked with a number of holes from 1 to 10.

Felt-tipped marker (optional).

Group size: Small group.

Procedure: Show the children a shoe and tell them it is worn out and has holes. Each child must count the holes in a shoe and put it in the pocket with the correct numeral. (This will tell the shoe repairer how many holes to fix in each shoe.)

For self-checking, write the correct numeral on the back of each shoe.

Questions: Can you tell how many holes are in this shoe without counting? Which shoe has more holes, this one or this one?

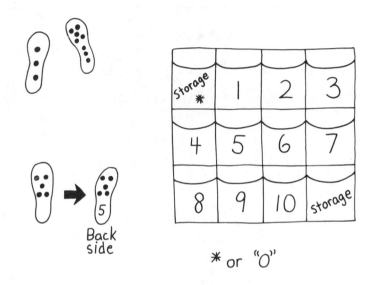

NUMBER MATES

Concept: Associate numerals 0 to 9 with the correct number.

Materials: Ten pieces of construction paper or large index cards.

Markers or crayons.

Group size: Class.

Procedure: Cut each piece of paper into two puzzle pieces. Be sure to cut each piece differently. On half the paper draw a set of objects; on the other half write the corresponding numeral.

To play, shuffle and distribute the cards. At a signal from you, each child tries to find the correct "number mate" to stand beside. Check for correctness by matching the two pieces together.

Variation: Let one child match the number mates as an independent activity.

HOW MANY BUTTONS?

Concept: Associate numerals with the correct number.

Materials: Ten spring-type clothespins, each marked with a numeral from 0 to 9.

Ten clothing cutouts, each with from 0 to 9 buttons.

Clothesline.

Group size: Small group.

Procedure: Each child takes a clothespin and pins the piece of clothing with the corresponding number of buttons on the clothesline.

NUMBER RUMMY

Concept: Associate numerals with the correct number.

Materials: Deck of cards, half containing numerals 0 through 9 and half containing pictures or drawings of the corresponding numbers of objects.

Group size: Two to four children.

Procedure: Shuffle the cards and deal five to each player. Place the remaining cards face down in the center of the table. Turn the first card of the stack over to make a discard pile.

The object of the game is to make as many pairs of numeral and number of objects as possible. In turns, each player draws a card from either the stack or the discard pile and then either plays a pair or discards one card. To play a pair, the player places face up a numeral card and a card with the corresponding number of objects; two 3's or two sets of four objects do not make a pair. When one player has run out of cards, the player with the most pairs is the winner.

NUMBER CONCENTRATION

Concept: Associate numerals with the correct number.

Materials: Deck of cards, half containing numerals 0 through 9 and half containing pictures or drawings of the corresponding numbers of objects.

Group size: Two to four children.

Procedure: Shuffle the cards and arrange them face down in rows. In turns, each child turns over two cards and names the numeral or number of objects on each card. If they match, the player keeps them. When all matches have been made, the player with the most cards is the winner.

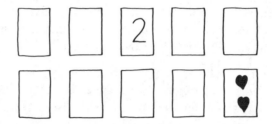

NUMBER NECKLACES

Concept: Associate numerals with the correct number.

Materials: Beads.

Lacing strings.

Number cards.

Strings or staples.

Group size: Small group.

Procedure: Give each child a lacing string and a number card. The child is to string the corresponding number of beads onto the string. When the necklace is correctly strung, tie or staple the number card onto it. Allow the maker to wear the necklace.

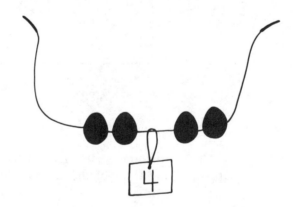

MUSICAL NUMBERS

Concept: Associate numerals with the correct number.

Materials: Pieces of construction paper, at least 9″ × 12″, each with a set containing from zero to nine objects.

Set of cards numbered 0 to 9 for each player.

Music.

Group size: Ten children.

Procedure: Tape the construction paper sets on the floor in a continuous path. Each child takes a set of number cards and stands on the path. As the music begins the children begin to walk around the path. When the music stops, each child must hold up the number card corresponding to the number of objects on the set underfoot. A player who holds up the wrong number is out of the game. The last player or players to remain will win.

POT OF CHIPS

Concept: Associate numerals with the correct number.

Materials: Pot of tokens or poker chips.

Deck of cards numbered 0 to 9.

Small pot or bowl for each player.

Group size: Two to four children.

Procedure: Shuffle the cards and place them face down in a stack in the center of the table next to the pot of chips. In turns, each child draws a card and turns it face up on the table. The player must then take the corresponding number of chips from the center pot and lay them on the table next to the number card. If the other players judge the number of chips to be correct, the child keeps them. If incorrect, the chips go back into the center pot.

When all cards or all chips have been played, the child with the most chips wins.

PEGBOARD NUMBERS

Concept: Associate numerals with the correct number.

Materials: Pegboards and pegs.

Nine cardboard templates to cover the pegboards.

Tape.

Number cards.

Group size: Small group.

Procedure: Cut a hole or holes in each template so that the first template will allow only one peg to be placed in the board, the second template to allow only two pegs to be placed, and so on up to nine pegs. (If desired, two or even three templates can be cut to fit onto one pegboard at the same time.) Tape the templates onto the pegboards.

To play, the child places pegs into the exposed holes and then matches the correct number card to the board. The game can be made self-checking by including the correct number on the back of the template or on the front under a "trap door."

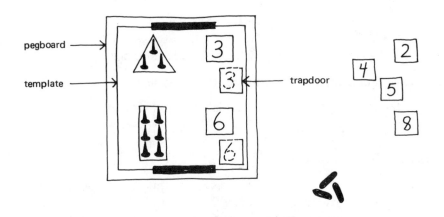

pegboard

template

trapdoor

NUMBER RUN

Concept: Associate numerals with the correct number.

Materials: Large flash cards, each with a set of from 0 to 9 objects.

Two sets of cards numbered 0 to 9.

Tape.

Group size: Small group or class.

Procedure: Divide the children into two teams. Place one set of number cards in a chalk tray or card holder for each team. Mark a starting line for each team several meters (yards) from the number cards.

To play, a player from each team stands at start. As you flash a set card, the two run for their number cards. The first one to hold up the correct card wins a point for the team. At the end of play, the team with the most points wins.

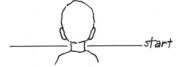

DOMINUMBERS

Concept: Associate numerals with the correct number.

Materials: Set of modified dominoes (see diagram).

        Masking tape or gummed labels.

        Marker or pen.

Group size: Two to four children.

Procedure: To make the dominumbers, put masking tape or a gummed label over one side of each domino. Mark each piece of tape with the numeral that corresponds to the set of dots it covers.

        Play the game according to the rules of regular dominoes, with this exception: to make a play, a set of dots must be matched to a numeral; two numerals or two sets of dots may not be matched.

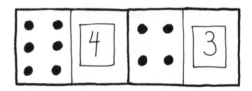

9.6   Ordering of numerals according to number

Given two sets, the child should determine the number (cardinal number) associated with each set and then decide which number is larger. Notice that the decision of which is larger is based on the judgment of which set has more objects. This information utilizes one-to-one correspondence.

POLKA DOT NUMBERS

Concept: Order numerals 1 to 9 according to the number of objects in the set.

Materials: Cards, cutouts, or wooden numerals 1 to 9.

        Forty-five tactile dots (felt, sandpaper, Velcro, putty-type plastic).

        Chalk ledge, wall, or tabletop.

Group size: Small group.

Procedure: Attach as many dots to each numeral as the numeral says. Beginning with 1, have the children sequence the numerals by finding the numeral with one more dot than the previous one.

STEPNUMBERS

Concept: Order numerals 1 to 10 according to the number of objects in the set.

Materials: Fifty-five snap-together cubes.

Stickers or masking tape.

Pen or marker.

Group size: Small group.

Procedure: Let the children help make the stepnumbers. Count one cube, put on a sticker, and mark it 1; count two cubes, snap them together, and mark the unit 2; and so on up to a unit of 10.

Ask a child to find the stepnumber with the fewest cubes, the "one." Ask another child to find the stepnumber with one more cube, the "two," and set it next to the one. Continue up to 10. When you are finished, you will have stepnumbers in a row.

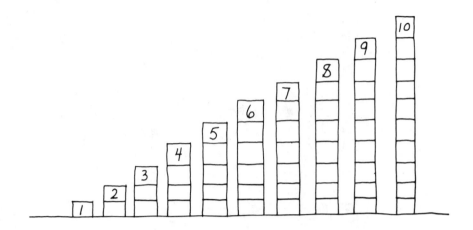

SKY TOWERS

Concept: Order numerals 1 to 10 according to the number of objects in the set.

Materials: Ten tagboard building cutouts, with from one to ten windows and with the number of windows printed on the door.

Chalk ledge or wall.

Group size: Small group.

Procedure: Tell the children that they are going to put the sky towers in a row, beginning with the fewest windows and going to the most. Ask a child to find the building with only one window; have the child put it at the left end of the chalk ledge. Ask another child which building has one more window than the first; let the child place the remaining buildings one at a time, next to the first until he or she finds the correct one. Continue up until 10.

Point out the numerals on the towers and have the children chant them from 1 to 10.

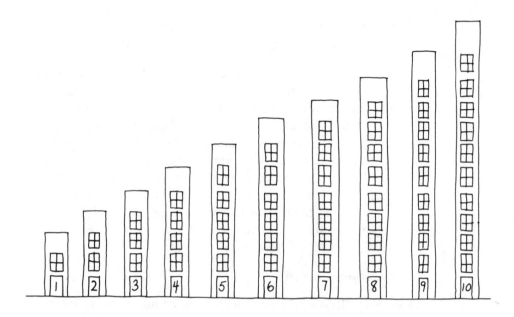

THE PROUD FLOWERS

Concept: Order numerals 1 to 3 according to the number of objects in the set.

Materials: Flannelboard.

Six identical felt flowers, each a bloom on a short stem.

Three felt flower pots, eyes optional.

Felt numerals, 1, 2, and 3.

Group size: Small group or class.

Procedure: Place felt pieces on flannelboard as you tell the following story:

"Once three flower pots sat in a window. (Place pots on board.) The first pot said, "I'm going to grow a flower!" And it did. (Place bloom.) It was a beautiful flower. When the next pot saw the beautiful flower, it said, "I want to be more beautiful than that pot. I will grow one more flower." And it did. It grew one flower to match the first pot (place bloom in direct line with bloom in first pot), and then it grew one more flower! (Place another bloom above first.) When the last pot saw this, it said, "Oh, I want to be the most beautiful flower pot! I will grow one more flower than this other pot." And it did. First it grew a flower to match both other pots. (Place bloom.) Then it grew another flower to match the second pot. (Place bloom)

And then it grew one more flower! "Now I am the most beautiful flower pot!" said the third one.

"Well, pretty soon the flower pots began to argue about which was the most beautiful. They made so much noise that Mrs. Harris came running to see what was wrong. When the flower pots told her, she exclaimed, "Oh, each one of you is just as beautiful as the other! You are all very beautiful, but you do have different numbers of flowers. I will put a numeral on each of you (place the correct numeral on each pot to stand for the number of blooms). This is how you will stay in my window: first, number 1; then, with one more, number 2; and then, with one more, number 3. How proud I am of all my beautiful flowers!" said Mrs. Harris.

And everyone agreed."

Variation: Illustrate story on chalkboard instead of the flannelboard.

THE RACCOONS' LUNCH

Concept: Order numerals 1 to 5 according to the number of objects in the set.

Materials: Raccoon puppet or stuffed animal (optional).

Five pieces of yarn or string.

Fifteen fish cutouts.

Sticky tape, tacks or pins to attach fish and strings.

Flannelboard, chalkboard, corkboard, or wall.

Numerals 1 to 5.

Group size: Class.

Procedure: Tell this story and assemble the fish lines as directed.

"One day some hungry raccoons went fishing for their lunch. The first one hung up his line (tack string to wall) and began to fish. He caught one fish and said, "This is enough for me. I'll just leave this fish on my line (attach fish). I have one fish so I'll mark it with a 1 (place 1 on line) while I go to wash my hands." And he did. Pretty soon the next raccoon came to hang up her line (attach string next to first one). She said, "That raccoon caught only one fish for his lunch. I'm hungrier than he is, so I'll catch one more." And she did. She caught one fish (attach fish) like the first raccoon; then she caught one more. She said, "I have two fish, so I'll mark my line with a 2 and then I'll go to wash my hands for lunch." And she did. (Continue story in same manner for raccoons three, four, and five.)"

When the raccoons come back, have the children give each raccoon his line of fish or match the raccoon to his line of fish. When the raccoons have their fish, announce that they are happy and will eat their fish.

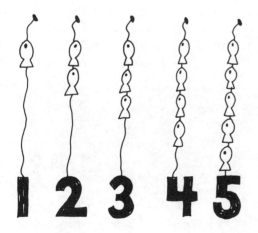

CHAPTER 10

Addition

10.1 Introduction

The activities involving addition are intended to be supplemental to a textbook series, not to replace the series. Highly motivational activities have been devised to provide addition fact practice as a means for participating in each activity. The sections have been separated into "sums to 5" and "other fact work." The primary reason for using sums of 5 as the separation point is that these "easy" facts are such that the cardinality of the set is instantly recognized by the eye whereas, when the cardinal number of the sum is larger than 5, an ordering principle must be used by the child to determine the sum.

It is important to encourage the children to count when confirming a response to an addition exercise. The teacher should take care to reinforce one-to-one correspondence when counting. Further, children should be allowed to use objects and materials as long as necessary when working addition problems.

A special note about working with an addend of 0 (zero). Initial work with addition should avoid use of this special case because the model involves an empty set. For the child needing a concrete model of the mathematical operation, the empty set contains no objects and the concrete learner is not cognitively able to work with this set. The teacher can avoid much of this

difficulty by making certain that success experiences with addition precede use of the special cases. Situations involving zero as an addend should come after introductory work with addition and be timed to correlate with the textbook introduction of zero as an addend. Different series introduce work with zero at different points in the curriculum, and the teacher should take special note of its placement.

10.2   Sums to 5

The "easy" basic facts involve sums of 10 or fewer and the "hard" facts sums between 11 and 18. However, in the set of "easy" basic facts, those sums between 6 and 10 require an ordering procedure to determine the total. The total for sums 5 or less are easily recognized by the child. The level of difficulty increases enough that it was decided to use the sum of 5 as a separation point for the chapter section.

SHAKE AND COUNT

Concept: Add sums to 5.

Materials: Oatmeal carton lid with divider.

Ten marbles.

Group size: One or two children.

Procedure: Place the diver in the carton lid securely with staples, tape or glue. Place the marbles in the lid. Allow a child to tilt the lid distributing the marbles in various combinations. Discuss how many are on each side of the divider and then make math sentences. Using the diagram, we might have many different equations all with the sum of 4.

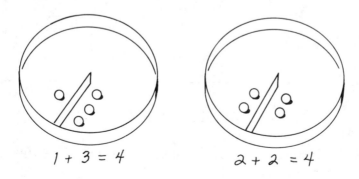

$1 + 3 = 4$ $2 + 2 = 4$

SUM EGGS

Concept: Show different addition sentences for the same sum.

Materials: Plastic eggs.

Small beads or chips.

Dittoed worksheets.

Chalkboard or chart paper.

Group size: Small group.

Procedure: Fill each egg beforehand with the same number of beads, for example, 5. Give each child an egg, and tell the group that you want to find as many ways to write the sum of 5 as you can. Let each child try dividing his or her beads between the egg halves and telling the combination. Record combinations on class chart and individual ditto sheets.

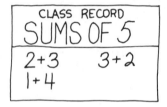

DUCK FAMILIES

Concept: Determine all possible combinations for a particular sum less than or equal to 5.

Materials: Cutouts of mother ducks each marked with a numeral from 1 to 5.

Cutouts of baby ducks each marked with a possible addition combination for the number on the mother duck (i.e., for 5 combinations would be 0+5, 4+1, 1+4, 3+2, 2+3, 5+0).

Group size: Two to four children.

Procedure: Have each child select a mother duck. Then have the child find all the baby ducks that have an addition fact that appears on the mother duck.

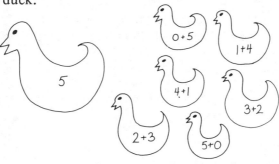

DAISIES

Concept: Identify sums for addition facts with sums to 5.

Materials: Daisy petals with addition problems.

Daisy centers with sums.

Group size: Two to four children.

Procedure: Have the children match the problems printed on each of the petals to the correct sum appearing on the center of the daisy. Petals can be color coded on the back for checking answers. All the petals for the number 5 could be marked red, all those for 4 could be green, and so on.

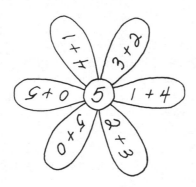

BEANBAG CLOWN

Concept: Add two numbers with sums less than or equal to 5.

Materials: Two beanbags.

                 Face target (see drawing).

Group size: Small group.

Procedure: Each child takes a turn throwing both beanbags at the clown face. The child then finds the sum of the two numbers on the spaces on which the beanbags landed. If a beanbag lands on a line, the player may choose which of the two numbers are to be used in the sum. If the sum is correct the player gets a point.

10.3   Fact work

The activities involving fact work are designed to reinforce and maintain skill knowledge with the 100 basic facts in addition. Few of these games are developmental in nature because the classroom teacher will have a text series or curriculum guide that develops the concept understanding. However, activities that provide varied settings aimed at maintaining and extending skills are contained in this section.

Many of the activities in this section may be used with the other operations, and the teacher should be cognizant of potential modifications and utilize these with other operations.

POUCH PROBLEMS

Concept: Find the correct sum given combinations with sums to 9.

Materials: Cardboard kangaroo drawing on which are pockets, each marked with a number 1 to 9 (see diagram).

Problem cards adding to sums up to 9.

Group size: One or two children.

Procedure: An addition fact is written on each card. The child places the card in the pocket having the correct sum.

Variation: Numbers and problems could be changed as children become adept at old problems.

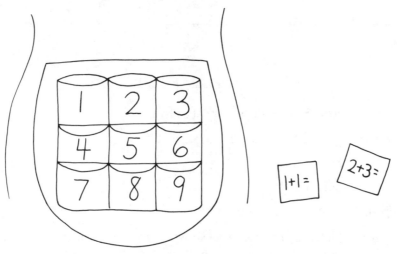

ADD AROUND

Concept: Add sums to 10.

Materials: Gameboard (see diagram).

Markers.

Spinner or one die.

Group size: Two to six children.

Procedure: Each child spins the spinner and then moves the correct number of spaces shown. The child will land on either a free space or a space with an addition problem. The child must answer the problem correctly or move back two spaces. The first child who makes it all the way around the board wins.

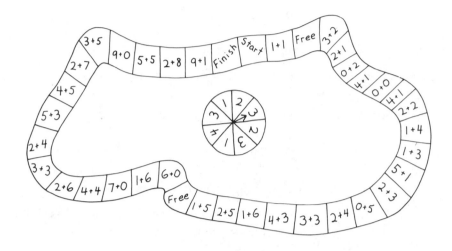

PROBLEM PUZZLE

Concept: Add facts with sums to 10.

Materials: Gameboard (see diagram).

              Marker.

              Scissors.

Group size: One to three children.

Procedure: Make a gameboard as shown with addition problems scattered randomly. Next cut the gameboard into pieces separating each problem from its answer. The children must put the problems together to reassemble the puzzle. The level of difficulty should be consistent with the children's ability. Any kind of problems—subtraction, addition, or multiplication—could be used.

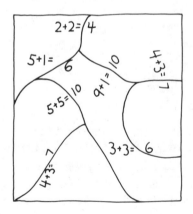

ADDING SHOES

Concept: Determine addition facts with sums to 10.

Materials: Shoe holder with pockets numbered from 1 to 10.

               Shoe cutouts marked with numerals from 1 to 5.

               Stapler (optional).

               Hole punch and yarn or string (optional).

Group size: One to four children.

Procedure: Mix all the left shoes into one pile and all the right shoes into another. Each child selects a left and a right shoe, adds the two numbers, and puts the pair into the pocket labeled with the correct sum.

               To control the combinations of addends, staple pairs of shoes together or punch holes and tie them together.

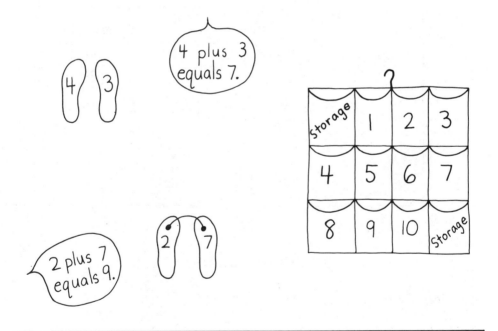

HOLIDAY DITTOS

Concept: Color sections of ditto using sums of addition problems as a guide.

Materials: Dittos.

               Crayons.

Group size: Class.

Procedure: Draw a ditto appropriate for the holiday. Divide the picture into irregular sections. In each section, place an addition fact. For each color to be used on the ditto decide on a sum, i.e., all problems having a sum of 8 should be colored green. Have the child work the problems and then color the picture using the key provided.

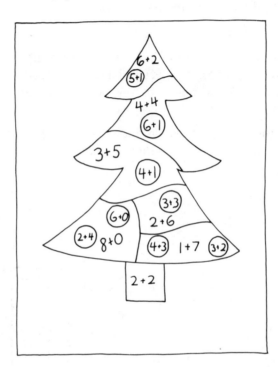

key

4 - Brown
8 - Green
6 - Red
7 - Blue
5 - Yellow

ADD THE ARROWS

Concept: Find sums to 10.

Materials: Tagboard.

Clear contact paper.

Grease pencil.

Group size: One to two children.

Procedure: Children follow the arrows adding the numbers and writing the totals in the squares.

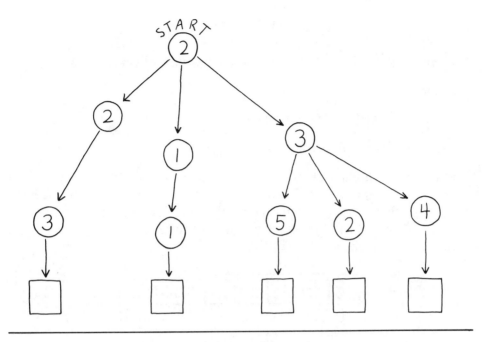

MAKE A BUG

Concept: Add sums less than 12.

Materials: Cutouts of bug parts (see diagram).

Dice.

Group size: Four to six children.

Procedure: Label the bug parts with numbers. Each child rolls the dice and adds the numbers. Then the child finds the part that corresponds to the sum. The first one to complete a bug is the winner.

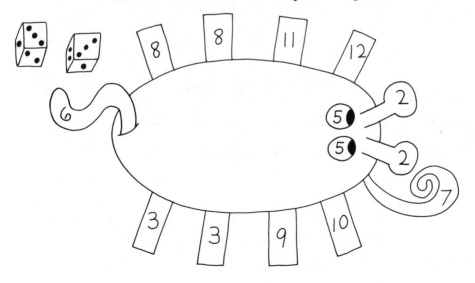

ROLLETTE

Concept: Add numbers whose sums are less than or equal to 12.

Materials: Dice.

                 Gameboard (see diagram).

Group size: Two to four children.

Procedure: Each child plays using the numbers on the row directly in front of him or her. The children in turn roll the dice, add the numbers, then cover the number on the row that is the same as the sum. The first child to cover all the numbers in the row is the winner.

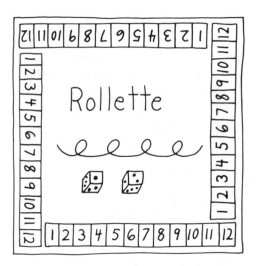

GRAPE BUNCH AGAIN

Concept: Add numbers to sums less than or equal to 12.

Materials: Grape gameboard (see diagram).

                 Markers.

                 Two spinners.

                 Chips or cover markers.

Group size: Two to six children.

Procedure: Taking turns, each child spins the spinners. If the sum of the numbers on the spinners is in the first bunch of grapes, the child may move there; if not he or she stays put. When a child lands on a number, that number is covered and may not be used again. Each child moves from bunch to bunch in this manner. When a child gets to the last bunch, the child gets one point and must spin a number back in the first bunch on the next turn. Play continues until all grapes have been marked out. Highest score wins.

Variation: Spinner numbers can be used for any function— addition, subtraction, multiplication. Choose problems that fit your children's level of ability.

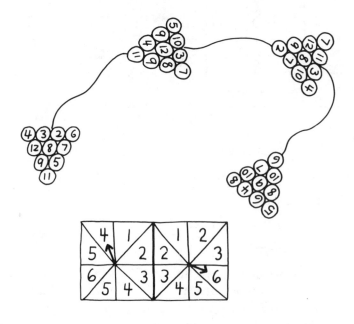

DOMINO LOTTO

Concept: Identify sums for addition facts up to sums of 12.

Materials: Set(s) of regular dominoes (12 dominoes per player).

Lotto cards, each with 12 spaces (large enough to hold one domino per space).

Group size: Two to four children.

Procedure: Number each space on the lotto cards with a numeral from 0 to 12. Be sure that each numbered space matches the sum of dots on a domino.

To play, turn all dominoes face down in the center of the table. Each player takes a turn drawing a domino from the pile and naming the sum of the dots aloud. If correct, the player matches it to the correct sum on the card. If incorrect, or if the child has no spaces with the correct numeral, the domino is returned to the pile. Play continues until one player covers all spaces on his or her card.

Domino	Lotta		
6	0	3	1
4	5	10	11
7	8	9	2

HORSE RACE

Concept: Problem solving using sums to 12.

Materials: Pictures of horses or toy horses in at least two colors.

Two dice.

Gameboard (see diagram).

Group size: Two children.

Procedure: Each player has two horses. The first child rolls the dice. He or she can move one horse for the sum of the two dice or both horses the number on one die. Players must get both of their horses around the track to win.

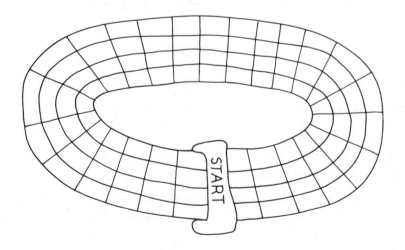

PROBLEM CARDS

Concept: Complete addition facts with sums to 10.

Materials: Transparent hard plastic strip or clear contact paper.

Problem cards.

Grease pencil.

Group size: Two to three children.

Procedure: Place the problem cards under plastic. The children can then use their pencils to write the answers on the cards. Problems may involve a missing addend or sum. The children can wipe off previous answers and then go on to other problems.

Variation: Have complete cards and cover the answers with cardboard. After the child answers, slide the cardboard over and check the answers.

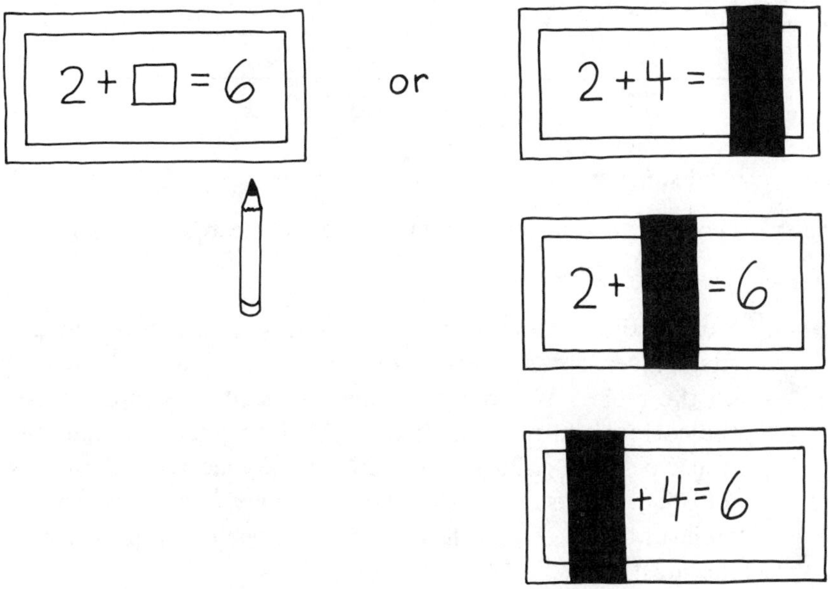

$$2 + \square = 6$$

or

$$2 + 4 =$$

$$2 + = 6$$

$$ + 4 = 6$$

BOWLING

Concept: Add sums to 10.

Materials: Ten potato chip cans.

Ball.

Group size: Two to four children.

Procedure: Line up the cans for bowling. Each child has two balls and rolls twice. The child counts the number knocked down on the first roll and adds that to the number knocked down on the second roll. Pins are not replaced between the first and second roll. The highest score wins.

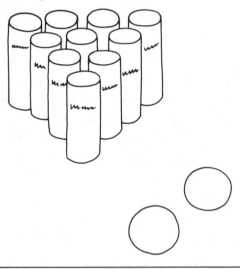

CARD SUMS

Concept: Add sums to 18.

Materials: Deck of playing cards, minus the picture cards and 10's.

Group size: Two to four children.

Procedure: Shuffle the cards and place them face down in a stack. The first player draws the top two cards and places them face up on the table. Without stopping to count, the child must say the correct addition sentence, i.e., "Two plus six equals eight." If correct, the child keeps the cards; if incorrect, the cards are returned to the bottom of the pile. Play continues around the table until all the cards are gone; winner is the player holding the most cards.

10'S COMPUTER

Concept: Use manipulative materials to show the regrouping of 1's to 10's in addition.

Materials: Large paper grid labeled "tens" and "ones."

Cubes or beads that snap together or other objects that can be bundled into groups of ten.

Cards of two-digit numbers.

Paper and pencil.

Group size: One to four children.

Procedure: Give each child two number cards that, when added, will require regrouping of 1's to a 10 (for example, 34 and 28). Place the cards beside the grid and ask the child to join and place the correct number of cubes on the grid to illustrate each amount. For 34, the child will place three 10's and four 1's; for 28 two 10's and eight 1's. Then have the child combine both groups of 1's; if there are enough to make a 10, make it and move it over to the tens' column. Combine both groups of 10. Record the problems worked on paper. If desired, give the player one point for each correct answer.

Variation: Use the grid to teach regrouping (borrowing) in subtraction problems. The grid can also be used to work two-place addition and subtraction problems that do not require regrouping.

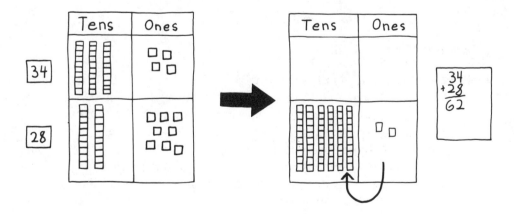

STORE ADDITION

Concept: Add sums of money.

Materials: Different canned goods (emptied from the bottoms).

Group size: Two to eight children.

Procedure: A small store can be arranged in the classroom. Each child might be given a certain amount of play money to make the game interesting. Each child goes shopping and must add up two or three items and state the total. The storekeeper should check for accuracy. Prices should be marked according to the level of the children. For young children, sums under 10 would be appropriate. If play money is used, practice in subtraction would also take place with making change.

ADDED ATTRACTION

Concept: Add sums to 20.

Materials: Gameboard (see diagram).

Markers.

Ten cards numbered 1 to 10.

Group size: Two children.

Procedure: Place one numbered card face up in the middle of the gameboard. Each child places a marker on start. A child begins by moving the marker one space and adding the number on the space to the number in the middle. If the child is correct he or she scores one point; if wrong, the child gets no points. Each child only moves one space forward during each turn. The winner is the one with the most points after both players have gone all the way around the track.

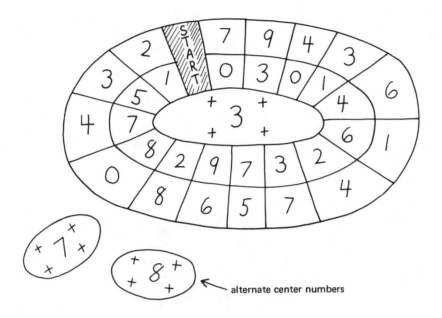

alternate center numbers

TOTAL THEM UP

Concept: Match addition facts with totals for sums to 20.

Materials: Gameboard marked with an even number of spaces, up to 20 spaces. Each space contains a numeral from 0 to 9 in a circle the size of chips used with the board.

Chips of one color.

Group size: Two to five children.

Procedure: Set up the gameboard with all the numerals covered with chips. One child thinks of a number that is less than 20 and tells it to the other players. That child then takes a turn uncovering two numbers and adding them. If the numbers total the chosen number, the child gets to keep the chips. Each child takes a turn voicing a number before turning over the chips. The game is played until all of the covers are removed.

④	①	⓪	⑧	⑨
②	⑤	①	③	④
⑦	④	⑥	②	⑤
⑧	⑤	⑨	⓪	⑧

MISSING ADDEND

Concept: Add sums to 18.

Materials: Two sets of cards marked 0 to 9.

Group size: Two to four children.

Procedure: Place cards in a deck facedown. One child picks two cards and looks at them. The child adds the card numbers and then shows only one card to the other children and tells them the sum of these two numbers. The children must guess the missing addend (the number that they cannot see). The first child who responds correctly gets to keep the cards. If the initial child gave a wrong sum for the two cards, he or she must return two cards to the deck. For example, if a child picked up a 4 and a 6, then he or she could show the 4 and say that the answer is 10. The others then try to figure out what the missing addend would be. However, if the child had given 4 and 11, then two of his or her cards should be returned to the deck.

Variation: Use this game with subtraction or multiplication.

OLD BACHELOR

Concept: Drill addition facts.

Materials: Deck of cards, half with addition problems and the other half with their corresponding answers plus one Old Bachelor card.

Group size: Two to six children.

Procedure: Shuffle and deal all the cards. In turns, each child picks one card from the player's hand to his or her left. When a player has a matching pair, the child places them face up. When all pairs have been matched, the player holding the Old Bachelor is the Old Bachelor!

COVER UP

Concept: Add sums to 12 recognizing possible sum combinations.

Materials: Gameboard (see diagram).

              Dice.

              Colored markers, a different color for each player.

Group size: Two to four children.

Procedure: Each player rolls the dice and adds to find the total. Using colored markers, the child covers those numerals that total the dice. If the child rolled an 8, 4 and 4 could be covered, or 6 and 2, etc. Once the numerals are covered, they belong to that child and cannot be used by anyone else. When the board is completely covered each child counts his or her markers. The one having the most markers is the winner.

Variation: (1) Instead of covering two numbers adding up to the total, the child can cover the total. If the child rolled 4 and 4, 8 could be covered. If 8 is already covered, the child can roll one die to add to the 8. (2) The game can also be played like tic-tac-toe, with the winner being the first child to get three markers in a row.

11	6	4	5	9	2
3	4	10	8	11	3
2	5	12	6	4	10
4	2	7	5	6	5
7	11	2	4	3	6
12	5	9	11	2	8
6	5	4	9	5	3
9	8	7	3	4	6

NUMBER BASEBALL

Concept: Addition facts with sums to 10.

Materials: A baseball gameboard.

Flashcards with addition problems to sums of 10.

Game markers.

Timer or watch with a second hand.

Group size: Two teams.

Procedure: One team is in the "field" while the other is at bat. The pitcher shows the flashcard to the first batter. The batter has an agreed upon amount of time in which to answer correctly (10 seconds at first). If the batter answers incorrectly, then a player in the field can attempt to answer the problem. If the field player answers correctly then the batter is out. Should the batter get the answer right, then a marker is advanced one base. Each correct answer for a batter moves him or her one more base until the child scores a run at which time the next batter takes a turn. The team with the most runs wins.

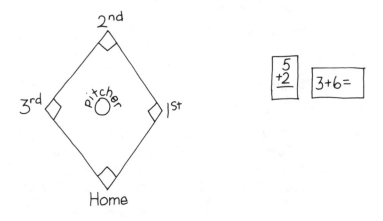

ADD AND GO FISH

Concept: Review addition facts.

Materials: Deck of cards minus the picture cards.

Group size: Two to four children.

Procedure: This game is played like the child's game "Fish." Deal out five cards and place the rest in a stack in the middle. One child asks another for a number. For example, if Joe asks Mike for a 7, Mike could give him a 7 or could give a 6 and a 1, a 4 and 3, etc. If Mike doesn't have a 7 or two cards that will combine to make a 7, he tells Joe to "go fish." Joe takes a card from the stack; if he gets a 7 he lays down his pair. If Mike gives Joe a 4 and a 3, Joe matches these cards with the cards from his hand that made 7 (say 2 and 5) and lays down the book of 7. When one player has played all the cards in his or her hand the game is over and that player is the winner.

HIGH ROLLER

Concept: Determine different facts for the same sum when the sun is less than or equal to 12.

Materials: Gameboards (see diagram).

        Dice.

        Enough markers for each child playing to cover a gameboard.

Group size: Two to four children.

Procedure: Each child is given a gameboard. The children take turns rolling the dice and covering that sum on the gameboard. An example would be a roll of 3 and 4. The sum is 7, so the child could cover any *other* combination with a sum of 7, such as 2, 5 (for 2 + 5) or 6, 1 (for 6 + 1).

7	3	7	4	2	9
3	10	5	11	9	6
5	6	2	8	7	10
4	8	7	12	12	11

RACE–A–RAMA

Concept: Review addition and subtraction facts up to 12.

Materials: Gameboard (see diagram).

        Markers.

        Two regular dice and one die marked with +'s and −'s.

Group size: Two to four children.

Procedure: Each child starts by placing a marker on the gameboard. One child rolls all three dice and makes a math sentence out of the numbers rolled. If the child rolls an addition sign, that child moves forward the sum; for a subtraction sign, the child moves backward the difference. The winner is the first person to make it around the gameboard in either direction.

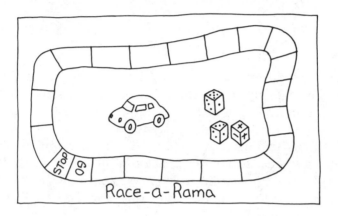

Race-a-Rama

SPINNER ADDITION

Concept: Review addition.

Materials: Spinner.

Group size: Two to six children.

Procedure: The children sit in a circle, each taking a turn spinning a number. The first child spins, then the second spins and adds his or her number to the first child's number. As each child spins, he or she must add the new number to the previous sum. A child who misses is out. Continue until there is a winner.

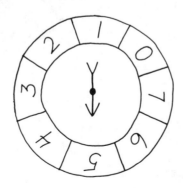

STACKING HAY

Concept: Determine different facts with the same sum where the sum is less than 12.

Materials: One barn for each player.

Two sets numbered 1 to 9 of cutouts of "bales."

Dice.

Group size: Two children.

Procedure: Give each child a barn. Spread the bales so that the numbers are face up in the middle of the playing area. Children take turns rolling the dice, counting their total, then finding the same total by adding the numbers on two bales. As a child finds two bales that add up to the same total as the dice, that child gets to put those bales in his or her barn. When all the bales are gone, the game is over and the winner is the one with the most bales in the barn. This procedure can be repeated over and over.

SUM–IT–UP

Concept: Add and subtract sums to 12.

Materials: Set of cards: four each 1 to 6, three each 6 to 8, two each 9 and 10, one each 11 and 12.

Gameboard (see diagram).

Group size: Two to four children.

Procedure: Deal the cards out equally. The first child lays a card under any number on the gameboard. The next child attempts to play a sum under two cards. For example, if the first child played a 4 under the 5, then the next child could play a 9 using addition (or a 1 using subtraction). If a child has the sum, he or she gets to keep the pair. If a child doesn't have the sum, he or she plays a card somewhere else (such as a 3 under the 11). The winner is the child with the greatest number of cards at the end of the game.

SUM-IT-UP											
1	2	3	4	5	6	7	8	9	10	11	12
				4							
				9							

ADDITION MOUNTAIN

Concept: Review addition facts.

Materials: Gameboard (see diagram).

Group size: Two to four children.

Procedure: Beginning at the foot of the mountain, the first child adds the two numbers and places the sum on the line (3 + 1 = 4). The next child places the sum of the 1 and the 6 on the line. Play continues until completely over the mountain. Using more than one mountain, teams may compete to see which one can cross the mountain fastest.

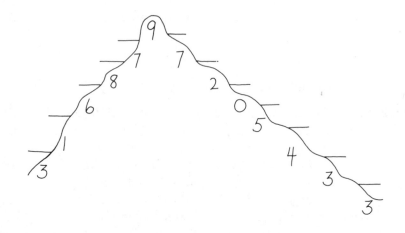

PINBALL

Concept: Add numbers to 500.

Materials: Shoebox top.

               Chip or marker.

Group size: Two to four children.

Procedure: The first child puts a chip on start and pushes it with a finger. The child then adds the number that the chip lands on to the total. The first one with a score over 500 wins. If the chip doesn't land on a score, the player may "shoot" again, but only two tries are allowed on each turn.

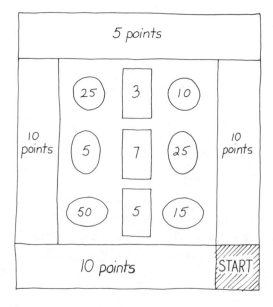

CHAPTER 11

Place Value

11.1 Introduction

Special attention is devoted to developing a conceptual understanding of place value as it is extremely important in work with borrowing in subtraction. It is no less important in addition; however, the borrowing involved in subtraction seems to require a better understanding of place value because it is more difficult to decompose a number than to increment it. The chapter sections are sequenced to develop understanding through introduction with concrete materials and consistent modeling.

11.2 Readiness activities with place value

Most of the activities in this section are of the "chip trading" variety. Initially, the focus is on the idea that one object can represent many of another object. In our number system, one position represents tenfold of the position on its immediate right.

Bottlecap trading is hard when you throw a zero.

BOTTLECAP SWAP

Concept: Exchange three tokens for a token of higher value.

Materials: Three different types of bottlecaps.

One die (numbered 0, 1, 2, 2, 3, 4).

Color coded gameboards, one per player (except the swapper).

Group size: Two to five children.

Procedure: Assign one player to be the "swapper." The swapper controls the giving and swapping of all the bottlecaps. Each of the other players begins with a blank gameboard. Designate each type of bottlecap a value. For example, each orange soda pop cap is worth one point, each root beer is worth three orange caps, each lemon lime is worth three root beer caps.

Each player rolls the die, receives that number of orange caps from the swapper and places the caps in his or her orange space (located at the right end of the gameboard). If the player has three orange caps, he or she gives them to the swapper in exchange for one root beer cap. When the player has three root beer caps, they are exchanged for one lemon-lime cap. Players continue to take turns rolling the die, collecting orange caps and swapping them for root beer and lemon-lime caps. The first player to accumulate ten lemon-lime caps wins.

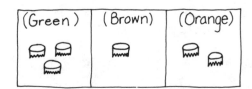

MONSTER FINGERS

Concept: Group objects by 10's.

Materials: Small objects to slip over fingers, 20 per child: rubber fingernails, thimbles, wide-necked balloons, plastic rings.

Tokens or small monster cutouts.

One regular or numbered die.

Group size: Small group.

Procedure: Start the game with all materials in the center of the table. Players will make a monster each time they win ten fingers.

In turns, each player rolls the die, takes as many finger covers as indicated, and slips them on his or her fingers. When the player's fingers are full of ten rings, they are exchanged for a monster cutout. At the end of the game the player with the most monsters wins.

Variation: Use toy rings and picture playing cards to make kings and queens.

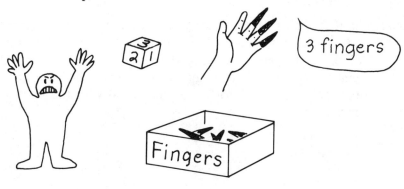

FIVE-BEAD BRACELETS

Concept: Group objects by 5's.

Materials: Lacing beads and strings.

Spinner or die.

Group size: Small group.

Procedure: Give each child a lacing string and tell the children that they are going to make bead bracelets. Each child spins the spinner, takes that number of beads, and strings them. Play continues around the table. When a string has five beads, the bracelet is finished and the player begins a new one. At the end of the game have each child tell how many bead bracelets he or she has made.

CHIPS

Concept: Group objects by 10's.

Materials: Poker chips.

Card deck with picture cards removed.

Group size: Small group.

Procedure: Shuffle the cards and place them face down in the center of the table. In turn, each child draws a card and wins that number of chips. Players must stack their chips in piles of ten. At the end of the game check the stacks. Any which do not have exactly ten must be forfeited. The child with the most stacks of ten wins.

TELEPHONE 10'S

Concept: Group objects by 10's.

Materials: Small chips or beans.

Spinner or dice.

Telephone cutouts with dialing holes marked, one per player.

Ditto sheets containing ten telephone outlines apiece.

Crayons.

Group size: Small group.

Procedure: Give each player a telephone cutout, a ditto sheet, and a crayon. Keep the chips in the center of the table. Tell the children that they are working in a telephone factory. Their job is to put the holes in the dials. Taking turns, each child spins a number, takes that many beans, and places each one in a dial space on his or her telephone cutout. When all ten spaces are filled, the child has made a telephone: the child removes the beans and colors one phone on the ditto sheet. Continue until all children have colored at least a few telephones. At the end, ask each child how many telephone "10's" were made.

POPCORN

Concept: Group objects by 10's.

Materials: Small paper bags, each marked "Ten."

Popped popcorn.

Play money dimes (optional).

Dice, regular or marked with numerals.

Group size: Small group.

Procedure: Tell the children that they are going to make bags of popcorn to "sell." Taking turns, each rolls the dice and takes that number of popcorn pieces. When a child has ten pieces, they are put in a bag marked "Ten." Each bag of ten may be exchanged with the storekeeper for a dime (optional). After all children have had several turns, ask each to tell how many "popcorn 10's" he or she made.

11.3   Place value involving 10's and 1's

The activities in this section focus on representing a number using concrete models based on the positional value of the system. Although values are increasing or decreasing in some of the activities, the operations (addition, subtraction) are not the objective, but rather the effect that these increases/decreases have on the values of the positions and their numerical representatives.

CUBE NUMBERS

Concept: Determine the 10's and 1's in any two-digit number.

Materials: Cards numbered from 10 to 99.

Snap-together cubes.

Paper bag.

Ditto sheets, chart paper, or chalkboard.

Group size: One to six children.

Procedure: Mix the numbered cards in a bag and let each child draw a number. Have the child count and take as many cubes as his or her card indicates. Then show the child how to take ten cubes and snap them together to make a "10." Ask the child to continue making as many 10's as possible. When finished, the child can tell you how many 10's and how many 1's that number made.

Record the number, the 10's, and the 1's on ditto sheets or the chalkboard.

Note: At first, keep the numbers below 50 for easier manipulation and eliminate zeroes to avoid the confusion that they can cause.

Variation: Use popsicle sticks or toothpicks and rubberbands instead of cubes.

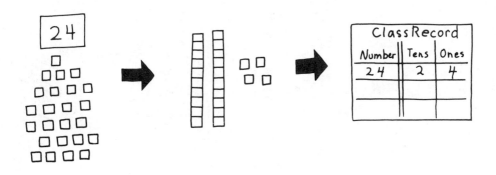

ROLL 'EM NUMBERS

Concept: Determine the 10's and 1's in any two-digit number.

Materials: Two regular dice or inch cubes marked with numbers 1, 2, 3, 4, 5, 6.

Snap-together cubes or popsicle sticks with rubberbands.

Ditto sheets, chart paper, or chalkboard.

Group size: One to six children.

Procedure: Designate one die as the "10's die" and the other as the "1's die." Have each child roll both dice and record the results on the record sheet. Then the child selects as many 10's and 1's from the pile as the dice indicate, counts all the cubes and tells and records what number they make.

Note: The activity proceeds more smoothly if a large pile of 10's and 1's has been made beforehand.

MAKING 10'S

Concept: Identify the meaning of "1's" and "10's."

Materials: Snap-together cubes or rubberbands and popsicle sticks, toothpicks, or rods.

Group size: One to six children.

Procedure: Show the children a single cube. Tell them it is a "1." Ask everyone to hold up a "1."

Next show them how to count out ten cubes and snap them together; call this a "10." Ask everyone to make a 10. Check for accuracy.

Let the children race each other to see who can make the most 10's in a period of time or until all possible cubes have been used. Each child can tell the others how many he or she made. Give direction such as, "Jose, hold up three 10's. Shonda, show me five 1's."

GUESSTIMATE ESTIMATE

Concept: Make two-digit numbers and recognize their value.

Materials: Cards numbered 0 to 9 with two or three cards of each number.

Group size: Two to six children.

Procedure: Deal two cards to each child. Tell each child to make a two-digit number with the cards. Each child then states whether his or her number will be the largest or the smallest. Children continue to hold their cards so that no one else can see them until all children playing have declared. Next all the children lay down their cards to find out whose predictions for the largest and the smallest two-digit numbers were correct. Give a point to the children who guessed correctly.

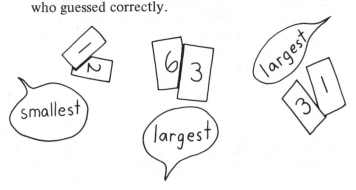

11.4   Place value involving 100's

This section extends the activities of the last section to include the 1,000's position. The teacher should refer back to activities in the last section and modify many of those for use with the 1,000's position. Likewise, if positions beyond 1,000's are desired, then many of these activities lend themselves to modification.

LEAPFROG 10'S

Concept: Use an abacus to show regrouping of 1's to 10's.

Materials: Abacuses, one per player (the abacus must have beads in rows of ten).

Two dice, each marked 0, 1, 2, 3, 4, 5.

Group size: Two to four children.

Procedure: Position each abacus on a stable surface to prevent jostling and push all beads to one side of the abacus. Each player takes a turn rolling the dice and pushing that number of beads in the first row across to the opposite side of the abacus. After all players have rolled and pushed beads for their *first* row, all roll again and push the rolled number of beads across in their *second* row. Continue rolling the dice and pushing the beads until all rows have been done for each player. Remember that for each roll of the dice a new row of beads is manipulated.

Next each player regroups his or her beads to see how many 10's he or she can make. For example, if the player's first three rows show 8, 6, and 9 beads, that child can "leapfrog" two beads from the second row to the first row to make a 10. (Do this by pushing two beads from the second row back to the start position and immediately pushing the corresponding two beads in the first row across to join the other eight beads.) On his or her next turn the child can "leapfrog" six beads from the third row to the second row to make another 10. Continue until all players have made as many 10's as they can. The winner is the player with the most leapfrog 10's.

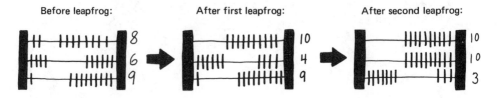

Before leapfrog: After first leapfrog: After second leapfrog:

CUT–AND–PASTE 10'S

Concept: Show the 10's and 1's in any two-digit number.

Materials: Duplicated worksheet (see diagram).

Scissors.

Glue or paste.

Group size: Class.

Procedure: Mark four or five spaces on a worksheet and write a two-digit numeral in each space. At the bottom of the worksheet put a cutout section of 10's and 1's.

To complete the worksheet, the child cuts out the correct number of 10's and 1's to illustrate each number and pastes them in the appropriate spaces.

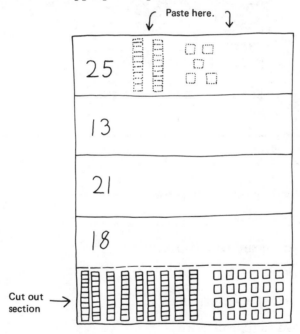

BLUE CHIPS–THE BEST

Concept: Group objects involving 10's and 100's.

Materials: Poker chips in three colors.

Gameboard (see diagram).

Spinner or dice.

Group size: Two to four children.

Procedure: Each child takes a turn spinning. The child may only take white chips with which to start. When the child gets ten whites the child may trade them in for one red. When the child gets ten reds, the reds can be traded for one blue. The winner is first who gets nine blues.

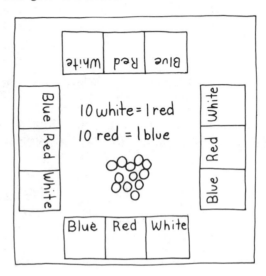

POTLUCK

Concept: Regroup objects to show 10's and 100's.

Materials: Three colors of poker chips.

Gameboard with two spinners.

Pot for chips.

Bank of exchange chips.

Group size: Two to six children.

Procedure: Each child begins with nine of the ones-unit chips, nine of the tens-unit chips and two of the hundreds-unit chips. One spinner should be used for the 1's while the other is used for the 10's. Have a pot of chips in the middle of the gameboard, and, as each child spins, he or she will remove the correct number of chips. For example, if a child spins one 10 and four 1's, the child takes 14 one-unit chips, then asks to "cash in" some chips. Assign one child as a banker who can cash in chips from the bank. The game is played until the pot is empty.

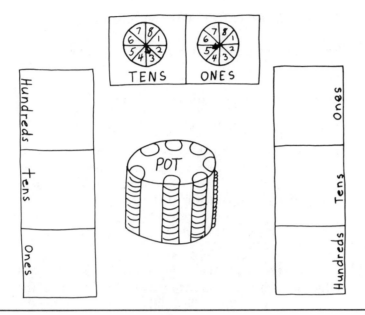

MONEY CHANGER

Concept: Exchange money for next higher unit using pennies, dimes, and dollars.

Materials: One red die and one blue die.

Play money—pennies, dimes, dollars.

Group size: Two to four children.

Procedure: One child is appointed money changer. The red die represents 10's (dimes) and the blue die 1's (pennies). Children take turns rolling the dice. The money changer gives each child the correct number of dimes and pennies indicated by the roll of the dice. The child then checks to see whether there are enough pennies or dimes to trade in to the money changer.

One important rule is that a child must cash in his or her money for the next higher unit. A player should never have over nine of a particular unit.

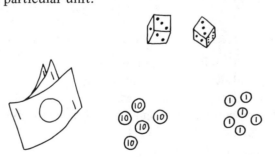

STRETCHED–OUT NUMBERS

Concept: Express number in expanded form and vice versa.

Materials: Large cards marked 0, 1, –, 9, 10, 20, –, 90, 100, 200, –, 900.

        Deck of small cards marked 50 to 999.

Group size: Small group of two teams.

Procedure: The large cards are placed along the chalk tray at the front of the room. A child draws a card from the small deck (say, 234). That child then goes to the board and arranges the cards to reflect the expanded form of the number.

| 200 | | 30 | | 4 |

This activity builds the child's confidence in understanding the value of each of the digits in their places; that is, the 4 tells the number of units, the 3 the number of 10's and the 2 the number of 100's. Later the child will understand the value of the places well enough to begin with the 2 (100's position).

Variation: The teacher says the numbers and the child must construct the number.

| 675 | | 600 | | 70 | | 5 |

11.5   Computation involving place value

These activities utilize symbols rather than values or materials to represent value in the positions. The teacher can generate many more of these activities if desired, but these three have been found to be quite useful.

FILL 'ER UP 10'S

Concept: Regroup ten units of volume into one ten of volume.

Materials: Two tall, thin jars (like olive jars).
        Two tall, wide jars (like pickle jars).
        Rice, cornmeal, sand, or water.
        One or two identical small cups for measuring.
        One or two dice marked 1, 2, 3, 4, 3, 2.
        Marking pen.

Group size: Small groups.

Procedure: On the tall, thin jars mark the level resulting from pouring in ten measuring cups of rice or water. On the wide jars mark the level resulting from pouring in ten thin jars of rice or water. (Marking each level of measure, not just the top level, is recommended.)

Divide the group into two teams that will race to see which team fills up its wide (10's) jar first. In turn, each team player rolls a die and pours that number of measuring cups into the thin jar. When it reaches its ten-cup mark, pour its contents into the larger jar and begin again. The first team to make its ten 10's (fill up its large jar) wins.

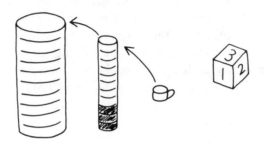

OVER THE HILL ON 50

Concept: Make a number of value near 50.

Materials: Cards numbered 1 to 9.

Place value boards with 10's and 1's (two sets).

Group size: Two children.

Procedure: Children take five turns drawing cards. As each draws a card it is placed either on the 1's or 10's, but once a card is placed it cannot be moved. The object is to try to get as close to 50 as possible. The one who must go over 50 loses.

Tens	Ones
2	8
1	9
	4

51!
Over the
hill!

999

Concept: Utilize place value to constitute numbers and perform column addition.

Materials: Three spinners.

Gameboard (see diagram).

Markers.

Group size: Two to four children.

Procedure: Have different colored spinners, one marked 1's, one 10's, and one marked 100's. On the gameboard have the units colored the same as their spinner. On the first round each child takes turns spinning all three spinners and then marks his or her progress on all three columns of the gameboard. Additional turns entail adding the newly spun numbers to the previous score. The winner is the first to reach 999.

Hundreds   Tens   Ones

WINNER		
9	9	9
8	8	8
7	7	7
6	6	6
5	5	5
4	4	4
3	3	3
2	2	2
1	1	1
O	O	O
Hundreds	Tens	Ones

CHAPTER 12

Subtraction

12.1 Introduction

Mathematical theory develops subtraction as the inverse operation of addition. It seems to be in vogue in the curriculum to present subtraction facts as the "opposite" of addition facts. Proponents and opponents of this approach justify their viewpoints including better pupil understanding of both operations and their inverse relationship in their arguments. However, pupil performance has not substantiated either conclusion. It seems that before a *relationship* can be well understood each of the components (operations) must be useful knowledge for the pupil. Subtraction facts should be introduced with modeled activities similar to those used with addition. Once subtraction is understood, the inverse relationship between addition and subtraction can be investigated. After a child learns the subtraction facts involving numbers to 5, it may be wise to develop the relationship of addition and subtraction. However, at the beginning, subtraction facts should be generated using real world examples, modeled concretely, and the facts internalized through practice. Once the facts are learned, the interrelationship of the operations can be presented and probably understood. The subtraction fact

$$\overset{\text{minuend}}{\searrow 5} - \overset{\text{subtrahend}}{3} \quad = \overset{\text{difference}}{2}$$

has a *minuend* of 5, *subtrahend* of 3, and a *difference* of 2.

Subtraction facts with minuends up to and including 5 should be learned first, then minuends less than or equal to 10, and last minuends to 18. The special case of subtracting zero should be timed to be introduced when your textbook series introduces subtraction with zero; different series introduce this work at different points in the curriculum. It is difficult for the child to work with a set of zero due to the fact that the concrete model contains no objects and the child in the concrete mode of learning views the set as not existing unless objects are present. This dilemma is difficult to deal with, but realizing that the problem exists gives the teacher one step up on those teachers not realizing that the problem exists. The reasonable remedy seems to be to delay work with the special case (empty set) until the child has had some successful experience with the subtraction operation.

The teacher should review activities in the addition chapter to determine those games that could apply to the subtraction operation using the same materials.

12.2   Subtraction fact activities

The reader is referred to the introduction to fact work with addition as most of those points are appropriate in introducing this section.

The activities in this section may involve the special case of zero, but the teacher should modify the activity should the children not be ready for its inclusion.

COUNT ENCOUNTERS

Concept: Drill subtraction facts.

Materials: Inch cubes.

Card deck of subtraction facts (minuend of 10 or less).

Group size: Two children.

Procedure: Each child is given ten cubes. The children sit facing each other. One child turns over the top card on the deck and the other child works the problem. In working the problem, the child may use blocks to generate the fact or recall it from memory. If correct, the child keeps the card; if incorrect, the card is returned to the deck.

$$6 - 2 = \square$$

SUBTRACTION FISH

Concept: Drill subtraction facts.

Materials: Pairs of cards, a subtraction sentence on one card and the correct answer on the other card.

Group size: Two to six children.

Procedure: Shuffle the cards and deal five to each player. Spread the remaining cards face down in a "pool" in the middle. Each child takes a turn drawing a fish from the pool and tries to make a pair. If a pair can be made, the player lays the cards face up; if not, the player must return one card to the pool. The winner is the player with the most pairs when all plays have been made.

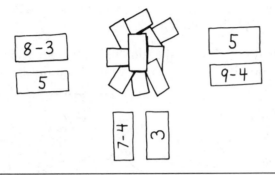

MATCH THE SOCKS

Concept: Drill subtraction facts.

Materials: Pairs of tagboard socks, each pair showing a subtraction problem and its answer.

                Spring-type clothespins or paper clips.

Group size: One to four children.

Procedure: Have a child or children "sort" the socks, clipping each problem to the correct answer.

PUZZLING PUZZLES

Concept: Drill subtraction facts.

Materials: Puzzle.

                Board on which to assemble puzzle with pieces outlined (optional).

Group size: Small group.

Procedure: Make a puzzle from a magazine picture by glueing it to cardboard and then cutting it into pieces, or use a commercially made puzzle. Mark the back of each puzzle piece with a subtraction problem. Mix the pieces in a box and let the children take turns drawing a puzzle piece. If the child gives the correct answer, he or she lays the piece in place. Play continues until the puzzle is complete.

Variation: Divide the children into two teams, each with its own puzzle, and race to see which team finishes its puzzle first.

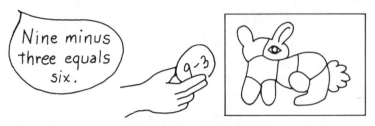

SPOT THE LEOPARD

Concept: Drill subtraction facts.

Materials: Gameboard with spotted leopard.

Circular playing cards, the same size as the leopard's spots, showing subtraction problems.

Group size: Two to six children.

Procedure: Number the spots on the leopard to correspond with the correct answers to the subtraction problems. Deal an equal number of spot cards to each player; set aside the remainder. Taking turns, players try to match their problem spots to the correct answer spots on the leopard. If a player places a spot incorrectly, it must be taken back and the player loses a turn. The winner is the first player to place all his or her spots correctly.

SHAKE UP

Concept: Subtraction with numbers less than 10.

Materials: Styrofoam hamburger box.

               Number sheet.

               Navy beans.

               Bag.

Group size: Two to four children.

Procedure: Glue the number sheet in the bottom of the hamburger box. Place two beans in the box. Then each child takes a turn closing and shaking the box. Then the box is opened and the numbers that the beans land on are used in a subtraction problem. (The smaller number is always subtracted from the larger one.) The game can be played as often as time allows. Each child should record the result of each subtraction and take that number of beans from the bag. At the end of the game, the winner is the child with the fewest beans. (Notice that this can provide skill maintenance with place value as the child uses groupings of 10's and 1's when keeping track of the beans.)

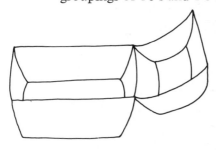

2	9	5	10	9	5	10	6
1	10	0	4	1	4	6	8
10	6	7	9	3	8	8	7
6	7	9	2	1	5	10	2
4	10	2	3	2	7	8	3
1	5	5	8	9	4	3	2
8	3	4	9	3	6	1	7
2	1	7	0	3	4	10	9

CLIMB UP OR DOWN THE LADDER

Concept: Compute using addition or subtraction.

Materials: Three spinners: two with numerals, one with +'s and –'s.

               Markers.

               Ladder gameboard (see diagram).

Group size: Two to six children.

Procedure: Each child begins at the bottom of the ladder. The child spins all three spinners and forms a math problem. If the problem is addition the child moves up the ladder two rungs. If it is subtraction, the child moves one rung down. If the child gives an incorrect answer, he or she moves two rungs down. The winner is the one who gets all the way to the top. Give an example of the marker movement before the game starts.

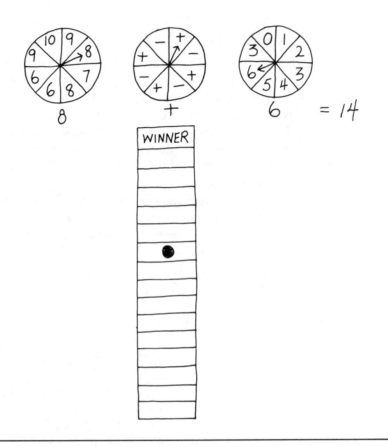

SOMETHING IS MISSING

Concept: Find the missing subtrahend in subtraction problems.

Materials: Two spinners on a gameboard (see diagram).

Answer cards, each marked with a numeral.

Group size: Two to four children.

Procedure: Position the spinners on the gameboard as in the drawing. The child spins both spinners and then must identify the *minuend* from the *subtrahend* and the *product*. The correct answer card is then placed on the gameboard. If you would like this game to be self-checking, write all possible problem combinations with any given minuend on the back of the answer card.

Variation: Move the spinners to different positions and change the sign to use the board for addition or multiplication.

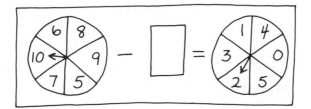

FOOTBALL

Concept: Drill with facts involving addition and subtraction.

Materials: Markers.

Football gameboard.

A deck of cards (each card has a subtraction problem).

Group size: Two to four children.

Procedure: Each team starts on the 50-yard line. The first team takes a turn drawing a card and answering the problem. If the child answers correctly the team moves 10 yards forward, if incorrectly 5 yards backward. To maintain "control" of the ball, the team must answer three out of four questions correctly. When the first team makes two consecutive errors, the other team gains control of the ball and begins drawing cards and answering. The team with the most touchdowns in the allotted time wins.

Variation: Include a die marked "+" or "−." When the die reads +, the ball moves forward; − indicates backward movement. When the child responds correctly, move 10 yards forward if die is + or 5 yards backward if the die is −. If the answer is incorrect move 10 yards backward.

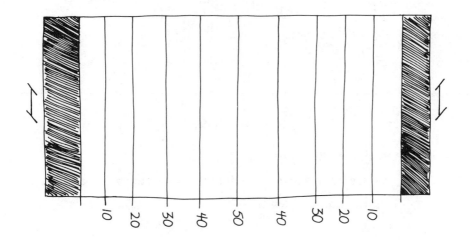

TREEHOUSE

Concept: Drill subtraction facts.

Materials: Gameboard and four markers or chalkboard and chalk.

Cards with subtraction problems.

Group size: Two to four children or teams.

Procedure: Draw a tree with a treehouse and four ladders. Each ladder should have the same number of rungs. Place the markers at the bottom of the ladders. Shuffle the cards and place them face down in a pile. In turn, each player takes a card and states the answer. If correct, the player moves a marker up one rung. The first player or team to reach the treehouse wins.

SECRET CODE

Concept: Review subtraction work.

Materials: A code book assigning each number a letter of the alphabet.

Subtraction problems.

Group size: Class.

Procedure: Assign number values to each letter such as a–1, b–2, c–3, etc. Put this in the code book. Give a series of subtraction problems to the children that when worked and translated in the code book will yield a message. The diagram is an example of this exercise. If the child solves the puzzle, he or she should receive some sort of reward.

Variation: Addition or multiplication problems could be used in place of subtraction.

$$
\begin{array}{c}
2 \\ -1 \\ \hline 1 \\ A
\end{array}
\quad
\begin{array}{cccccc}
18 & 13 & 8 & 10 & 15 \\
-2 & -4 & -3 & -7 & -10 \\
\hline
16 & 9 & 5 & 3 & 5 \\
P & I & E & C & E
\end{array}
\quad
\begin{array}{cc}
16 & 9 \\
-1 & -3 \\
\hline
15 & 6 \\
O & F
\end{array}
$$

$$
\begin{array}{ccccc}
22 & 23 & 12 & 9 & 26 \\
-2 & -5 & -5 & -8 & -6 \\
\hline
20 & 18 & 7 & 1 & 20 \\
T & R & E & A & T
\end{array}
\quad
\begin{array}{cc}
12 & 21 \\
-3 & -2 \\
\hline
9 & 19 \\
I & S
\end{array}
\quad
\begin{array}{cc}
18 & 20 \\
-3 & -6 \\
\hline
15 & 14 \\
O & N
\end{array}
$$

$$
\begin{array}{ccc}
21 & 14 & 10 \\
-1 & -6 & -5 \\
\hline
20 & 8 & 5 \\
T & H & E
\end{array}
\quad
\begin{array}{cccc}
7 & 10 & 19 & 22 \\
-3 & -5 & -0 & -11 \\
\hline
4 & 5 & 19 & 11 \\
D & E & S & K
\end{array}
$$

COUNT DOWN

Concept: Subtract one- and two-digit numbers.

Materials: Gameboard (see diagram).

Two dice.

Four markers.

Group size: Two children.

Procedure: Both players start at 100 on the gameboard. The first player rolls the dice and adds the two numbers. That player then subtracts this number from 100 and places one marker on 10's place and one on the 1's. For example, to make 89 one marker would be on the 80 and one marker on the 9. Each child takes a turn until a player reaches zero.

START	
100	9
90	8
80	7
70	6
60	5
50	4
40	3
30	2
20	1
10	0

---

100 DOWN

Concept: Practice subtraction with two-digit numbers with occasional borrowing.

Materials: Pencil.

Paper.

One die marked in red with 1, 2, 3, 1, 2, 3, on faces.

One die marked in green with 2, 3, 0, 2, 4, 1 on faces.

Group size: One to three children.

Procedure: Beginning with 100, the child throws the dice and constitutes a number using the red die for the 10's digit and the green die for the 1's value. The child then subtracts the number thrown from the 100, yielding a new number. The child then repeats the procedure and subtracts the number from the last result. Players take turns in rotation, and the first child to reach zero wins. The player does not have to score zero exactly; for instance, if the child has a score of 23 and throws 34, then he or she has wiped out the 23 and is assumed to have zero left.

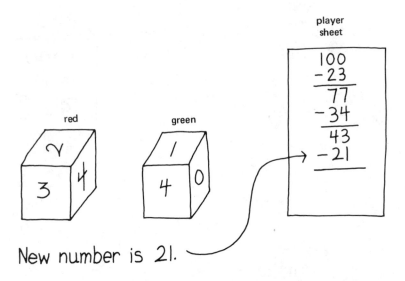

New number is 21.

ZERO WINS

Concept: Practice subtraction with two-digit numbers involving borrowing from the 100's and 10's places.

Materials: Pencil.

Paper.

One die marked in red with 1, 2, 3, 7, 8, 9.

One die marked in green with 6, 7, 8, 5, 8, 1.

Group size: One to three children.

Procedure: The child begins with 1,000. The child throws the dice and constitutes a number that is subtracted from his or her score. The number is constituted with the red die representing the 10's digit and the green die the 1's digit. The number is then subtracted, and the new score is used on the player's next turn. The first player to reach a score less than 10 wins.

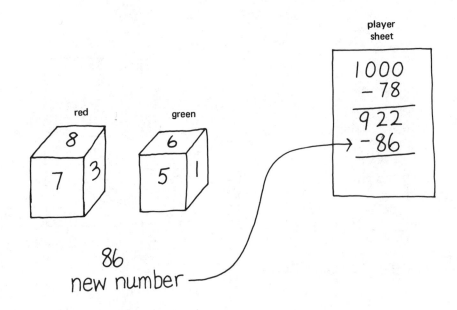

CHAPTER **13**

Multiplication

13.1   Introduction

Multiplication facts should be systematically introduced, generated, and internalized. When generating the facts, you should model them using real world examples of sets of equal number. Special note should be made regarding the use of 1 and 0 as factors.

First, the use of 1 (one) as a factor violates the model of putting together (unioning, if you will) sets of equal number. For example, the model of $2 \times 3 = \square$ is

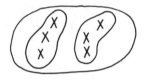

Two groups of three

However, the model of $1 \times 3 = \square$ is

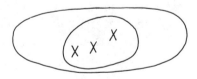

The child is faced with a single set, although the operation means unioning multiple sets of equal number. Suffice it to say that this special case causes some children difficulty.

The use of 0 (zero) as a factor only increases the difficulty. The use of the empty set with concrete learners is a contradiction from the beginning. Assuming for the moment that the child comprehends the empty set, consider modeling $3 \times 0 = \square$

3 x 0 =

Three sets of zeros yields zero

The model is consistent, but what about

0 x 3 = □

Zero sets of three

This fact cannot be modeled, and it is suggested that some discussion involving money and people be used to generate the fact. For instance, 3 x 0 = □ could be interpreted as three people with zero dollars yields zero dollars. Then the next fact 0 x 3 = □ would be $3 given to zero people yields zero dollars altogether. Needless to say, work with these special cases should be delayed until the child understands the multiplication operation and has been successful with it. The introduction of special cases should be timed to introduction in your text series as different series approach the special cases at different times in the curriculum.

13.2   Multiplication fact activities

The reader is referred to the introduction of the fact work with addition, as the same basic comments apply to multiplication. Activities from both addition and subtraction chapters should be reviewed to obtain additional games that could be used with multiplication. If special cases are used in activities in this section, the teacher should include the facts only if the children are ready; otherwise drop them from use and play the game with the remaining facts.

BUNNY HOP

Concept: Represent multiplication concept pictorially.

Materials: Tagboard for number line (contact paper to cover).

Blank playing cards with facts and concepts (see diagram).

Group size: Three to five children.

Procedure: A player's card is constructed by cutting a piece of cardboard (or tagboard) long enough to draw a number line of length 30.

The deck is made up of two types of cards: multiplication fact cards and multiplication concept cards (as indicated below). All cards are shuffled together and placed face down in the middle of the table. The child turns the top card face up and responds according to the type of card drawn (see diagram). If correct, the child scores a point. Play proceeds until the deck is exhausted. The child with the most points wins.

The deck can consist of those facts the teacher decides to include. At first use 2 and 5 facts, then include 3, 4, and 1 facts. It is difficult to use this with facts beyond 5's due to the length of the number line necessary. It is also of questionable importance at that point.

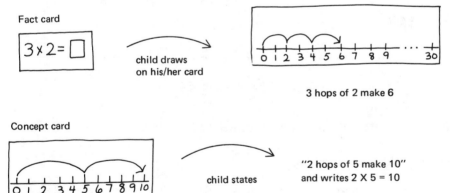

Fact card

3 x 2 = □

child draws on his/her card

3 hops of 2 make 6

Concept card

child states

"2 hops of 5 make 10" and writes 2 X 5 = 10

MULTIPLICATION TRAIN

Concept: Use cubes to show multiplication problems.

Materials: Inch cubes, snap cubes, or snap beads.

Cards with multiplication problems.

Group size: Two teams.

Procedure: Shuffle the cards and place them face down in a pile. A player from the first team pulls the top card, reads it, and makes an array of cubes to show the problem. If correct, the child uses those cubes to begin building the team's train. Teams alternate drawing cards, making arrays, and adding the cubes to their trains. An incorrect display forfeits the cubes and that team's turn. At the end of play the team with the longest train wins.

correct display

team train

LEAPFROG TIMES

Concept: Use abacus to compute multiplication facts.

Materials: Abacuses, one per player.

Cards with multiplication problems (1 X 1 to 5 X 5).

Group size: Small group or class.

Procedure: Show the first player a multiplication problem, for example, 5 x 3. The player displays five rows of three beads on an abacus. At the cue, "leapfrog," the player exchanges beads from one row to the next as many times as possible to consolidate them (into 10's and 1's) and then states the product. A correct answer earns one point. The winner is the player with the most points.

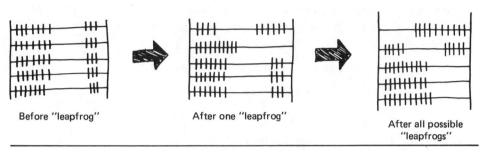

| Before "leapfrog" | After one "leapfrog" | After all possible "leapfrogs" |

SAMMY SNAKE

Concept: Match addition, subtraction, or multiplication problems with the correct models.

Materials: Snake puzzle (see diagram).

Group size: Two to four children.

Procedure: Cut out the snake so each piece will fit only in its correct spot. Have the children assemble the snake. Problems can be all of one type or a selection of different operations. Have the problems at an appropriate level for your children.

Each piece should have a problem written symbolically and the answer to a problem presented pictorially.

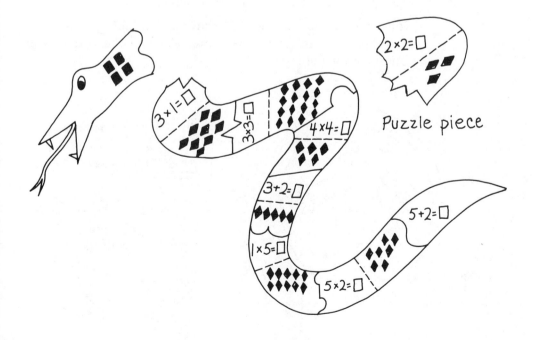

Puzzle piece

MULTIPLICATION ROBOT

Concept: Drill multiplication facts.

Materials: Two heavy cardboard or tagboard circles at least 10″ in diameter (pizza wheels are excellent for this—cut a 1″ border off one wheel).

    Colored felt-tipped markers.

    Brass brad paper fastener.

    Cloth, cellophane, or masking tape (optional).

Group size: One child or small group.

Procedure: To construct, draw a robot on one pizza wheel as illustrated. Cut out the eyes and nose; cut around the mouth partially so it can be lifted up. (Reinforce the fold line with tape if desired.) Note that the smaller the robot's head, the more problems will fit inside. Place the robot circle over the blank circle and attach them together at the center with the paper fastener. In the eye blanks, write two multipliers (3, 5); under the nose, the sign (×); and under the mouth, the correct answer. Turn the wheel slightly and continue writing problems until the circle is full.

To use, the child looks at the multiplication problem and says the answer. To self-check, the child lifts the mouth for the correct answer. If used as a group game, the children can alternate turns and earn a point for each correct answer. Many problem wheels can be made and interchanged.

Note: Wheels can be made for addition and subtraction as well as for practice in mixed operations (be sure the correct sign appears in the nose space).

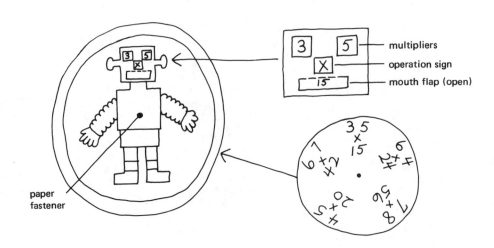

DEALER'S CHOICE

Concept: Multiply two numbers less than 10.

Materials: Multiplication flash cards.

Answer cards.

Group size: Three or more children.

Procedure: One child holds all the flash cards. The answer cards are spread out so all of the other children playing can see them. The child holding the flashcards will flip one card over at a time. The other children try to find the answer. The first child to find the answer card gets to keep it. The child having the most answer cards at the end of the game is the winner.

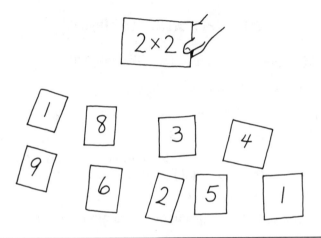

HOCKEY

Concept: Drill multiplication facts.

Materials: Hockey gameboard marked with central starting space and an equal number of spaces to each goal.

Two chips, coins, or other "pucks."

Flash cards with multiplication problems.

Die or spinner marked 1, 2, 3, 1, 1, 2.

Group size: Small group or class.

Procedure: Divide the group into two teams. Shuffle the cards and place them face down in a pile. Place both pucks on start. Players alternate choosing a card and saying the answer; if correct, the die is thrown to see how many spaces the puck advances. The team scoring the most goals wins.

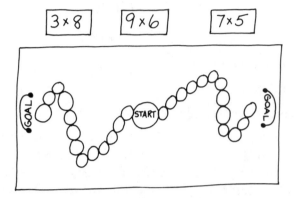

MULTIPLICATION DOMINOES

Concept: Multiply numbers matching like products.

Materials: Cardboard dominoes (at least 30).

Group size: Two to six children.

Procedure: Each child picks five dominoes. The rest of the dominoes go in a bone pile. The first child lays out any domino he or she wishes; the next child must lay a domino that has the same product as the first.

Variation: Use addition or subtraction dominoes.

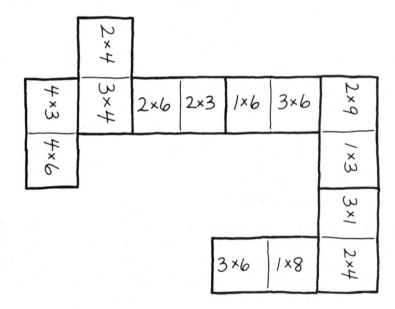

TIC–TAC–TIMES

Concept: Drill multiplication facts.

Materials: Gameboard with tic-tac-toe grid, one per pair of players.

Cards with multiplication problems (mark 0 on back of half of the deck and X on back of other half).

Group size: Two, four, six children or more.

Procedure: Shuffle the X cards and the 0 cards separately. Let one player have X's and the other 0's. In turn, each draws a card; if answering correctly, the player may place the card on the grid. If incorrect, the player must return the card to the bottom of the pile and lose a turn. Continue until one player makes three marks in a row.

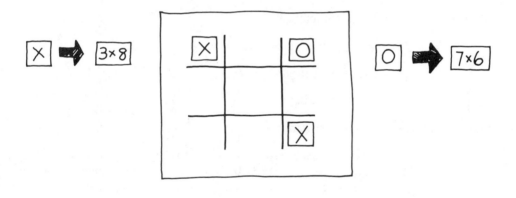

FROGS IN THE LILIES

Concept: Drill multiplication facts.

Materials: Plastic or posterboard mat with lily pads.

Two beanbag "frogs."

Group size: Small group or a class.

Procedure: Number the lily pads. Divide the children into two teams. In turn, each player tosses the frogs onto two lily pads, multiplies the two numbers, and states the answer. If correct, score a point for the team. Continue the game as long as desired. The team with the most points wins (and may hop about saying "Ribbet, ribbet").

RING TOSS

Concept: Review multiplication facts.

Materials: Pipe cleaners twisted into rings.

Dowel rods on a target board.

Score sheet (see diagram).

Group size: Two to five children.

Procedure: Each child throws two rings and multiplies the two numbers they land on, then records the score on the score sheet. Tossed rings that miss the dowels can be assigned a number value, i.e., each miss equals 2. Every child has five turns and adds the numbers of these turns together for a final score. The player with the most points wins.

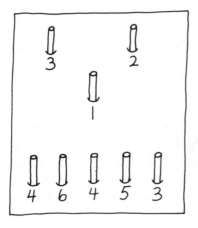

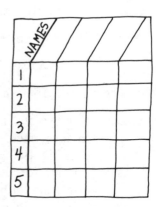

WIPE OUT

Concept: Multiply two numbers less than 10.

Materials: Cards with multiplication problems or multiplication flash cards.

Gameboards (see diagram).

Markers.

Group size: Four to six children.

Procedure: Each child should have a playing board and some markers. The first child turns over a card and solves the problem. That player then looks for that product on his or her gameboard. If it is uncovered, the player may put a marker on it. When the player board is covered, the game is over. The game can be played like Bingo, with winners having a row across, down, or diagonally covered.

12	5	3	10	20
36	27	6	21	16
9	18	Free	24	35
36	25	8	32	20
15	4	56	28	12

MULTIPLICATION TABLE GAME

Concept: Multiply two numbers less than 10.

Materails: Multiplication table.

Cards with products written on them.

Group size: Two to four children.

Procedure: Each player is dealt five cards. To begin play, the top card on the deck is turned over and played on the appropriate square (say, the 30 card is turned over and played on the 6 x 5 position). The players in turn must play a card adjacent to a card already on the board, so that the second player plays the 25 card on 5 x 5. The next player must place a card next to one of the cards on the board.

Each time a player makes a play he or she gets five points (reinforces counting by 5's). If a player cannot make a play adjacent to a card on the board, that player draws a card and the next player tries. Play continues until one player has played all cards or until no player can make a play. At the end of play, each card remaining in a player's hand subtracts one point from that player's score. Highest score wins.

Variation: This may also be used in addition or subtraction. Or, when the first round is over, all remaining cards are discarded and five new cards are dealt to each player from the deck.

X	1	2	3	4	5	6	7	8	9	
1										
2										
3										
4				16	20	24				
5				20	25	30				
6				24	30	36				
7										
8										
9										

CARDS

CHECKERS

Concept: Drill multiplication facts.

Materials: Checkerboard.

Checkers or milk jug lids.

Group size: Two children.

Procedure: Mark numerals on either the red or black squares, whichever will be played. Mark other numerals on the checkers.

Play as in regular checkers; however, when a player lands on a new space, that player must multiply together the number on the checker and the number in the space and name the correct answer. If incorrect, the player moves the checker back to its original position and loses a turn.

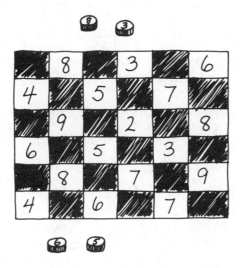

CONCENTRATION

Concept: Drill multiplication facts.

Materials: Deck of regular playing cards, with or without picture cards.

Group size: Two to six children.

Procedure: If playing without picture cards, remove them and set them aside. If playing with picture cards, assign them a number you wish to drill, i.e., all picture cards are 9's.

Shuffle the deck and lay the cards face down in rows of eight. Each player takes a turn exposing two cards. If the player says the correct multiplication sentence, he or she may keep the cards and take one extra turn. If incorrect, the cards are turned face down and the next player proceeds. When all cards are gone, the player with the most cards wins.

Note: This game may be modified to use any basic operation.

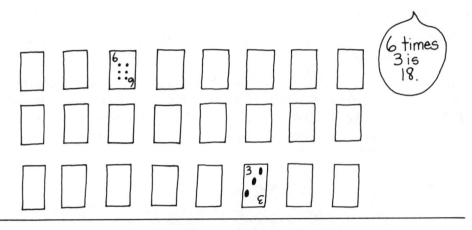

WHAT DID I DO?

Concept: Recognize the operation used with two numbers.

Materials: Two set of cards numbered 0 to 9.

Group size: Teams of two to six children.

Procedure: One child at a time picks up two cards and adds, subtracts, or multiplies mentally. The player then shows the cards to the other children and says the "answer is" and states it. The child who then can tell what he or she did—added, subtracted, or multiplied—to get the answer gets to keep the cards.

CHAPTER 14

Patterns

14.1   Introduction

Each of the pattern activities included in this chapter has logical rules that can be discovered. Just as there are rules in multiplication or in measuring, there are rules in making the included patterns. Encourage the child to detect the pattern rule(s) and then follow the rules in continuing or completing the pattern. Visual or auditory discrimination skills are developed in the process. Note that patterns are imposed by the designer. As a designer, the child identifies a set of rules that can logically be duplicated.

The teacher must take care not to confuse sequencing with seriating. Seriation builds on a property of the construct such as light-red, red, bright-red, whereas sequencing builds on continuation of a pattern such as red, blue, green, red, blue, _____ .

14.2   Patterns with objects

The activities in this section involve exact duplication of a pattern using objects. At first the child should be presented with a pattern using objects from the child's environment. The child should be presented a card with a picture of the pattern to be duplicated, and objects should be drawn so that, when the child fits the real world object onto the pattern card, the object exactly fits in the picture space. As the child gains experience with duplicating patterns, then a scaled drawing of the pattern should be presented and the child is to duplicate the pattern without the objects fitting exactly on the picture. This requires a higher level of cognition on the part of the child and is prerequisite to completing activities in other sections in the chapter.

NECKLACES

Concept: Follow given pattern to make a bead necklace.

Materials: Beads of assorted colors and shapes.

Lacing strings or rods.

Pattern cards with pictures of bead patterns.

Group size: Four to six children.

Procedure: Have the child look at a bead pattern and reproduce the pattern in the correct order on a string. You might need to say, "Where is the knot on the pattern card?" "What bead should go next to the knot?" "Put that bead on your string so it will be next to the knot." "What bead goes next to that bead on the pattern card?" "Put it on your string."

The task may be made easier by (1) drawing the pattern cards exactly to the scale of the beads and letting the child match the correct beads onto the pattern card before stringing or (2) limiting all beads on a pattern card to only one shape, thus requiring only color sequencing. The task may be made more difficult by (1) drawing the pattern cards smaller than the beads or (2) having the child reverse the order of the pattern card on the string.

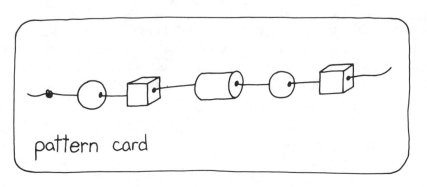

pattern card

SET THE TABLE

Concept: Copy a pattern to arrange dishes on a placemat.

Materials: Toy dishes, at least two of each piece (plates, cups, saucers, forks, knives, spoons).

Small cards picturing different place settings.

Group size: One to four children.

Procedure: Arrange one set of dishes and silverware on a placemat. Have the child arrange another place setting in the same order. Begin with only a few items and increase the number as the child gains skill with the activity.

For a more difficult task, the child may try to reproduce the place setting shown on the pattern card. You might need to say, "Where did I put my cup?" "Put your cup in the same place on your placemat." "Did you put your spoon where I put mine?" "How could you move your spoon to look like mine?" "How could I move my spoon to look like yours?"

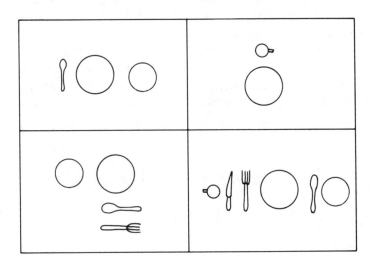

SANDWICH

Concept: Order sandwich items to build a sandwich.

Materials: Cutouts of different sandwich materials (either cutout pictures or hand-drawn ones or foam slices).

Group size: Two to four children.

Procedure: Allow the children to build many different kinds of sandwiches. Next have them continue a pattern. For example, build a very tall sandwich with "baloney and cheese" alternating slices and ask what would come next.

14.3 Patterns with shapes

Although the activities in this section involve concrete materials, the materials are more mathematical in form (shapes versus toy dishes). The use of mathematical shapes seems to be more difficult for many children. At first present pattern cards on which the shapes are to be placed directly. Work the patterns with children or allow one child to generate a pattern and see if the other children can continue the pattern. This helps the children discover the rule for the pattern.

Patterns can demand various levels of ability. The pattern activity may require that the child is to (1) only identify the rule, (2) continue a pattern once or to a predetermined point, (3) develop an original pattern, or (4) identify errors in a pattern. Some activities from each of these types should be provided in the child's curriculum.

READY FOR SHAPES

Concept: Order shapes according to a shape pattern.

Materials: Cutouts of shapes.

Group size: One or two children.

Procedure: Have the children match your pattern. Begin simply. Ask the children what comes next and then next. Work from both directions in setting up a pattern.

FEEL SHAPES

Concept: Reproduce the pattern of shapes by feeling (not seeing) the shapes.

Materials: Feel box.

Shapes made from cardboard, clay, or plastic.

Masking tape to hold down the shapes.

Group size: One or two children.

Procedure: Place two or more shapes in a row in the box using masking tape to hold the shapes in place. The child should not be able to see the pattern. Have the child put a hand in the box and find the shapes. With duplicate shapes, have the child put them in order in front or on top of the box so that they duplicate the order of the shapes in the box.

Child places these shapes on top.

DETECTIVES

Concept: Match shape patterns and identify a missing shape.

Materials: Shapes (various colors and sizes optional for more difficult activities).

Envelopes with shape patterns on the outside.

Group size: One or two children.

Procedure: Enclose in each envelope the shapes that a child will need to match the shape pattern drawn on the envelopes. Have the child select the pattern that he or she wishes to match.

Ask the child to place the shapes on the envelope pattern. If a child can do this, then have the child match patterns next to the envelope.

Take one shape out of the envelope. Let the child identify which shape is missing from the pattern.

Variation: Include in each envelope enough shapes to match the envelope pattern and reproduce it continuing the pattern once.

SHAPE PATTERN WORKSHEET

Concept: Construct a pattern or continue a pattern using two or more shapes.

Materials: Worksheet (see diagram).

Group size: Any size group.

Procedure: Ask a child to name the given pattern. Have the child point to a place where a shape is missing and name what shape should be there. Have the child draw in the shape that is missing (if child cannot draw the shape, have that child use templates or paper cutouts).

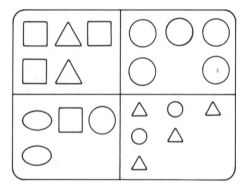

14.4   Patterns with colors

Color patterns continue to reinforce and expand a child's recognition of colors. A child uses logic to order colors by one or more rules. Color shades need not be a factor in making a pattern, as they were in the seriation chapter.

Color media offer enticing and unlimited ways to make patterns in artwork and game making. Allow children to design their own games on paper, sharing them with others. Help every child to generate a pattern and use as many as possible in classroom activities. Display them on bulletin boards.

BLOCK PATTERNS

Concept: Match a given pattern of objects.

Materials: Blocks or cubes of different colors, at least two of each color.

Group size: Small group.

Procedure: Place some blocks in a pattern. Give the child a group of blocks and have the child copy the pattern. Say, "What block did I put first? Can you find one just like it? What block comes next in my row? Can you put one just like it next to your first block? Do our rows look the same?"

Variation: The child copies the pattern from a pattern card by first placing the blocks directly on the card and then in front of the card.

RALLY 'N RETRIEVE

Concept: Recall verbal order of sizes (or colors) and construct the order.

Materials: Three objects of three sizes or colors, i.e., blocks, cups.

Group size: Any size group.

Procedure: Line the objects up on a table or chalk tray. Have the children face the objects.

Call one child to get the objects in a given order. Have the child listen to the complete order. Next let the child bring the objects back, handing them to you in the order you called. "Bring me red, blue, and green."

Variation: Set out more than three objects or spread the objects throughout one end of the room, so that the child must look for the objects and remember the sequence.

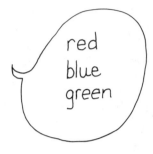

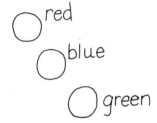

LEGGY MONSTER

Concept: Construct and continue a color pattern.

Materials: Gameboard (see diagram).

Poker chips or other color chips.

Group size: Two or three children.

Procedure: Attach 2, 3, or 4 legs to the monster depending on how many colors are going to be in the pattern. Explain that as the monster walks, it leaves footprints the color of its feet. Point to the monster's feet, calling off the pattern that they will make, "green, red, blue, green, red, blue, ...". Have one child start the pattern by placing a chip on the first square. Alternate children until there are no more squares left.

COLOR CARDS

Concept: Construct and continue a pattern of colors.

Materials: Fifteen cards: five red, five yellow, and five blue.

Group size: Two children.

Procedure: Divide the cards between two children. They can place the cards face up on the table or hold them so that they can see each card. Put the odd card on the table. Have the children take turns adding to the row of cards, making a pattern. Help with the first pattern duplication. If a child cannot add a card to the pattern then the other child does until the pattern ends.

Use two colors and only ten cards if a three-color pattern is too difficult.

Variation: Have a child match a pattern of colored cards.

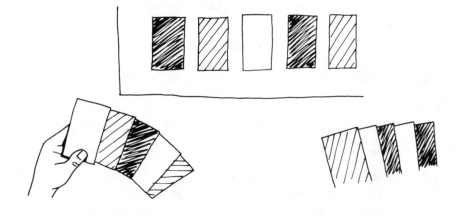

COLOR STRIPS

Concept: Order two or more colors in a pattern.

Materials: Paper strips (colored).

Paste.

White paper.

Group size: Any size group.

Procedure: Allow the children to choose from two or more piles of strips. Help each child begin by taking an equal number (two or three are good to start with) of strips of each color.

Demonstrate how to set up a pattern on a piece of paper prior to pasting. Have each child construct a pattern, check it, and then begin pasting.

This is a good activity to have children help each other on, as patterning with colors can be very difficult for some children.

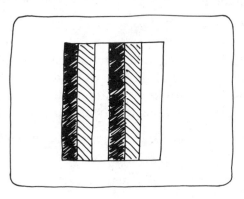

COLOR CHIPS

Concept: Construct a pattern using three or more colors.

Materials: Tic-tac-toe gameboards.

Color chips, i.e., poker chips, or worksheets and crayons.

Group size: Any size group.

Procedure: Begin a pattern on a gameboard or ditto sheet. Let each child fill out the remainder of the board with chips on the colored squares. Color in circles on the worksheet variation.

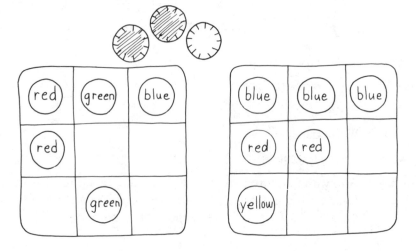

MARBLE EGGS

Concept: Match patterns in an egg carton with colored marbles.

Materials: Marbles, at least two of each kind.

              Egg carton.

Group size: One or two children.

Procedure: Arrange one row of marbles in a color pattern. Have the children find a marble that is the same color as in the first space. Continue throughout until both rows are identical. Begin the order from left to right.

              Variation: Use numerals instead of colors.

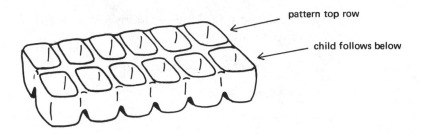

pattern top row

child follows below

LOLLIPOPS

Concept: Identify and duplicate a color pattern.

Materials: Paper cut in lollipop shapes with designs (see diagram).

              Crayons.

Group size: Any size group.

Procedure: Show the front and back of a lollipop with one side colored in a design. Explain that the colors on one side will come through to the other side so that the back must be colored in the same pattern as the front.

              Let the children duplicate a given pattern or make their own. Have them find someone else with the same pattern.

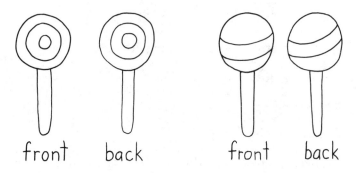

front   back   front   back

RAINBOW FLOWERS

Concept: Construct a pattern using three or more colors. Match duplicate color patterns.

Materials: Flowers drawn on paper (see diagram).

                Crayons, paint, or chalk.

                Scissors (optional).

Group size: Any size group.

Procedure: Show the children the flowers. Ask them to color the flowers so that they look alike using two or more colors on each flower. They may cut out the flowers and duplicate the pattern of color on the back of the flower.

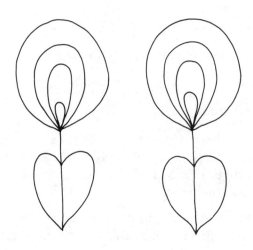

PEGBOARD PATTERNS

Concept: Reproduce a pattern on a pegboard.

Materials: Pegboard.

Pegs or golf tees.

Group size: One or two children.

Procedure: Have a child make a pattern on one line of the pegboard. Let the second child match the pattern of the first child.

Variation: Use a pegboard that has holes all the way through the board. Let the child copy or make a pattern stringing colored yarn through the holes in the board.

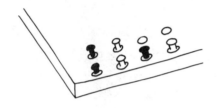

T-SHIRTS

Concept: Identify and duplicate a color pattern.

Materials: Paper cutouts shaped like T-shirts with one side colored.

Group size: Any size group.

Procedure: Show the front and back of a T-shirt cutout. Have the children make the same color patterns on the back as on the front.

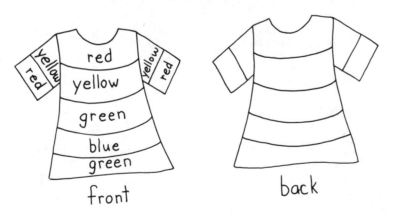

POKER CHIPS

Concept: Order poker chips according to color.

Materials: Poker chips or colored marbles.

Group size: Two or three children.

Procedure: First have the children match your pattern with their own. Begin very simply using two colors such as red and green. Play it like a game. Allow the children to make patterns and you match them. After several times of matching, ask the children what would come next. Use simple patterns to begin with, then more difficult ones using both number and color.

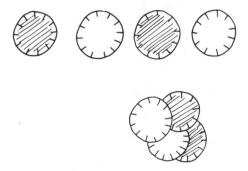

TIE DESIGN

Concept: Continue the order of a pattern of three colors.

Materials: Paper with tie drawings (see diagram).

Group size: Any size group.

Procedure: Show a tie with a pattern of two or more colors. Ask which color comes next in the pattern. And then which comes next. Have the children duplicate and finish a tie or make their own patterns.

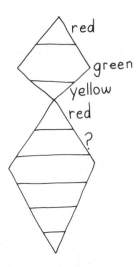

red
green
yellow
red
?

PLEXIGLASS DESIGNS

Concept: Continue patterns drawn on glass.

Materials: Plexiglass or glass with edges taped (do not allow glass to be used unless on a table).

Crayons.

Alternative: Use clear acetate covers with wax crayons.

Pattern cards to be slipped under the glass (optional).

Group size: One to three children.

Procedure: Draw a beginning pattern on glass and have the child finish the pattern. Or place a pattern card under the glass and have the child match the pattern by coloring on the glass. Using pattern cards might be easier as they could be made up ahead of time and changed rapidly to meet children's ability level. Use unfinished pattern cards next and let the child try to finish them.

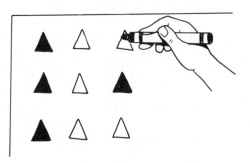

MARBLE PINBALL

Concept: Order marbles in a pattern of colors.

Materials: Box lid.

              Pencil with eraser.

              Paired colored balls or marbles.

              Plastic eggs or paper cups.

Group size: One or two children.

Procedure: Cut six holes in the box lid, three on each side. Glue the plastic egg halves or paper cups under the holes to hold the marbles when they are dropped into the holes. Use the pencil to shoot marbles into the holes. Put three marbles into the holes on one side (one marble per hold). The child must duplicate the order of colors by shooting the remaining marbles into the pockets opposite the given order.

              Variation: Number the marbles or balls with indelible ink. The child must drop the marbles into the holes in the numerical sequence 1 to 6.

14.5   Auditory patterns

Auditory patterns contribute to a child's mathematical abilities. For instance, numerous auditory patterns can incorporate quantity as a factor of the pattern, i.e., 2 claps/3 claps/2 claps/3 claps. Auditory memory is exercised in identifying and duplicating logical patterns. Motor coordination is necessary in combining an auditory pattern and reproducing it physically.

Word patterns, as in poetry, highlight mathematical contributions to the language arts.

CLAP YOUR HANDS

Concept: Imitate a sequence of sounds by hand clapping.

Materials: None.

Group size: Any size group.

Procedure: Clap out a rhythm; have the children try to imitate it.

The rhythm can be varied by alternating claps and pauses, by fast and slow claps, by loud and soft claps.

NONSENSE WORDS

Concept: Repeat a pattern of nonsense words.

Materials: None.

Group size: Four to six children or class.

Procedure: Call out a chant of nonsense words. Have the children try to imitate it. Allow the children to "play" with made-up words. Begin very simply and work toward the complex. If the children have trouble, rhythmic clapping by the children helps.

Variation: Allow the children to make up new patterns.

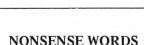

Boo coo coo ...
Boo coo moo ...
Boo coo moo moo ...
Boo coo moo too ...

Mmmmm . . .

Concept: Recall and duplicate a pattern of sounds.

Materials: None.

Group size: Any size group.

Procedure: Ask the children to repeat the sound you make (m, r, s, f). Say, "Can you make this sound?" "Can you make it last a long time? A short time?" Make a sound pattern mmmm–mm–mmmm–mm. Have the children try to duplicate it.

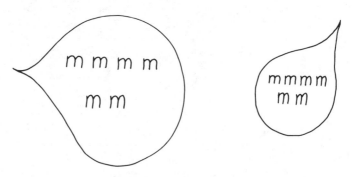

14.6 Patterns of action and time sequences

Patterns using an order of actions in time are less arbitrary than other types of patterns presented in this chapter. Habits within a culture dictate appropriate activities over periods of time, i.e., there are three meals a day—breakfast, lunch, and dinner. Yet, there still may remain some variation that leads to evaluating the logic of the actions and making revisions or allowances where a new rule or new interpretation of an old rule would make a change acceptable. Identifying the logic behind activities and predicting what will happen next from given information extends mathematical abilities. The probability of an act occurring is a factor in deciding how to predict an occurrence.

ACTION

Concept: Order and duplicate a set of actions.

Materials: None.

Group size: Any size group.

Procedure: Have one child stand up in front of the others and either do three things following adult directions or using his or her own ideas. Have other children tell the order of the child's actions and then try to duplicate them.

JUMPIN' ALONG

Concept: Jump in a pattern according to a model.

Materials: None.

Group size: Class

Procedure: Demonstrate the pattern that the children will jump. You might use, feet together, feet apart, feet together, feet apart, etc. Start with very simple patterns such as this one. Gradually increase the difficulty such as feet together, together, apart. You can add other movements such as feet to the side or front. The difficult patterns would be adding arm movements to coordinate with the pattern of the feet.

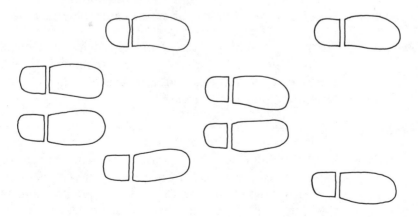

STORY LINES

Concept: Arrange events in time sequence by order of occurrence.

Materials: Sequenced story cards or cartoon or comic strips.

Group size: Any size group.

Procedure: Have the children talk about what comes first in the story, what comes second, and so on. It might help to have the children sequence a story they've heard before. Show the children the story cards and have them talk about what happened first, next, and so forth. Have the children place the cards in order. Allow the children to work individually on other story sequences.

NEXT

Concept: Order pictures of things or actions according to time.

Materials: Pictures of things in a time sequence such as apple from whole to just the core, Christmas tree untrimmed to completely trimmed, flower from a seed growing to a flower, getting ready for school, preparing a meal.

Group size: One or two children.

Procedure: Have a child place the picture cards of a familiar activity in correct time order. There may be some variation in the way in which children decide to order the pictures and as long as they can justify that sequence it is acceptable.

 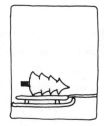  

HOW DO WE DO IT?

Concept: Perform steps of an action in proper time sequence.

Materials: None.

Group size: Any size group.

Procedure: Have a child pantomime in correct order a sequence of steps to a familiar task, for example, getting dressed.

For a child who needs help, say, "When you get dressed for school, what do you do first?" "What do you put on first? What do you put on next?" "Then what do you put on?"

Suggestions for sequences:

playing ball	setting the table
eating breakfast	building with blocks
washing hands	going to bed

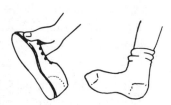

BURNING CANDLE

Concept: Order pictures of a burning candle.

Materials: Small birthday candle.

Matches.

Pictures of stages of a candle burning.

Group size: Any size group.

Procedure: Have the children observe a small candle burn from a whole one to nothing. Have the children discuss what they saw first, next, and so forth. Show pictures or drawings of candles burning and talk about what was first, second and so forth. Place the pictures in the order they decide. (Help guide them, if needed.) This could be a science lesson on observation and on what happens to burning things.

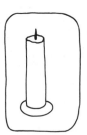

GROWING UP

Concept: Arrange people pictures in order by age, from youngest to oldest.

Materials: Pictures of people of different ages.

Group size: Small group.

Procedure: Have a child arrange the pictures in age sequence, from youngest to oldest. For a child who needs extra help, say, "Let's look at these pictures. Which one shows the youngest person?" "Yes, it's the baby. Put it first." "After a baby grows awhile, what would it look like next?" "Yes, a little boy. Put that picture next."

Variation: Arrange family members by age. You may have children bring in pictures of their families and order them from the youngest to the oldest.

Appendix

Activity Index

The purpose of this index is to help the instructor locate appropriate activities to fit specific needs. Two kinds of information are contained in the index. The first is the level of difficulty of each activity in terms of whether it uses manipulation of concrete materials, manipulation of pictures or semiabstract materials, or abstract concepts independent of objects or pictures. Activities utilizing concrete materials are the easiest and are generally used to introduce new concepts. Pictorial or semiabstract activities represent the next level of difficulty and are meant to aid a more sophisticated and generalized understanding of concepts. Abstract activities are, of course, the most difficult. Mastery of abstract ideas represents the highest level of mathematical thought.

The second type of information in the index deals with the type of response or skill needed by the child to participate in each activity. The checklist indicates which type of stimulus—visual, auditory, tactile/kinesthetic—the child receives. Also indicated is the type of response the child is asked to make: vocal, gross motor, or fine motor.

The instructor can use this chart to help select appropriate activities for children with special needs. For a nonverbal child, for example, activities requiring motor responses would be selected and those requiring vocal responses would be limited. A partially sighted child would benefit more from tactile experiences and less from visually oriented activities. A child who learns best through the auditory/vocal channel would learn best from activities involving auditory/vocal modes. The teacher should modify the activities to meet the child's learning style, not vice versa.

| | | Mode of Activity | | | Response of Child | | | | | | |
| | | | | | Input | | | Output | | | |
Chapter 2. TOPOLOGY		Concrete (objects)	Semiabstract (pictures)	Abstract (symbols)	Visual	Auditory	Tactile/Kinesthetic	Verbal	Gross Motor	Fine Motor	Writing
Proximity (near, far)											
11	The Hot Seat	X			X			X	X		
11	Beanbag Buddies	X			X		X		X	X	
12	Magic Shoes	X			X	X			X		
13	Playground Directions	X				X			X		
14	Monster, May I?	X				X		X	X		
14	Marble Game	X			X		X		X	X	
15	Card Sharp	X	X		X	X			X		
16	Point to a Picture		X		X	X		X	X	X	
17	Jug Pictures		X		X			X	X		
17	Detective		X		X	X		X			
18	Earth and Sky		X		X		X	X		X	
19	Worksheet: Near and Far		X		X	X					X
19	Draw a Duplicate	X	X		X	X					X
20	Dot Pictures		X		X						X
Separation											
21	Buttons	X			X	X	X			X	
22	The Little Engine that *Could*	X			X			X		X	
22	The Oatmeal Tunnel	X			X		X	X		X	
23	The Orange that Separates	X				X	X	X	X		
24	Glued People	X				X	X		X		
24	Yarn Runners	X			X	X	X		X		
25	Join 'Em Up	X				X	X			X	
26	Kissing Cousins		X		X					X	X
26	Twins		X		X	X				X	
Separation and order											
27	Checkers	X			X					X	
28	Juggler	X	X		X					X	

Chapter 2 (cont'd)		Mode of Activity			Response of Child						
					Input			Output			
		Concrete (objects)	Semiabstract (pictures)	Abstract (symbols)	Visual	Auditory	Tactile/Kinesthetic	Verbal	Gross Motor	Fine Motor	Writing
29	Choo Choo Train	X			X	X			X	X	
29	It's a Grape Day!	X			X	X		X		X	
30	Hip Connected to the Thigh	X				X		X	X		
31	Make a Face		X		X	X				X	
31	Body Beautiful		X		X		X			X	
32	Clown		X		X		X			X	
33	Build the House		X		X		X			X	
Enclosure (open, closed)											
36	Walk the Shape	X			X		X		X		
36	Bean Bag Maze	X			X				X	X	
37	Rope Maze	X			X		X		X		
38	Out or In—Who Will Win?	X			X	X		X	X	X	
39	Bean Bag Rally	X			X		X	X	X		
39	Big Mouth		X		X		X			X	
40	Blind Man's Shapes	X				X	X	X		X	
41	Open or Closed	X			X		X	X		X	
42	Geoboards	X	X		X	X	X			X	
42	The OK Corral	X	X		X		X			X	
43	Keep Your Pet in the Yard		X		X					X	
44	Lion Maze		X		X	X					X
45	Open-Closed Concentration		X		X					X	
46	Mailcarrier in Your Area		X		X		X			X	
47	Barefoot Baby	X	X		X					X	
48	Hop Home	X	X		X					X	
49	Open-Closed Worksheet		X		X	X					X
49	Holes		X	X	X					X	X
50	Holes in Your Name		X	X	X						X
51	Draw It Again, Sam		X		X						X

| | Mode of Activity | | | Response of Child | | | | | | |
| | | | | Input | | | Output | | | |
Chapter 2 (cont'd)	Concrete (objects)	Semiabstract (pictures)	Abstract (symbols)	Visual	Auditory	Tactile/Kinesthetic	Verbal	Gross Motor	Fine Motor	Writing
52 Hidden Pictures		X	X	X	X				X	X
Surrounding by a boundary (inside, outside)										
53 Rope Shapes	X			X	X			X		
54 Animals Playing	X	X		X	X	X			X	
54 Farm Fences	X			X	X	X			X	
55 Hungry Monster	X	X		X	X		X		X	
56 Inside–Outside Concentration		X		X					X	
Surrounding on a line (betweenness)										
59 You're Among Friends	X			X	X		X	X		
59 Between You and Me	X			X	X		X	X		
60 Between the Puddles	X			X	X		X	X		
61 Baby Bear		X		X	X				X	
62 Bears' Return		X		X	X				X	
63 Haunted House		X		X	X				X	
64 Skyscrapers	X			X	X				X	
65 Necklaces	X			X	X	X			X	
66 Jewelry Worksheet		X		X	X					X

Chapter 3. SHAPE	Mode of Activity			Response of Child						
				Input			Output			
	Concrete (objects)	Semiabstract (pictures)	Abstract (symbols)	Visual	Auditory	Tactile/Kinesthetic	Verbal	Gross Motor	Fine Motor	Writing
Shape readiness										
69 Shape Goes Around the Outside	X			X	X	X	X		X	X
70 Shape Walk	X			X	X	X	X	X		
71 Tricky Shapes	X			X		X			X	
71 Shapeboard	X	X		X					X	
72 Shape Box	X			X		X			X	
72 Look Alikes	X			X		X			X	
73 Shape Hunt	X	X		X	X	X		X		X
Naming and discriminating shapes										
75 Circle Song			X		X	X	X	X		
76 Just a Rollin' Along	X			X		X			X	
76 Circle Stacks	X			X		X			X	
77 Square Song			X		X	X	X	X		
78 Body Squares	X			X		X		X		
78 Triangle Song			X		X	X	X	X		
79 Oval Song			X		X	X	X	X		
80 Turkey Eggs	X			X				X	X	
80 Rocks	X			X		X			X	
81 Rectangle Song			X		X	X	X	X		
82 Feed the Rhino	X			X					X	
82 Humpty Dumpty's Wall	X			X		X			X	
83 Postcards	X			X		X		X	X	
84 Shape Match	X			X	X		X		X	
85 Shape Match-Ups		X		X					X	
85 Shape Scopes		X		X			X		X	
86 It's in the Bag	X			X		X			X	
87 *Aiken Drum*		X	X	X	X		X			
88 Nameshapes		X		X			X		X	

Chapter 3 (cont'd)	Concrete (objects)	Semiabstract (pictures)	Abstract (symbols)	Visual	Auditory	Tactile/Kinesthetic	Verbal	Gross Motor	Fine Motor	Writing
	Mode of Activity			Response of Child — Input			Response of Child — Output			
89 Finger Shapes		X		X		X	X		X	
89 Now You See It, Now You Don't		X		X	X		X			
90 Can Shuffle	X			X			X	X		
91 Shape Run	X			X	X		X	X		
92 The Not Game	X	X		X	X	X	X	X		
92 Pop-Up Shapes	X	X		X			X		X	
93 Match Me		X		X					X	
94 Shy Shapes		X		X			X		X	
94 Sherlock Shapes	X		X		X		X			
95 Beat the Clock			X	X	X		X			
96 Shake a Shape		X		X			X		X	
96 Treasure Hunt		X		X					X	
97 Flower Garden		X	X	X						X
98 X Marks the Shape		X		X					X	
Drawing shapes										
100 Scribble	X			X						X
100 Size Scribbles	X			X						X
101 Stir a Circle	X					X		X	X	
102 Clean Scribbles	X			X		X		X	X	
103 Coordinated Circles			X	X		X		X	X	
104 Headbands	X			X		X				X
104 Wave Notes	X			X	X	X			X	X
105 Rain			X	X	X	X			X	X
106 Streets		X		X	X					X
107 Clay Play	X			X		X				X
107 Glue Templates		X		X		X	X			X
108 Jar Lid/Milk Carton Templates	X			X		X				X

| Chapter 3 (cont'd) | Mode of Activity | | | Response of Child | | | | | | |
| | | | | Input | | | Output | | | |
	Concrete (objects)	Semiabstract (pictures)	Abstract (symbols)	Visual	Auditory	Tactile/Kinesthetic	Verbal	Gross Motor	Fine Motor	Writing
109 Box and Can Collages	X	X		X		X				X
110 Fingerpaint Shapes		X		X		X			X	
110 Air Shapes			X	X		X			X	
111 Guess the Shape			X	X			X		X	
112 Curves and Zigzags	X			X		X			X	
112 Don't Fall Off the Sidewalk		X		X		X				X
113 Copycat		X		X		X				X
113 Dot to Dot	X			X		X				X
114 Listen and Do		X		X	X					X
115 Transparencies		X		X			X			X
115 Shape Memory		X	X	X						X
116 Badges		X		X	X				X	
117 Signs		X		X	X					X
Constructing with shapes										
118 Greeting Cards		X		X					X	
119 Shape Man		X		X					X	
119 Shape Mobiles	X			X					X	
120 Shape Reflectors	X			X		X	X		X	
121 Shape Sculpture	X			X					X	
122 Glitter Shapes		X		X					X	

| | Mode of Activity | | | Response of Child | | | | | |
| | | | | Input | | | Output | | | |
Chapter 4. COLOR	Concrete (objects)	Semiabstract (pictures)	Abstract (symbols)	Visual	Auditory	Tactile/Kinesthetic	Verbal	Gross Motor	Fine Motor	Writing
Color readiness (matching without naming)										
124 Canned Colors	X			X					X	
125 Color Cards	X	X		X					X	
126 Color Collections	X	X		X	X		X			
127 Color Recall	X	X		X	X		X		X	
127 House Flowers	X			X					X	
128 Dogs' Suburb	X			X					X	
129 Flash a Color	X			X					X	
Naming colors										
130 Hat Parade	X			X	X		X			
131 Same Name	X			X	X		X			
132 The Red Coat	X			X	X		X			
132 Color Favorites	X			X	X		X			
133 There Goes Matt	X			X	X		X	X		
134 Red Sled	X			X	X		X		X	
134 Yellow Jello	X			X	X		X		X	
135 Blue Brew	X			X	X		X		X	
136 Green Bean	X			X	X		X		X	
137 Orange Orange	X			X	X		X		X	
138 Violet Pilot	X			X	X		X		X	
138 Xylophone	X			X	X		X		X	
139 Brown Clown	X			X	X		X		X	
140 Purple Turtle	X			X	X		X		X	
140 White Kite	X			X	X		X		X	
141 Black Sack	X			X	X		X		X	
142 Hop and Stop	X			X	X			X		
143 Color Creations	X			X	X		X		X	

Chapter 4 (cont'd)	Mode of Activity			Response of Child						
				Input			Output			
	Concrete (objects)	Semiabstract (pictures)	Abstract (symbols)	Visual	Auditory	Tactile/Kinesthetic	Verbal	Gross Motor	Fine Motor	Writing
144 Rainbow Puzzle	X			X	X		X		X	
144 Color Book		X		X	X		X		X	
145 Color Towers	X			X	X		X		X	
146 Color Land		X		X	X		X		X	
147 Frame Colors	X			X	X				X	
147 Fishing for Colors	X			X	X				X	
148 Collected Colors	X			X	X		X		X	
149 Blue Cat?		X		X	X					X
149 Home Sweet Home		X		X	X				X	
150 Color Call	X			X			X			
Recalling colors										
151 Color Commentary	X			X	X		X			
152 Colors Away	X	X		X	X		X		X	
Shades and blends										
153 Shades		X		X	X				X	
153 Off Colors		X		X	X				X	
154 Painter's Delight	X			X	X		X		X	
155 Drops of Color	X			X	X		X		X	
155 Master Mixers		X		X	X		X		X	
156 Iced Colors	X			X	X		X			

	Mode of Activity			Response of Child						
				Input			Output			
Chapter 5. SIZE	Concrete (objects)	Semiabstract (pictures)	Abstract (symbols)	Visual	Auditory	Tactile/Kinesthetic	Verbal	Gross Motor	Fine Motor	Writing
General size (big, little)										
158 Size It Up	X			X	X	X			X	
159 Roll-A-Way	X			X	X		X	X		
159 Binocular Watch	X			X	X		X	X		
160 Find a Big One	X			X	X	X		X		
160 Big and Little	X			X	X		X		X	
161 Big Shape, Little Shape	X				X	X			X	
162 Fit a Pocket	X			X		X	X			
162 Nails and Screws	X			X	X	X			X	
163 Nuts and Bolts	X			X	X	X			X	
163 How Big?	X		X		X			X		
164 Magnifying Wonder	X			X	X		X		X	
165 Gardeners	X			X	X	X	X			
166 Big People, Little People		X		X	X					X
166 Animal Sounds		X	X	X	X		X			
Length (short, long, tall)										
167 Buildings	X			X	X		X		X	
168 Back to Back	X			X	X			X		
169 Superperson	X			X	X	X	X	X		
169 Wiggly Worms	X			X	X		X		X	
170 Lines			X			X	X			
171 Rods	X			X	X	X	X		X	
171 Snakes 'n Snails	X			X	X		X		X	
Width (wide, narrow)										
172 Rivers		X		X	X		X		X	
173 Noodles	X			X	X		X		X	
174 Designer Stripes		X		X	X		X			X
174 Wide Space, Narrow Space			X	X	X			X		

| | Mode of Activity | | | Response of Child | | | | | | |
| | | | | Input | | | Output | | | |
Chapter 5 (cont'd)	Concrete (objects)	Semiabstract (pictures)	Abstract (symbols)	Visual	Auditory	Tactile/Kinesthetic	Verbal	Gross Motor	Fine Motor	Writing
Thickness (thick, thin)										
175 Thread and Rope	X			X	X		X			
176 Candles	X			X	X	X	X		X	
177 Animal Tails		X		X	X		X			X
177 Pencil-Eating Parrots	X	X		X	X	X	X		X	
Volume (empty, full)										
178 Rice Jars	X			X	X		X		X	

	Mode of Activity			Response of Child						
				Input			Output			
Chapter 6. CLASSIFICATION	Concrete (objects)	Semiabstract (pictures)	Abstract (symbols)	Visual	Auditory	Tactile/Kinesthetic	Verbal	Gross Motor	Fine Motor	Writing
Classifying objects that belong together										
181 Coat Box	X			X				X		
182 Emergency Vehicles	X			X	X			X	X	
183 Doll House		X		X	X		X		X	
183 Go-Togethers		X		X	X		X		X	
184 Papa Bear, Mama Bear and Baby Bear		X		X	X				X	
185 Animals' Homes		X		X	X				X	
186 Dress-Up		X		X	X				X	
186 Cookie Sort	X			X	X				X	
187 What's Cookin'?		X		X	X				X	
Classifying objects into disjoint (separate) sets										
188 Color Clothes	X			X	X			X		
189 Holiday Cleanup	X			X	X			X		
189 Bird Families		X		X	X				X	
190 Crayons Beyond Repair	X			X	X	X			X	
191 Jobs	X			X	X				X	
192 Color Baskets	X			X	X				X	
192 A Three-Ring Circus	X			X	X				X	
193 Color Cars	X			X	X				X	
193 Sort the Objects	X			X	X	X			X	
194 Bottle Caps	X			X	X				X	
195 Nuts	X			X	X				X	
195 Super Seeds	X			X	X		X		X	
196 Rock Hound Collections	X			X	X	X	X		X	
197 Sizable Groups	X			X	X	X			X	
197 The Great Outdoors	X			X	X		X		X	

Chapter 6 (cont'd)	Concrete (objects)	Semiabstract (pictures)	Abstract (symbols)	Visual	Auditory	Tactile/Kinesthetic	Verbal	Gross Motor	Fine Motor	Writing
	Mode of Activity			**Response of Child**						
				Input			**Output**			
198 Sugar and Salt		X		X	X		X		X	
199 Float or Sink	X			X	X		X		X	
199 Hot and Cold		X		X	X		X		X	
200 Are You Attracted to a Magnet?	X			X	X		X		X	
201 House Hunt	X			X	X		X		X	
202 Nails	X			X	X	X	X		X	
202 The Button Box	X			X	X				X	
203 Coin Cuties	X			X	X	X	X		X	
204 Color Cubes	X			X	X		X		X	
204 Find-a-Shape	X			X	X	X			X	
205 Mail Shapes		X		X					X	
206 Shape Flowers	X	X		X		X			X	
206 Sort-a-Shape	X	X		X		X			X	
207 Off to See the Shape Whiz		X		X			X		X	
208 Plaids and Stripes and Silly Dots		X		X					X	
209 Same and Different Game		X		X					X	
210 Sleepers and Crawlers	X	X			X		X	X		
211 You Are Not . . .			X		X		X			
211 A TV Survey			X		X		X			
212 Food Groups		X		X	X		X		X	
213 By Land, Sea, and Air		X		X	X				X	
213 To the Zoo or to the Farm	X	X		X	X		X		X	
214 Categories Galore		X		X	X				X	
Classifying objects into intersecting sets (multiple factors)										
215 People Blocks		X		X	X		X		X	
216 Attribute Blocks	X			X	X	X	X		X	

	Mode of Activity			Response of Child						
				Input			Output			
Chapter 6 (cont'd)	Concrete (objects)	Semiabstract (pictures)	Abstract (symbols)	Visual	Auditory	Tactile/Kinesthetic	Verbal	Gross Motor	Fine Motor	Writing
216 What Color Is Your Shirt?	X			X	X		X	X		
217 What Do I Look Like?	X			X	X		X	X		
218 Find a Secret Object			X	X			X			
219 Clothes in Season		X		X	X				X	
219 Matrix Board		X		X	X		X		X	
220 Wild Things		X		X	X		X		X	
Classifying objects with an inclusion relationship										
221 Toys and Dolls	X			X	X		X		X	
222 Birds and Animals	X			X	X		X		X	

| | Mode of Activity | | | Response of Child | | | | | | |
| | | | | Input | | | Output | | | |
Chapter 7. SERIATION	Concrete (objects)	Semiabstract (pictures)	Abstract (symbols)	Visual	Auditory	Tactile/Kinesthetic	Verbal	Gross Motor	Fine Motor	Writing
Size (little, big)										
226 Big 'n Little	X			X					X	
227 Stack It Up	X			X		X			X	
228 Fit-Togethers	X			X		X			X	
228 Sizing Up Beanbags	X			X		X			X	
229 Puppets	X	X		X	X		X	X		
230 Follow the Fish	X			X		X			X	
230 Pie Angles	X			X	X				X	
231 Lollipops	X			X		X			X	
232 Growing Neighborhoods	X			X		X			X	
232 Bigger and Bigger	X			X	X	X			X	
233 Circles	X			X	X	X			X	
233 Squares	X			X	X	X			X	
234 Ranging Rectangles		X		X		X			X	
234 Angles		X		X		X			X	
235 Animal Kingdom			X		X		X			
Size (length)										
236 Straws	X			X		X			X	
237 Shoes in a Row	X			X					X	
237 Hot Dogs and Buns	X			X					X	
238 Record a Jump	X			X	X			X	X	
239 Rockets	X			X		X			X	X
240 Stair Steps	X			X	X		X	X		
240 Heights		X		X			X			
241 Guess My Rule	X		X	X			X			
242 Longer and Longer		X		X		X			X	
Size (width)										
243 Ribbons	X			X					X	

Chapter 7 (cont'd)	Mode of Activity			Response of Child						
				Input			Output			
	Concrete (objects)	Semiabstract (pictures)	Abstract (symbols)	Visual	Auditory	Tactile/Kinesthetic	Verbal	Gross Motor	Fine Motor	Writing
243 Skinny Pencils, Fat Pencils	X			X					X	
244 Dowels	X			X		X			X	
244 Line Drawing	X	X		X		X				X
Color shades										
245 Matching Paint Chips	X			X					X	
246 Paint Chips	X	X		X	X				X	
247 Shady Eggs	X	X		X					X	
247 Shade Collectors		X		X					X	
Tactile										
248 Jars	X				X	X			X	
248 Water	X				X	X	X		X	
249 Fabric Squares	X			X		X			X	
249 Toothbrushes	X			X	X	X			X	
250 Sandpaper	X	X		X	X	X	X		X	
250 Water Jars	X			X					X	
251 Hard and Soft	X				X	X	X		X	

| | Mode of Activity | | | Response of Child | | | | | | |
| | | | | Input | | | Output | | | |
Chapter 8. NUMERALS	Concrete (objects)	Semiabstract (pictures)	Abstract (symbols)	Visual	Auditory	Tactile/Kinesthetic	Verbal	Gross Motor	Fine Motor	Writing
Chanting numerals										
254 Pantomime Counting		X	X	X	X		X	X	X	
255 Carnival Counting	X		X	X	X		X	X		
256 Ten Little Indians			X		X	X	X		X	
257 A Pig Alive			X		X	X	X	X	X	
258 Two Ears, Two Eyes	X		X	X	X	X	X	X	X	
258 What You Count Is What You Get	X			X	X	X	X		X	
259 Build a Tower	X		X	X	X		X		X	
260 Number Echo			X		X		X			
260 A Moving Chant			X	X	X			X		
261 Chant a Rhythm			X		X		X	X		
261 Parade March			X	X	X		X	X		
262 Chant and Freeze			X	X	X		X	X		
263 Numeral Train			X	X	X		X	X		
263 Stubborn Donkeys			X		X		X	X		
264 Helpers	X		X	X			X		X	
264 Snack Server	X			X	X		X		X	
Numeral recognition										
266 Palmed Number			X	X		X	X			
266 Age Necklace	X			X	X	X			X	X
267 Glitter Numbers		X		X		X	X		X	
268 Hide-a-number	X			X	X			X		
268 Over and Over			X	X			X			
269 Number Puzzle			X	X		X	X		X	
270 Number Train			X	X		X			X	
271 Number concentration		X		X			X		X	
271 Number Walk			X	X	X		X	X		

| | Mode of Activity | | | Response of Child | | | | | | |
| | | | | Input | | | Output | | | |
Chapter 8 (cont'd)	Concrete (objects)	Semiabstract (pictures)	Abstract (symbols)	Visual	Auditory	Tactile/Kinesthetic	Verbal	Gross Motor	Fine Motor	Writing
272 Number Necklaces			X	X	X		X			
273 Grocery Store	X		X	X	X		X		X	
273 Numeral Windows			X	X			X		X	
274 Fish in a Bucket	X		X	X			X		X	
275 Stand-Up Match			X	X	X		X	X		
276 Number Pockets			X	X					X	
276 Who Has My Number?			X	X	X		X	X		
277 Numeral Characters			X	X	X	X	X			X
278 Numerals in a Shoe			X	X	X		X			
278 Match a Hatched Numeral			X	X	X		X		X	
279 6 and 9			X	X	X		X			X
279 Magic Numerals			X	X	X		X		X	
280 Pick a 3, 5, or 8		X	X	X	X		X		X	X
281 Floored Numerals			X	X	X		X	X		
282 Show and Tell a Numeral			X	X	X		X			
282 Number Patterns			X	X			X		X	
283 Ordered Numbers			X	X	X		X		X	
283 Next Numeral			X	X	X		X			X
Numeral writing										
284 Frames			X	X	X		X			X
285 Fun with 1, Then to 9			X	X	X		X			X
287 I.D. Cards			X	X	X		X			X
287 Using Numerals			X	X	X				X	X
288 Place and Time			X	X	X				X	X

		Mode of Activity			Response of Child						
					Input			Output			
Chapter 9. NUMBERNESS		Concrete (objects)	Semiabstract (pictures)	Abstract (symbols)	Visual	Auditory	Tactile/Kinesthetic	Verbal	Gross Motor	Fine Motor	Writing
Sets											
290	Roped Sets	X			X	X	X	X	X		
291	Making Sets	X			X	X	X	X		X	
292	Flannel Sets		X		X	X	X	X		X	
292	Shape Sets	X			X	X	X	X		X	
One-to-one correspondence											
293	What's Mine Is Mine	X			X	X	X	X	X		
294	Snack Match	X			X	X	X	X	X		
295	Animal Tag		X		X	X	X		X		
295	Circle Sets	X			X	X	X	X	X	X	
296	Shape Partners		X		X	X	X	X	X		
Equivalent sets											
297	Musical Chairs	X			X	X		X	X		
298	Is There Enough?	X			X	X		X	X	X	
299	Hats and Workers		X		X	X		X	X		
300	Feed the Animals	X	X		X	X		X		X	
300	More Shapes, Fewer Shapes	X			X	X	X	X		X	
301	Striped Shoes	X			X			X		X	
Numerals for numbers											
302	Worn Out Shoes, Holey Shoes	X	X	X	X	X		X		X	
303	Number Mates		X	X	X	X				X	
304	How Many Buttons?	X	X	X	X	X				X	
304	Number Rummy		X	X	X	X		X		X	
305	Number Concentration		X	X	X	X				X	
306	Number Necklaces	X		X	X	X		X		X	
306	Musical Numbers		X	X	X	X		X	X		
307	Pot of Chips	X		X	X	X		X		X	
308	Pegboard Numbers	X		X	X			X		X	

| | Mode of Activity | | | Response of Child | | | | | | |
| | | | | Input | | | Output | | | |
Chapter 9 (cont'd)	Concrete (objects)	Semiabstract (pictures)	Abstract (symbols)	Visual	Auditory	Tactile/Kinesthetic	Verbal	Gross Motor	Fine Motor	Writing
309 Number Run		X	X	X	X		X	X		
310 Dominumbers		X	X	X	X		X		X	
Ordering of numerals according to number										
310 Polka Dot Numbers		X	X	X	X	X	X		X	
311 Stepnumbers	X		X	X	X	X	X		X	
312 Sky Towers		X		X			X			
313 The Proud Flowers		X	X	X	X		X			
314 The Raccoons' Lunch		X	X	X	X		X			

| | Mode of Activity | | | Response of Child | | | | | | |
| | | | | Input | | | Output | | | |
Chapter 10. ADDITION	Concrete (objects)	Semiabstract (pictures)	Abstract (symbols)	Visual	Auditory	Tactile/Kinesthetic	Verbal	Gross Motor	Fine Motor	Writing
Sums to 5										
317 Shake and Count	X		X	X	X	X	X		X	
318 Sum Eggs			X	X	X		X		X	
318 Duck Families		X	X	X					X	
319 Daisies		X	X	X					X	
320 Beanbag Clown		X	X	X	X	X	X	X		
Fact work										
321 Pouch Problems			X	X					X	
321 Add Around			X	X	X		X		X	
322 Problem Puzzle			X	X	X		X		X	
323 Adding Shoes			X	X	X		X		X	
323 Holiday Dittos		X	X	X	X					X
324 Add the Arrows			X	X	X					X
325 Make A Bug	X	X	X	X	X		X		X	
326 Rollette		X	X	X	X		X		X	
326 Grape Bunch Again			X	X	X		X		X	
327 Domino Lotto		X	X	X	X		X		X	
328 Horse Race	X	X	X	X	X		X		X	
329 Problem Cards			X	X	X					X
329 Bowling	X			X	X	X	X	X		
330 Card Sums		X	X	X	X		X		X	
331 10's Computer	X		X	X	X	X			X	
332 Store Addition	X		X	X	X		X		X	
332 Added Attraction			X	X	X		X		X	
333 Total Them Up			X	X	X		X		X	
334 Missing Addend		X	X	X	X		X		X	
335 Old Bachelor			X	X	X				X	
335 Cover Up		X	X	X	X		X		X	

| | Mode of Activity | | | Response of Child | | | | | | |
| | | | | Input | | | Output | | | |
Chapter 10 (cont'd)	Concrete (objects)	Semiabstract (pictures)	Abstract (symbols)	Visual	Auditory	Tactile/Kinesthetic	Verbal	Gross Motor	Fine Motor	Writing
336 Number Baseball		X	X	X	X		X		X	
337 Add and Go Fish		X	X	X	X		X		X	
338 High Roller		X	X	X	X				X	
338 Race-a-Rama		X		X					X	
339 Spinner Addition			X	X			X		X	
340 Stacking Hay		X	X	X	X		X		X	
340 Sum-It-Up			X	X					X	
341 Addition Mountain		X	X	X	X		X		X	
342 Pinball			X	X	X		X		X	

	Mode of Activity			Response of Child						
				Input			Output			
Chapter 11. PLACE VALUE	Concrete (objects)	Semiabstract (pictures)	Abstract (symbols)	Visual	Auditory	Tactile/Kinesthetic	Verbal	Gross Motor	Fine Motor	Writing
Readiness activities with place value										
344 Bottlecap Swap	X	X		X	X	X	X		X	
344 Monster Fingers	X	X		X	X	X	X		X	
345 Five-Bead Bracelets	X		X	X	X	X	X		X	
346 Chips	X	X	X	X	X	X	X		X	
346 Telephone 10's	X	X	X	X	X	X	X			X
347 Popcorn	X	X	X	X	X	X	X		X	
Place value involving 10's and 1's										
348 Cube Numbers	X		X	X	X	X	X		X	X
349 Roll 'em Numbers	X		X	X	X	X	X		X	X
350 Making 10's	X		X	X	X	X	X		X	
351 Guesstimate Estimate			X	X	X		X		X	
Place value involving 100's										
352 Leapfrog 10's	X		X	X	X	X	X		X	
353 Cut-and-Paste 10's	X		X	X	X	X			X	
353 Blue Chips – The Best	X		X	X	X	X	X		X	
354 Potluck	X		X	X	X	X	X		X	
355 Money Changer	X	X	X	X		X	X		X	
356 Stretched-Out Numbers			X	X	X		X		X	
Computation involving place value										
356 Fill 'er Up 10's	X		X	X	X				X	
357 Over the Hill on 50			X	X					X	
358 999			X	X		X			X	

Chapter 12. SUBTRACTION	Mode of Activity			Response of Child						
				Input			Output			
	Concrete (objects)	Semiabstract (pictures)	Abstract (symbols)	Visual	Auditory	Tactile/Kinesthetic	Verbal	Gross Motor	Fine Motor	Writing
Subtraction fact activities										
360 Count Encounters	X		X	X	X	X	X		X	X
360 Subtraction Fish			X	X	X				X	
361 Match the Socks			X	X					X	
361 Puzzling Puzzles	X		X	X	X		X		X	
362 Spot the Leopard			X	X	X		X		X	
362 Shake Up	X		X	X	X	X	X		X	
363 Climb Up or Down the Ladder	X		X	X	X	X	X		X	
364 Something Is Missing			X	X	X		X		X	
365 Football	X		X	X	X		X		X	
366 Treehouse	X		X	X	X	X	X		X	
366 Secret Code			X	X			X		X	
367 Count Down	X		X	X	X		X		X	
368 100 Down			X	X					X	X
369 Zero Wins			X	X					X	X

| Chapter 13. MULTIPLICATION | Mode of Activity | | | Response of Child | | | | | | |
| | | | | Input | | | Output | | | |
	Concrete (objects)	Semiabstract (pictures)	Abstract (symbols)	Visual	Auditory	Tactile/Kinesthetic	Verbal	Gross Motor	Fine Motor	Writing
Multiplication fact activities										
373 Bunny Hop		X	X	X	X		X		X	X
373 Multiplication Train	X		X	X	X		X		X	
374 Leapfrog Times	X		X	X	X		X		X	
375 Sammy Snake		X	X	X		X			X	
376 Multiplication Robot		X	X	X	X		X		X	
377 Dealer's Choice			X	X					X	
377 Hockey	X		X	X	X		X		X	
378 Multiplication Dominoes			X	X					X	
379 Tic-Tac-Times	X		X	X			X		X	
379 Frogs in the Lilies		X	X	X			X	X	X	
380 Ring Toss	X		X	X			X	X	X	
381 Wipe Out			X	X	X		X		X	
381 Multiplication Table Game			X	X	X				X	
382 Checkers			X	X			X		X	
383 Concentration		X	X	X	X		X		X	
384 What Did I Do?			X	X			X		X	

Chapter 14. PATTERNS	Mode of Activity			Response of Child						
				Input			Output			
	Concrete (objects)	Semiabstract (pictures)	Abstract (symbols)	Visual	Auditory	Tactile/Kinesthetic	Verbal	Gross Motor	Fine Motor	Writing
Patterns with objects										
385 Necklaces	X			X	X	X	X		X	
386 Set the Table	X			X	X	X	X		X	
387 Sandwich	X			X	X		X		X	
Patterns with shapes										
388 Ready for Shapes	X			X	X	X	X		X	
388 Feel Shapes	X			X	X	X	X		X	
389 Detectives	X			X	X	X	X		X	
390 Shape Pattern Worksheet		X		X	X		X			X
Patterns with colors										
391 Block Patterns	X			X	X	X	X		X	
392 Rally 'n Retrieve	X			X	X	X	X		X	
392 Leggy Monster	X	X		X	X		X		X	
393 Color Cards	X			X	X		X		X	
393 Color Strips	X			X	X		X		X	
394 Color Chips	X	X		X	X		X		X	
395 Marble Eggs	X			X					X	
395 Lollipops	X	X		X	X					X
396 Rainbow Flowers	X	X		X	X				X	X
397 Pegboard Patterns	X			X					X	
397 T-Shirts	X			X	X					X
398 Poker Chips	X			X	X		X		X	
398 Tie Design		X		X	X		X			X
399 Plexiglass Designs		X		X	X		X			X
400 Marble Pinball	X			X	X				X	
Auditory patterns										
401 Clap Your Hands	X			X	X				X	
401 Nonsense Words			X	X	X		X			

| Chapter 14 (cont'd) | Mode of Activity | | | Response of Child | | | | | | |
| | | | | Input | | | Output | | | |
	Concrete (objects)	Semiabstract (pictures)	Abstract (symbols)	Visual	Auditory	Tactile/Kinesthetic	Verbal	Gross Motor	Fine Motor	Writing
402 Mmmmm . . .			X		X		X			
Patterns of action and time sequences										
402 Action	X			X	X			X	X	
403 Jumpin' Along	X			X	X			X		
404 Story Lines		X		X	X			X		
404 Next		X		X	X		X		X	
405 How Do We Do It?	X			X	X	X	X	X	X	
405 Burning Candle	X	X		X	X		X		X	
406 Growing Up		X		X	X		X		X	

Webster Groves Presbyterian Nursery School
45 W. Lockwood
Webster Groves, MO   63119